From the Ashes
of My Dreams

From the Ashes of My Dreams

Ed Smith

Flanker Press Ltd.
St. John's, Newfoundland
2002

National Library of Canada Cataloguing in Publication Data

Smith, Ed, 1940-
From the ashes of my dreams / Ed Smith.

ISBN 1-894463-27-7

1. Smith, Ed, 1940- --Health. 2. Quadriplegics--Newfoundland and Labrador--Biography. 3. Authors, Canadian (English)--20th century-- Biography. I. Title.

RC406.Q33S64 2002   362.4'3'092   C2002-901827-7

Printed in Canada by Robinson-Blackmore

Typing: Gail Turner

First printing May 2002
Second printing July 2002

Flanker Press Ltd.
P O Box 2522, Stn C,
St. John's, Newfoundland, Canada, A1C 6K1
Toll Free: 1-866-739-4420   Telephone: (709) 739-4477
Facsimile: (709) 739-4420   E-mail: info@flankerpress.com
www.flankerpress.com

ED SMITH CAN BE REACHED AT:
4 Brinex Avenue
Springdale, NF
A0J 1T0

www.edsmithbooks.net

Author's Note

This book has been written with the help of several people. Two in particular stand out.

My daughter, Jennifer, who was in the accident with my wife and me, had the foresight to keep a journal which she made available to me when I began writing this story. I recognized immediately that her unique insights could be best expressed in her own words. The sections under her name, therefore, are her writing with practically no editing from me.

Especially for the first few months of my rehabilitation, I was often unaware of my condition and what was going on around me. What I do remember is usually clear and vivid, but there are gaps in my memory. Only Marion, my wife, can speak with any accuracy to the details of those times. Thus the sections under her name, although my words and writing, are largely based upon her recollections and reactions.

As well, Jennifer spent many hours on the manuscript utilizing her skills as a professional editor. Marion has always been my primary editor and continued in that role for this book.

Those people with whom we came in contact professionally have been given pseudonyms. Family and friends are afforded no such luxury.

This book is intended to be futuristically productive rather than historically unkind.

For Marion

1

I am conscious only of noise.

I know the Ford Explorer is out of control and plunging down over the embankment because of the noise. The rattling and banging as the vehicle bounces over ground and rocks and trees is deafening. I can see nothing from my prone position in the rear except roof padding. Then I close my eyes tightly. Curiously, I feel no movement, no sense of being thrown around. I know when the vehicle comes to rest because the noise is over.

There is a great silence. I open my eyes and discover several things at once. The upper half of my body is outside the side window and lying on the ground. My right arm is on fire. Already there are excited voices as other motorists climb down from the highway to where we are. I realize we are upside down because lying on my back I can look up and see the wheels. Then a voice comes from inside the car.

"Okay, I'm all right. Is everyone else okay?"

It is the take-charge mode of my youngest daughter's voice. Almost immediately, I hear my wife's response.

"I'm okay." A slight hesitation. "Ed?"

"Yes, I'm fine." And enormously relieved that we have all lived through this with hopefully nothing more than a broken arm.

Men are clambering down over the side of the road and through the snow. They gather around and prepare to lift me completely out of the car. The fiery pain in my right arm is increasing, if that's possible, and I ask them not to touch it. It seems to be broken in several places. And then I'm aware of something else.

"I can't feel my legs." It's a matter-of-fact statement, said to no one in particular. None of the men say anything so I feel obliged to say it again.

"I can't feel my legs." Again, no one seems to notice.

I hear Jennifer trying to get to me through the inside of the car.

"Don't move him," she calls. "Don't move him." She, at least, has heard me.

"We can smell gasoline," a male voice answers. "This thing could explode any minute." And they continue their efforts to get me away from the car.

This time Jennifer's voice is a shout.

"Do not move him!"

The men stop trying to move me. But now I have another concern.

"Is my wife out of the car?"

Jennifer is kneeling beside me on the ground.

"Yes, Dad," she says, "Mom is okay."

Moments pass like lifetimes, like milliseconds. People are talking above me, but no one seems to be talking to me, lying down here on the ground, on the snow. I seem to be a bit player in some vague drama, and I have the ridiculous feeling they've forgotten all about me. Jennifer is talking to me, asking me questions. Am I answering her? I don't know.

Then Marion is bending over me.

"You'll be okay, my love." But there is no conviction in her voice and I know she's only trying to comfort me.

"No, no!" I say desperately, trying to reach out to her, trying to make her understand. "It's not okay. I can't feel my legs. I can't feel anything."

Which is not exactly true, since the fire in my right arm is burning almost out of control. But it is nothing compared to the fear now rising rapidly in my throat, threatening to overcome me, to suffocate every other feeling, every other thought.

"It's okay, Ed, it's okay."

Marion's words cut through the thick, heavy panic that lies on me, surrounds me, engulfs me. And although I know it's not okay, her voice reaches out and touches me. The fear that gripped me only moments ago like a giant bird of prey slowly releases me from its clutches.

I can't feel my legs. The impossible thought remains, but the great bird is gone. It's only when the words are spoken, I realize, that I'm seized by the talon-fear. I won't say them aloud again.

I hear the voices of many people. Something is being placed around my neck, and I'm in an ambulance. I know it's an ambulance because of the flashing lights which mean someone is hurt or sick or having a baby. I hope, as I always do when I hear the siren and see the flashing lights, that it's a baby.

Someone is asking me if I can feel this or that, but I don't know if I'm responding. I'm on a table and I see Marion and a man who seems to be talking to me or perhaps to Marion. I'm not sure because everything is getting fuzzy and then there is nothing.

<u>Jennifer</u>

I'm not sure if I was reading my first-year-law contracts book or dozing, but I wasn't looking at the highway. First I felt the car drift. That's what made me look up. One side of the car was already over the edge of the road. I looked at Mom, half amused, to tease her about having let the car move out of the lane.

Mom was turning the wheels in the direction of the drift, and for a moment it worked. We began moving toward the centre of the highway.

Then we slid again. We were still on the ice. We were out of control with no way to stop, no way to slow down, no way to put the VCR on pause while we figured out what to do.

There was a moment when we left the road the second time, when I knew there was no going back.

The car was going too fast, the trees too close. Somehow, some way, we were going to crash. Crash hard. There was no way out.

I waited.

Waited to see what our lives would be. In all my twenty-seven years, it was the most helpless feeling I've ever known. I was a passenger in this Greek drama. Enormous forces of fate, weather, physics, all at work in a careening, screeching, warp-speed sequence with us at its centre, motionless, waiting.

I don't remember an articulate thought. Just the waiting. Waiting for pain. Waiting for a tree through the windshield, the crunch of the roof on my head, the screaming sound of metal as it impaled me. I couldn't protect myself from the assault because I didn't know how it would happen. I just knew that it would. That my body would be mutilated. That there would be pain.

It seemed Mom and I were at the centre of the vortex, with the back of the car spinning around creating centrifugal force. The force of the slide whipped the back around, turning us facing the way we came. It felt like a stately, graceful, inevitable arc, pushing us over. As the car started to flip, I raised my hands to the roof as though to brace myself from hitting the ceiling.

Then we hit.

Hard, so hard. The crash felt solid. I don't know how to describe the force. Greater than anything I've ever felt. The tail of the car whipped a bit more. Then we were still.

It took a second to realize nothing else was going to happen. I was hurt, but not badly. Nothing had pierced my skin. First order of business, status report.

"I'm okay," I called. Mom answered, "I think I'm okay." Then Dad, "I'm okay."

A miracle.

I heard people running toward the car. Yelling about gas. We had to get out.

I became aware of my surroundings. It was dark. We were upside down. I was hanging in the seat belt. I couldn't see anything. I couldn't get out. I could hear people trying to get Mom's door open, people talking to Dad, shouting about gas, about getting away from the car.

I was trapped. I tried to find the door handle, tried to find the seat belt buckle. Mom called to me that the ignition was still on. Tried to roll down the window. I couldn't find the button. I found the seat belt buckle, but it wouldn't release me. Somehow, I had to relieve the tension on the seat belt. I reached over my head and braced myself off the ceiling, then traced my finger back along the belt and pushed the button. It released. I fell, head first, to the roof of the car, now the floor of the car. I was completely disoriented.

The first thing I saw, in the Between Time, was Dad. Light was pouring in through the broken window, pouring over Dad's body, on his back, out in the snow. I'll see that vision to my dying day, may it be many decades from today.

There were men helping him. One man had his hands under Dad's armpits, pulling him from the car.

I shouted, "Don't move him! Don't move him! I'm trained for this. I can help him."

I tried to crawl between the seats, but something was in my way. I realized Dad was blocking the window, anyway. I tried to open the door, but the car was up against the trees and I could only open it a crack. I could hear people trying to get Mom's door open, Dad telling people to help us, shouting about the gas.

I called again, "Don't move him. I can't get out of the car. If you can get me out, I can help him."

A man left Dad's side and came to help me. I could feel the blow to my head and shoulders. It occurred to me vaguely that I shouldn't move until I'd been X-rayed in case my neck was broken. Only vaguely. Not enough to keep me from getting to Dad.

He asked if Mom was out of the car yet. If I was okay. About the gas.

"Better get me out of here," he said. "I don't want to be near this thing when she blows."

I refused. I don't know why. I knew there was gas. I thought Dad was fine, I really did. He looked fine. He sounded fine. So why wouldn't I let people move him? And why did anyone listen to me? I'd just crawled out of a car wreck on my hands and knees, a young woman, disoriented, hurt.

I told a man to get an ambulance. He said his wife had already gone. I sent him for boards to put under Dad's head and neck.

I started checking Dad for injuries. I had no idea what I was doing. I knew there was an order of things I was supposed to follow, but my mind was blank. Completely calm. Completely blank.

First I checked Dad's skin. Warm and dry. Any trouble breathing? No? Good. Pulse steady. Scan for blood, none visible.

I bumped his arm and he cried out in pain. He said he thought it was broken. People were milling around. I felt his arm, but couldn't find a break. The other arm was good. I moved to the stomach. Internal injuries? I raised his shirt and undid his pants. Loosen the clothing. That sounded right. How do I search for internal injuries? I couldn't remember. I looked for bruising, pooling of blood. Nothing. Gently I pushed on his stomach.

"Does that hurt?"

"I can't even feel it."

I don't know why I didn't pick up on that. I thought he meant I was pushing too gently for him to feel it. I should have known then. Maybe he just didn't seem hurt that badly. I was being cautious, after all. And there was clearly nothing wrong with him. I was just following some crisis autopilot. But I should have known then.

I was really worried about Mom. She was still trapped in the car. Should I go to her? But she hadn't sounded hurt, and other people were helping her. People better suited to prying open a door. If I left Dad people would try to move him. Where were those boards to support his head?

I just kept talking calmly to Dad, reassuring him. Trying to soothe the panicked sound in his voice.

"You're okay," I said. "Your heartbeat's even, circulation is good. Your fingernails are pink. That's all great. I don't see any blood, just two little cuts on your face. Don't worry. Mom's fine. She's getting out of the car now. Yes, I'm fine, too. Perfect. Not a scratch. I'm just going to check your legs now for injuries. Does this hurt?"

It's hard to write the next line. My pen moved twice, three times toward the page. Each time I hesitated.

That question marked the end of the Between Time and the beginning of the After Time. After everything changed.

When I asked that question, we were all still okay. When Dad answered, everything was terribly wrong. The Before Time was gone forever.

So many people milling around. So much snow. My knees must have been cold, but I don't remember. Numb, I guess, inside and out. No aches, no pain, no fears. Just motion, endless motion. And stillness, endless stillness. Endless. Forever.

"Does this hurt?" I asked again, feeling Dad's ankle. His legs were scrunched up against the frame of the car. An awkward angle, I thought, but best not to change the alignment of his back by straightening them.

"I can't feel anything."

I traced my way up his legs. No obvious wounds. There was blood on his upper thigh. I touched it.

"You've got blood on your leg. Does this hurt?"

"I can't feel anything."

I remember being vaguely aware that there was blood on my fingers. Bright. Red. How strange, to have your fingers covered in someone else's blood. Your father's blood.

I continued the body survey, this time for sensation. No feet, no legs, no stomach. Wait. Try this the other way round. Head, yes. Arms, yes. Shoulders, yes. Chest, no. Go back. Upper chest, yes. Lower chest, no.

My God.

I don't remember being upset. I rechecked the vitals. All good. I kept talking to Dad, reassuring him.

"Just tell me I'm not paralyzed."

I didn't miss a beat.

"Believe it or not, Dad, there are more important things right now. Your breathing, your circulation, blood loss and shock. And all those things on you are good. Those are the things that can really get us in trouble. And you're doing great. You don't have any problems there at all."

Mom appeared. Dad looked up at her.

"I think I'm paralyzed."

I remembered the gas. The ignition was on, but the engine was off. It seemed the lesser of the two evils. I told Mom to wrap some boards in blankets and hold them next to Dad's head to keep him from moving. She looked worried. I felt perfectly calm. I wonder why.

I kept checking Dad's vitals and reassuring him.

Checking, rechecking, keeping him warm. Stop moving your head. Keep it absolutely still.

Mom was kneeling by Dad's head, holding the boards. Her eyes met mine. She was worried. Silent, unsoothable worry.

The firefighters arrived. I gave them a quick rundown on our status. They listened curiously, as if they half wondered who the hell I was and how I got there first.

Mom. She said she was okay but would she lie? I checked her vital signs, surveyed for blood, breaks, pain, shock. She smiled when I checked her fingertips for blood flow. Like it was silly. I didn't care. Then I checked myself.

So calm. I remembered my St. John Ambulance course. The instructor said we might think we wouldn't remember what to do. But don't worry, he said, in a crisis it will all come back to you. God, I thought, I hope so. I hope I took care of him okay. I pray I didn't make a mistake.

I looked down at Dad, still on his back in the snow. At the firefighters kneeling over him where I used to be. At the blood on my fingers.

2

<u>Marion</u>

For a moment I felt the peculiar floating motion of a vehicle out of control on a slippery highway. I knew we had hit black ice, that most treacherous of all road hazards, and a quick surge of panic rose from wherever it is that panic lies when it isn't clawing at your throat. But a part of me remained cool and reasoning. I kept my foot off the brake, as I had been told a thousand times to do, turned the wheels in the direction of the skid, and waited.

I felt the wheels make contact with the pavement again and with a sigh of relief began to get the Explorer under control. But the respite was tragically brief. We hit another patch of ice, and the SUV turned completely around. It struck the road shoulder going backwards still at highway speed, and I knew the accident was inevitable.

"I'm going to die," I thought to myself. "I wonder if it'll hurt."

The next thing I was aware of was hanging upside down suspended in my seat belt. Before I had time to wonder if Jennifer, sitting in the front seat beside me, had been hurt, I heard her call out that she was okay. As I replied that I was okay, too, I thought of Ed lying in the back of the Explorer and wearing no seat belt. For a long, agonizing moment there was only silence. In that moment, I died the proverbial thousand deaths, thinking the worst that, not belted in, he would have been thrown around like a rag doll. Or thrown out of the vehicle to be crushed under it, or smashed against the rocks.

When Ed had decided in Gander to lie down out back, I tried to talk him out of it. Like everyone else, we had all been conditioned to wear the belts and felt uncomfortable and insecure without them. But Ed had insisted he was in too much pain to sit up, and stretched himself out on a makeshift bed we finally set up for him.

He had been in terrible pain in his lower back all through Christmas, so much so that he was, for the first time in twenty-six years, unable to play piano for our annual Christmas Eve carol sing. We urged him all through Christmas to go see about it, and finally he made an appointment with our doctor for Monday, January 5. Against the wishes of the whole family, he decided to go to Gander for the trustee-staff Christmas dinner of his health care board on Friday, January 2.

"I'm chair," he said, "so I should be there."

Now here we were on Saturday, January 3, 1998, upside down in some trees, and listening desperately for the sound of his voice.

"I'm okay."

When it finally came, the relief threatened to choke me as much as the panic had a few moments ago.

Someone was pulling the door open and releasing me from the seat belt apparatus and helping me out of the vehicle. Several men were already standing around Ed, who was half in and half out of the car. Jennifer was kneeling by his side.

"He says he can't feel his legs," I heard someone say, but everything was confused and the words had no immediate impact on me.

It must have been longer, much longer, but it seemed only moments before the ambulance arrived and then the police. Later we learned that the ambulance and the police had already been dispatched to an accident a few miles back, and had continued on to us when no one there was seriously hurt. The Badger Fire Chief had been attending a funeral in the cemetery a kilometre or so from the town, and was on the scene almost immediately. Ed would no doubt say that if you're going to be killed, it might as well be near a cemetery.

Jennifer and I climbed aboard the ambulance with Ed, a paramedic and a doctor. As the ambulance was turning around to get back to the hospital in Grand Falls-Windsor, I remembered the comment about Ed's legs. But even now I was sure that Ed was in shock and didn't know what he was saying, or else the problem was temporary. It wasn't until I asked the doctor about it that I realized something could be very seriously wrong.

"Ed evidently said something about not being able to feel his legs," I said. "Could that be a temporary thing?"

"I don't know," he replied, and I realized he was avoiding looking at me directly. "It's difficult to say right now."

He could have said, "Oh, I'm sure it's nothing serious," or "He'll probably be fine," or "There's nothing to worry about yet." But he didn't. Despite the shock I was in, a part of me knew why. I glanced at Jennifer, but she had either not overheard or was keeping her feelings to herself. Ed seemed to be conscious, but totally unaware of where he was or what was happening.

In the emergency room of the hospital, a young doctor named Harrison examined Ed carefully. He kept poking him with something sharp and asking Ed if he could feel it. As his hands moved higher up Ed's body, my heart sank lower with each negative response.

"We'll have to take some X-rays to be sure how serious it is," Dr. Harrison said, but there was nothing in either his face or his voice to give me hope.

While we were waiting for the X-rays, I called our daughter, Kathy, in Springdale, told her about the accident and asked her to make sure the rest of the family was told. Then Jenny and I sat and waited. I don't remember what we talked about or if we talked at all. Both of us were still in shock. It seemed to be forever but actually it was a little over an hour before the doctor reappeared. We didn't have to ask the question.

"I have bad news," he said. "He has a spinal cord injury. He's paraplegic."

The stark reality of the words hit us both like a giant fist. Ed, who loved to wander around the ponds in spring searching for trout; Ed, who spent every possible moment in the fall and winter hiking his rabbit trails; Ed, who loved being out on the salt water in his boat looking for mackerel feeding on the surface; Ed, who was so healthy and in such good shape; Ed would never walk again?

It was too much to take in all at once. It would take days and weeks for the full impact of this to strike us. But in the emergency room of the Central Newfoundland Hospital, there was no escaping the unbelievable, crushing words.

"He has to be transferred to the Health Sciences Centre in St. John's," the doctor said, "so arrangements have to be made for that."

In my confused state of mind, I didn't know what to do next. Then I remembered that the CEO of the hospital, Don Keats, was a friend of Ed's so I called him for advice. Again, I don't remember the exact details, but I do know that Don arrived almost immediately and supervised the details of getting us to Gander and on to St. John's. Jennifer, in the meantime, had to go back to Springdale with Rod, Kathy's husband, because there was no room for her in the air ambulance plane.

No one was thinking of anyone except Ed at this point, so Jennifer and I paid no attention to our own injuries. Jennifer had examined me briefly at the accident scene and I had only a few bruises. We were to learn weeks later that Jennifer was not only suffering from the trauma of the accident and the shock of her father's injuries, but also she had a concussion, a sprained wrist, a lot of bruising and a neck injury as well.

Jennifer

I can still see Mom standing at the head of Dad's bed as they prepared to take him for X-rays. She was half-dressed from her own checkup. Pants on bottom. Blue gown on top. Holding a hospital mobile phone in her hands. Hovering. As they took Dad for X-rays, Mom leaned over and kissed him, then quietly touched his hair.

That's when I knew. My parents haven't kissed in front of me in fifteen years. Something was wrong. Odd, isn't it. Until that moment I wasn't upset, wasn't consciously worried. But then my throat constricted, my eyes started to tear. I had to escape to a private place to compose myself. I found a bathroom, splashed water on my face. Stared at my own reflection in the mirror and said out loud, "Come on, Jennifer. You're supposed to be cool in a crisis. Hold it together."

While we waited for the X-ray results, Mom and I paced the hospital hallways. Sometimes we joked and laughed. A nurse showed us to the waiting room, but there was only one empty seat. A sea of blankly curious faces stared back at us. Their eyes followed us from the seats, peered out from examining rooms. An elderly man sat in the hallway in a wheelchair, watching.

The doctor came. The results were in.

"I have bad news. It's a spinal cord injury. He's paraplegic."

Straight. To the point.

Mom put her hand over her eyes, bowed her head and started to cry. I put my arm around her shoulders. It was so soon. It had been barely an hour since the Before Time. A time when this only happened to other people. Nameless, faceless people.

"Will he ever recover?"

The doctor hesitated.

"We know you can't say for sure, but what do you think? What's your best guess?"

"I don't think he'll ever walk again." The doctor spoke slowly and watched Mom carefully. She continued to cry.

"Why couldn't this have happened to me? I could cope. Ed doesn't know how to cope."

I knew what she meant. I knew she was right. I knew it didn't matter.

We hugged. The two of us. In that strange hospital. Surrounded by strangers. Strangers watching us, inserting themselves into the most screamingly painful, earth-shattering hour of our lives.

Looking back, I feel horror remembering our movements. Not because we fell apart. Because we coped. I called people on the phone. Mom asked what happened next. We offered to give blood. We paced the hallways, waiting for Dad to come back on the stretcher from X-rays. Brave, strong Mom, asking the doctors about air ambulances and helicopters. Coping. Moving forward. Doing what had to be done.

It's horrible that we kept moving, meeting the challenges. By rights, the world should have stopped at that moment while we sank to our knees and wailed in grief. While we adjusted to the crisis. While the numbness wore off and the pain set in.

We were less than an hour from home.

Mom should have gone to her Girl Guide meeting. Dad should have checked out his bad back, bottled his blueberry wine. I should have flown back to law school and written my exams. Instead, we walked the halls of that hospital, waiting for Dad to come back so we could tell him he was paralyzed. Waiting for Kathy and Aunt Marilyn to arrive so we could shatter their world with words. Organizing and planning the details of our new life, being smart and strong and capable in the face of the unfixable, uncopable, unplannable.

I remember looking back into those stares of the people in the waiting room. They knew that something bad had happened. That we were the reason all those nurses and doctors were there. I stared back, remembering the times I'd been on their side of this exchange, wondering what was going on on my side. I didn't expect I'd ever know. I imagined myself behind their eyes, looking at us. Pacing the hallway, arms folded, holding back tears, eyes red. I'd never be on their side again. In this game, you only trade places once.

The elderly man still sits in his wheelchair. My God, that will be my father. Sitting to one side, talking to no one. I know this reality; I don't need to see it. Not now. Not before I'm ready. Take it away. Wheel away, old man, into someone else's nightmare. Don't be there every time I open my eyes and drag my head from the sand.

I walk past into Dad's room. He's back. Does he know yet? I asked the doctor. His eyebrows raised. I had to tell him, he said, of course he knows. I stopped. I hadn't expected that. I'd been waiting for the family conference where the doctor delivered the news and we all... what? I didn't know. I look past him into Dad's exam room. For the first time I didn't want it to be real. To see Dad's eyes, knowing. Would I panic? Would I cry? I squared my shoulders.

"Hi, Dad."

"Hi, honey."

I stroked my fingers through his hair.

"That feels nice," he said.

Medical people were milling around, getting Dad ready for transfer to St. John's. I needed fresh air. Mom had disappeared. Probably crying somewhere by herself so I wouldn't see and be upset. As if I don't know. As if I'm not already upset. As if this will be okay if neither of us shows our pain in front of the other.

I fold my arms against the cold and walk toward the sliding doors of the emergency room. They part for me. Making way for my pain, just as the nurses, doctors and waiting room people do. They don't avoid me, even ask how I am at times. They don't seem to expect an answer. It's a gesture. I move past, as the sea of people parts for me. I don't feel any emotions, but still I can feel the tears lurking in the background, waiting for their chance. The three of us are alone here in this strange place. It feels more real than anything I've ever known. Each moment and detail vivid, etched. And yet, it's too intense to last. We can't keep this up forever. Soon we'll go back to our other life.

The sliding doors close behind me. I'm on the curb. I look toward the parking lot for familiar faces. None. Don, who towed Dad's Explorer to the garage, is there.

He ambles up to me. Points to my face. "That's a heck of a shiner." I smiled. I guess it was weak. He put his hand on my shoulder. Looked at me kindly. "Everything's fine," he said. "Your Dad's okay."

I turned, looked at him, said the words for the first time, shaking my head slowly.

"No. He's not."

Later, much later, as we left the emergency ward, following Dad's stretcher out the door on his way to the ambulance, I took one last look at the old man in the wheelchair. He met my eyes.

Then he leaned forward, stood up and walked away.

I didn't want to leave the hospital. Standing on the curb, watching the ambulance pull away, I knew someone was going to try and make me leave.

Something had gone wrong. I used to have things to do. People were counting on me. Life and death decisions. Now I'm being shepherded, ordered around, cared for, controlled, separated from the sequence. No! Stop! If I can't keep moving I'll fall apart. If you love me give me back some control. Let me deal with this. Face it. Move forward. I have two choices. Surf the wave or drown in it. Don't let me drown. Don't hold my head still, under the water, until the last pocket of air slips from my lungs, sealing my fate.

Aunt Marilyn wants me to leave. I knew she would. I'm not ready. Right now this nightmare is contained in this hospital. Now it starts to leak. To the car, the highway, the house, to neighbours, to tomorrow. When I wake up tomorrow, how long before I remember?

I didn't ask for this. But now it's all I have. I'm separated from the sequence. Now they're separating me from the place.

I look around for alternatives. None.

I leave. I pack the baggage I'll carry forever, and walk into the world. The future.

3

Marion

By the time the ambulance reached Gander, the next-closest thing to a blizzard was well underway. The plane was waiting for us on the open Tarmac, and the ambulance personnel had a real problem in the snow and wind trying to get Ed up into it.

Ed had been given enough sedative to knock out a horse, so he was completely unaware. It was just as well. He was so claustrophobic that flying in the best of times was nothing short of a nightmare for him. The nurse, Doreen Wriggit, told me that his fingers were squeezing her hand each time she spoke to him. I was hoping he wouldn't wake up completely until we were on the ground.

Mercifully, we were able to taxi into a hangar out of the storm at the St. John's airport. An ambulance driver came aboard the plane and after conferring briefly with Doreen shouted to the other driver out in the hangar.

"This fellow's got a C6 break and he's paralyzed."

Doreen was furious. She crawled over me in her haste to get to the driver, making hand motions for him to stop. It was highly inappropriate that other people in the hangar should learn about Ed's condition that way, even before we got him to the hospital. Even more important, we didn't know how close Ed was to consciousness, or what his reaction might be to hearing this being shouted. The ambulance driver was unrepentant.

"He's got to find out about it sometime," he said flatly.

The ambulance carried us to the Health Sciences Centre which includes the largest hospital in the province. Ed was immediately taken for tests and still seemed to be out of it. The rest of that long, first night is a blur. I called my friend, Kay Bradley, who is like a sister to me, and she came to the hospital immediately. Ed's sister, Pat, and her daughter, Jackie; my brother, Fred, and his daughter, Sian, were all waiting for us when we arrived. Ed was taken for X-rays and a CT scan, and from there to a special care room around 3:00 A.M.

When they had put him to bed, I went in to see him once more before leaving the hospital. He was naked except for a sheet that came up to his waist, and he was shivering with cold. I went out to see the nurse about some blankets.

"Ed is very cold," I said. "I'd like to get a blanket for him."

"You'll have to wait until we finish report," she said, "and then we'll look after it."

I was given a copy of the hospital regulations. They didn't seem all that important at that point.

I went back to Ed's bed. He was absolutely perishing. Sian was wearing a long winter coat and we covered him with that. When I was sure he was relatively comfortable, I went back to Kay's house and fell asleep in my clothes.

At eight, I was back in the hospital to make sure Ed knew I was there. Apart from everything else, his acute claustrophobia would make the small, curtained-off cubicle almost intolerable. Perhaps my being there would make a difference.

A nurse met me at the entrance to the ward and handed me another copy of the regulations.

"Visiting hours don't start until eleven," she said, barring my way.

I told her who I was.

"I just have to let him know I'm here," I explained.

"It makes no difference. You cannot go in there at this hour."

I tried again to be reasonable.

"My husband is claustrophobic. I don't know how the trauma of the accident will affect his being in a small space like this. It may make him much worse. Whatever, if he knows I'm here he'll probably handle it better."

The nurse was unmoved.

"You cannot go in there until eleven o'clock."

My brief flirtation with patience ended abruptly. "My husband is in there. He has just suffered a major injury. He is also claustrophobic. He will need to know I'm here. I am going in."

And with that I walked around her into the room and over to Ed's bed. He was conscious and so thirsty he could hardly speak. They had screwed some kind of apparatus into his skull designed to keep his neck and head from moving around. Whether because of that or the confined space or both, he had an almost pathological fear of being left alone, but I assured him I would be right outside and that seemed to calm him a little. When I came out, I was given a third copy of the regulations.

Promptly at eleven, I was back in the room and stayed there until eleven that night. At Kay's, I again simply fell on the bed exhausted in mind and in body. My only thought was to be in Ed's room as early as possible next day.

The next morning was a repeat of the one before. The nurse kept telling me I was breaking the rules, and gave me yet another copy of the appropriate regulations. I told her I knew I was breaking the rules and I was sorry about that, but nothing would keep me from letting Ed see that I was there. Again, I went in, gave him a drink, spoke to him for a few moments and went outside to await the appropriate time for visitors.

As I entered the room at eleven, another nurse looked out from behind the curtain of one of the other beds. She spoke immediately and without any greeting.

"The nursing station is being swamped with calls," she said. "You have to do something about it."

I didn't quite understand what she meant.

"But I have no idea who's calling. How can I stop them if I don't know who they are?"

The nurse didn't answer and disappeared behind the screen, leaving me still wondering what I could do. When I told Fred about it, he immediately went to the hospital administration and stated his view that this was their concern and not one they should be calling on a family member

to correct. I believe they resolved the problem by not for-
warding calls to the nursing station from the switchboard
and refusing to give out any information on Ed.

That worked fine until our son, Rob, tried to get in to
see his father. Rob had been home in Iqaluit only a few days
from having spent Christmas with us when Kathy called him
with the news. He had immediately jumped the earliest aircraft and was in St. John's the next day. He came directly to
the hospital and, not knowing the logistical problems they
were having, asked the person at the nursing station how Ed
Smith was doing. She told him she wasn't allowed to give
out any information on Mr. Smith.

Rob was a bit taken aback by that, but thought he'd try
again and asked what room Mr. Smith was in. The woman
told him she wasn't allowed to give out that information,
either. Poor Rob was already very upset and getting more so
by the minute.

"But I'm his *son!*" he pleaded.

"Oh," she said, "I didn't know. Of course I'll tell you
where he is." And she did.

It was clear to me that Ed could not be left alone at
night. He was paralyzed, after all, although we didn't know
to what extent. The various machines hooked up to other
patients were noisy enough that he couldn't be heard if he
were to choke on something or call out. I asked the nurse
about it.

"Having someone stay here overnight is quite impossible," she said. It was a response I should have expected.

"It doesn't have to be one of the staff," I pointed out.
"We'll pay for a private duty nurse. Or one of the family or
a friend could be with him."

"I'm sorry," the nurse said, "but that's against regulations."

I wasn't about to give up.

"Is there someone else I can talk to about this?"

"Yes," she said. "You can speak with the supervisor
when she comes in tomorrow."

The next morning the supervisor called me into her
office. As I walked down the hall I was expecting that she
wanted to respond to my request for a private duty nurse for
Ed at night. I also thought she might be interested in how I

was doing and if there was anything I needed. Instead, I was asked to sit down in a chair across from her desk and was read the riot act.

The same theme was repeated and hammered at me for forty-five minutes. I was breaking the rules. Rules were there for a reason. Rules could not be ignored. If everyone was allowed to break the rules, there would be chaos. Over and over, on and on. I tried to break into the lecture and explain that I knew all that, but felt I had no choice. Perhaps there was some compromise we could reach, perhaps...

But she wasn't listening at all. I was presented with another copy of the rule book, and dismissed.

Less than three days ago I'd been the driver in a terrible car accident that had left my husband paralyzed. I'd gotten practically no sleep and was still in the clothes I'd been wearing at the time. No one on that staff had asked if I needed help or counselling or even if I'd been injured in any way. Instead, all I got was grief for not complying with their stupid rules. I found a chair in a small waiting area, sank into it and cried as though I would never stop.

I didn't see the woman approach, but suddenly she was speaking to me and handing me a piece of paper.

"This is my name and address," she was saying. "I live just around the corner from the hospital. If you ever need to talk to someone or have a cup of tea, I'll be there."

And she was gone as quickly and as quietly as she appeared.

I've always responded to kindness emotionally, especially when I'm down, and this brought on a whole new spell of crying.

If my face hadn't been in my hands, I might have seen the supervisor, accompanied by a man, sail by and on into Ed's room. I couldn't help but notice, however, when she returned a few moments later, bent over me anxiously and asked if I was all right.

Where was that change of heart coming from?

"No," I replied, still weepy and too upset to observe the niceties of language, "but I was okay before you started shitting on me."

"I really didn't mean to do that," she said, sincerity and tenderness dripping from every syllable. "Can I get you a cup of coffee? Is there anything at all I can do for you?"

I was totally astonished. A half-hour ago she was about to toss me out of the building and now she's a combination of Florence Nightingale and Mother Teresa. It made no sense, but I was too weary to try understanding it.

"No," I said again. "I'm going in to see my husband."

"That's fine," she said with a smile. "Just let me know if you have a problem."

Mentally shaking my head, I almost bumped into the man coming out of Ed's room. He smiled and walked on by.

Ed was barely able to speak. His voice was thick, his breathing ragged and he spoke in broken phrases. Even so, he was still trying to find a spark of humour even in this situation. I can't reproduce his speech but I could certainly understand what he was saying.

"Hello," Ed said. "Where have you been?"

"Outside. I see you had a visitor. Who is he, anyway?"

"Oh, no one of any importance. I don't know him that well, but we've met at a few meetings. Nice of him to come down and see me." All said with no little difficulty.

"Okay, but who is he?!"

"You mean you really don't know?"

I had a feeling Ed was playing one of his little games.

"No! I don't know. Tell me who he is!"

Ed let a moment or two pass before answering. He was enjoying this, even with a broken neck.

"He's Dr. Jerry Barton, the medical director of this great institution."

From then on, I had no problem seeing Ed whenever I wanted to. I tried not to be obtrusive or get in anyone's way, but I was in the room at eight each morning and didn't leave until almost eleven at night. No one questioned me or asked me to leave or was anything but pleasant. And best of all, we were permitted to have someone sit by Ed's bed all night.

I asked our daughter, Kathy, to remain in Springdale for a few days to handle things at that end. There were people to be called and our house made secure. We had left home at the height of the Christmas season expecting only to be gone overnight. The place was an absolute war zone with the trappings of the season strewn everywhere. We were going to be gone a long time and someone had to try to bring some order to our cluttered home. It had to be someone close enough to us to know what to do and that someone was obviously Kathy. She agreed to stay but she was most unhappy about it.

"I'd be satisfied if I could only talk to Dad," she said. "Can't you put him on the phone?" She so desperately wanted to talk to her father that I knew something had to be done.

The problem was that there were no phone jacks in the special care room and Ed certainly couldn't be moved. We talked to the staff about it and they said it was simply not possible for Ed to phone Kathy. They were reckoning without my brother, Fred.

Fred likes to say that nothing is impossible; some things just take longer than others. It was Fred who now came to the rescue. For the better part of a day he worked on the 'impossible' problem. He consulted with Newtel. He scrounged up phone lines and somewhere found a phone. With Rob and his cousin Gavin's help he laid a line from the special care room across the corridor and to a phone jack in another room. Then he had Rob and Gavin stand on the wire crossing the corridor so that no one would trip over it. Fred wasn't worried that someone might break a neck. He just didn't want the phone line pulled out of the jack.

Finally everything was ready. I lifted the receiver and heard a beautiful dial tone. A moment or two later Ed was talking to Kathy and I knew she'd be fine from then on.

Two days later they still hadn't decided what to do with Ed. The neurologist was at a loss to understand why he was paralyzed because the injury to his vertebrae wasn't severe enough to cause it. A second CT scan solved the mystery. The spinal canal through which the spinal cord runs is abnormally narrow in Ed. A trauma from which anyone with a normal spine would have walked away caused him to be paralyzed for the rest of his life.

I asked Dr. Goodwin if not wearing a seat belt would have contributed to the injury.

"Not at all," he said. "Your husband has been leading a charmed life. Almost any blow would have had a similar result—riding a snowmobile, falling on ice in your driveway—anything. The vertebrae had only to move slightly and the spinal cord would have been damaged. If he had been wearing a seat belt, chances are the whipping around of the vehicle would have had the same result or worse."

We were given two choices. One was to put Ed in traction and wait for the vertebrae to heal, a process that would take several months. The other was to operate now and fuse the vertebrae with a sliver of bone taken from his hip.

I asked if there would be any risk with surgery. Yes, Dr. Goodwin said, any invasive procedure carries risks, primarily from infection, but no more in Ed's case than any other. Could the surgery cause further paralysis? At this point I was still thinking paraplegia because the nurse in the airplane had said repeatedly that Ed was squeezing her hand. No, he said, there was no risk of that in this case. I talked it over with Fred and decided on surgery.

As might be expected, Ed was restless the night before his operation. Jennifer and Robbie wanted to stay with him all night so that one of them would always be awake if their father wanted something. To put it mildly, they had an active night. Ed wanted to have poetry read to him, he wanted to sing songs and have them sing songs to him. I guess he was doing everything he could to keep his mind off surgery.

Finally, Jennifer found somewhere to lie down for a nap, leaving Robbie to entertain his father. They were in the middle of a reading or a song or something when Ed said suddenly, "I'm running a fever."

Rob looked at him closely and felt his hands.

"No, Dad," he said, "you don't have any fever."

"Yes I do," his father said. "Feel my neck."

When the children were small, Ed could always tell if they had a fever or not by placing his hand on the back of their necks. He was amazingly accurate.

Rob felt his neck.

"No Dad," he said again, "you don't have a fever."

"You don't know anything. Call Jennifer. She'll know I have a fever."

"I can't call Jennifer, Dad. She just went for a nap. She's really tired. But I'm telling you, you don't have a fever."

"What do you know? Jennifer will know I have a fever. Call Jennifer."

This went on for some time until finally Rob had no choice but to go wake up Jennifer.

"I know I have a fever but Rob says I don't," Ed said when she came into the room. "Would you put your hand on my head and tell him?"

So Jennifer dutifully placed her hand on his face and neck.

"No, Dad," she said, "you don't have a fever."

"Okay, my dear," Ed said, "if you say so."

Rob was really rotted.

"I tell him time after time he doesn't have a fever," he said grinning, "and he doesn't believe me. I'm staying up all night with him, too, and he won't believe me. Then Jennifer comes in and says once that he doesn't have a fever and he believes her. What am I, chopped liver?"

On Wednesday morning they wheeled Ed into the operating room.

4

My bed is rushing down a corridor at great speed. I know I'm on a bed, but I don't think to wonder why because this is a dream, and things just happen in dreams.

I'm in a large white chamber. There are ledges of different heights, one of which I'm standing on and looking around to see what kind of place this is. It seems to be made of snow because nothing else is that white. I have the distinct impression that someone else is here, but I can see no one. The chamber itself and its ledges keep changing and undulating, although they never seem to lose shape.

Some people are standing around me and trying to push something long and slippery down my throat, but it doesn't seem to be going where it should. It doesn't hurt, but I know something's wrong.

"It's not working," I say, "it's not going in there properly."

"It's not going in there properly," a voice directly above my head is saying. I want to tell him I just said that, but now they're trying to get this thing down my throat again, and it still won't go.

"It's still not in there right," I say to the voice above me, and again my words are echoed.

"It's still not in there right."

I hear another voice, and yet another, but I can't hear what they're saying. Only the voice directly above me is clear.

"Let's try it one more time," I say to the voice above me.

As I knew it would, the voice repeats what I've said, except slowly and still more slowly. "Okay, now let's... try... one..."

I am suspended in a soft, fluid cloud of shades and shapes and nuances of sound. Phantom and shadow drift in and out, there but not there, real but not real. Voices with no words, rising and swirling around me like the liquid voices of the sea. Flowing and ebbing, ebbing and flowing. I float, I drift, I sink, I rise. I have no sense of time or place. I don't know where I am. I know only that I am here. I have no curiosity about where 'here' might be, or what it might be. I am waiting to be born. I am waiting to be.

Suddenly, I'm slipping, falling, sinking into a great darkness. Fire leaps out of the blackness, like the flames from a thousand midnight bonfires, and completely engulfs me. There is no sensation of burning. I'm conscious only of the dark and the paradoxical flames.

A moment, an eternity, passes before I feel myself being lifted out of the pit and into a purgatory of warmth and confusion and dreams. In another moment, another eternity, I'm being lowered again into the black inferno. Again I'm lifted. Again I'm lowered. Over and over, lifted and lowered and lifted.

I begin to hear Marion's voice, coming towards me from a great distance. She tells me she loves me. She says everything will be okay.

Then a different voice, a friend's voice, reciting lilting words, lulling me, willing me into drifting peacefully among the shadows and the sounds that are my world. The word-music whispers from somewhere close by.

On either side the river lie
Long fields of barley and of rye,
And through the fields the road runs by
On down to Camelot.

Gradually shapes grow more distinct and voices clearer. The voices of my family, the shapes of other people, emerge from out the amniotic mist in which I am suspended. They call to me and I struggle to respond. I see them clearly now, waiting anxiously for me to join them. I try harder but nothing happens.

The voices and the faces tell me it's all right. But it isn't all right. I can't respond. I can't communicate. I can't speak.

Marion

We were all in the family room outside the ICU waiting for the surgery to be over. Ed's parents, his sister, Jennifer, Robbie and me, and some others I don't remember. Actually, we had begun waiting up on the fifth floor near the special care room. There was a small lounge area on that floor, and it was here that we kept our vigil in the days and nights prior to the surgery. We believed that Ed would be brought back to his room after the operation and were quite surprised when he was taken to the intensive care unit.

We were each reacting differently to the tragedy now stalking our family. Some of us were talking quietly. Ed's father just sat there, his face a sombre mask, speaking only when spoken to. I could only guess what he and Ed's mother must be going through. The family room was crowded, mostly with friends of Ed's parents but also with friends of ours. Some of them just stood there as though they were at a funeral.

I had no sense of the passing of time, but finally the doctor on duty in the ICU came out to talk with us.

"The operation went well," she said, "although we're still not sure of the extent of the paralysis. Hopefully, he'll have some use of his hands. We also had to perform a tracheotomy because the anesthetist couldn't get the breathing tube down his throat."

"He's not doing well coming out of the anesthetic," she went on. "Perhaps you can talk to him and calm him down a little."

I wanted very much to see Ed, but I didn't know what to expect and tried to steel myself for whatever lay ahead.

He didn't look as bad physically as I feared. His face and neck were badly swollen and there was some bruising. But it was his eyes that I will never forget. They were wide open and wild and filled with terror. He was flailing his arms around his head and trying to tear out the tubes. Only the trach in his throat was keeping him from screaming out loud, although there was no doubt about the words his mouth was forming.

"Help me, help me!" he was pleading and, "Kill me, shoot me! Please shoot me!"

Over and over I told him I loved him, and that I would always be with him and we would still have a good life together. Gradually his eyes grew less wild and his arms stopped flailing. Later after the immediate family had been in to see him he finally closed his eyes and rested.

For the next several hours he drifted in and out of consciousness, and his times of alertness increased until we knew he was fully awake and understood where he was and what had happened. In the meantime, the staff in the ICU was just wonderful. Except for the necessary two visitors at a time rule they allowed us to come and go pretty much as we pleased, and took time they probably didn't have to explain what was happening to Ed. They certainly helped make a difficult time for us much easier than it might have been.

Jennifer

I'm sitting on a chair next to Dad's bed in the intensive care unit. Aunt Pat is standing next to me, and there's an intern at the foot of the bed writing notes on his chart. Dad is asleep. Every moment he's asleep we offer up silent thanks. When he's awake he mouths words to us such as "Help me," or "Shoot me," or just over and over "Help."

One of the most difficult parts of this ordeal is looking into my father's eyes and telling him I'm sorry, but I can't help him. I can't get him up. I can't take the tubes out. I can't shoot him and put him out of his misery.

He's going insane and I can't do anything to help him. I feel powerless and despondent, then I remember that it must be only a fraction of a thousandth of what he's feeling. He's going insane.

This has always been my father's nightmare. Just a few weeks ago Robbie and Dad and I had another of those continual conversations where Dad said he'd hate to be helpless. He'd rather be dead. Just don't let him have a stroke and not die.

Mom wasn't hurt much in the crash. She's a little sore but no impact injuries. I have a concussion, a sore shoulder, a bruised knee and miscellaneous aches and bruises.

Dad's neck was broken on impact. He has no sensation below his armpits. He can move his shoulders and elbows and has some movement in his wrists. He can't use his hands at all. He can't sit up. He can't roll over. He can't cough. He can never be left alone again.

He's quadriplegic.

He's sleeping, or more accurately drugged, in the bed beside my chair, and he has no idea I've just written a word that will change his life. For the first fifty-seven years of his life he was healthy and active, a big man, 6'2" and over two hundred pounds. He'll spend whatever years he has left in a wheelchair and that's the way he'll be defined forever.

"Ed Smith? Oh yes, fine fellow. Quadriplegic, you know."

ICU is pretty sunny today. There are about eleven beds in the room and six are occupied. Everyone seems sicker than Dad, which gives us a lot to be grateful for. The first night we were here Mr. Norman died in the bed next door. I'd like to say it was an earth-shattering event but it wasn't. The curtains were drawn, a lot of people bustled about, we couldn't get Dad's nurse's attention to move him to a more comfortable position, then people drifted away. It wasn't until I heard someone say to call the family and a minister that I suspected he'd passed away.

I guess people die all the time in ICU. Marcy Greene is brain-dead now. Alden Fancy is on a "Do Not Resuscitate" order. Mr. Matthews disappeared somewhere. I've come to realize that more often than not people come to intensive care to die.

I was worried that Dad would panic if someone died in the bed next door, but I don't think he even knew it happened. For all the understated quality, I don't think I'll forget it.

Good night, Mr. Norman, wherever you are.

Almost without warning, I am out of the mist. Without being told, I know where I am and why. I remember the accident and that I couldn't move my legs. Somehow I understand that nothing has changed.

Nothing has changed. My legs won't move. Dear God, my legs are dead! Does anyone know? I try to tell them. I try to scream it out so that they understand. I can't move my legs! But I can't scream. I open my mouth and nothing happens. The scream stays inside me and I can't get it out. It's growing and building and bursting inside me but I can't get it out. I must scream, I must scream!

The panic passes and the scream dies, still inside me.

For the moment I am composed, and I must hang onto that. I try to speak in normal tones, but again nothing happens. I can feel the panic moving deep inside me, ready to rise and engulf me again and I fight it down. But what's wrong? Why can't I even speak? Marion, where's Marion? She'll know. She'll tell me. I search around the bed and the people there, and suddenly there she is, standing close to me, her hand on my forehead.

"You'll be all right, my love," she's saying. "Nothing important has changed. I love you."

It's not the answer I'm looking for, but it's the one I need. I feel calmer and I can listen to what she's saying. And I can see the others, too, my adult children, my parents, my sister. They're all here. They shouldn't know I'm afraid. I've got to show them I'm not afraid.

Jennifer

Gumpy and I just sang Dad to sleep. First, Gumpy sang a beautiful song I didn't know. It was touching and bizarre at the same time. For the first time since the crash, Dad had a positively beatific look on his face. Still, he had a feeding tube running out of his nose and a Minerva brace up under his chin, and all the monitors whirring behind him. On the other side of the curtain behind us a nurse was literally shouting at another patient.

"David! David! DAVID! Move your feet! MOVE! Move your feet, David!"

In the midst of this raucous disorder and tragic injury, Gumpy was softly serenading his son, my father, into a peaceful sleep. It was beautiful. A beautiful island in a sea of chaos.

Marion tells me I've had a tracheotomy but it's only temporary and when it comes out I'll be able to speak. But I have things I need to say now. I'm thirsty. I'm too warm. I'm too cold. Don't leave me alone. I try to mouth the words, and sometimes I can make them understand that I need water or another blanket.

Jennifer suggests running down through the alphabet letter by letter, and me clicking my tongue when they come to the appropriate letter. This is a long and frustrating process, especially when I get confused halfway through what I want to say, but it's the only method we have for now.

The one thing I desperately need them to understand is how terrified I am of being alone without Marion or at least another family member being near me. But Marion already knows and there is never a moment without a member of the family or a close friend being near my bed. I have a vague but certain memory of Kathy, one especially difficult night, somehow finding room to get into my bed with me and wrapping her arms around me until I am quiet. She stays there the whole night.

Marion, it seems, is always there.

Through the haze of drugs and pain I hear someone singing. It's Jennifer and my father and it's beautiful. Then Father sings one of his favourite songs, "Makushla." He used to sing it to us when we were small. Did I ask him to sing it now? I don't remember and it doesn't matter. I am a child again being comforted by the sound of my father's voice telling me there are no monsters under the bed. I believe him and fall asleep.

"It's a great day to be on the water, my son."

I know what he means. Dawn is a pink promise on the eastern horizon. The lights of Musgravetown twinkle from astern growing fainter in the slowly lightening sky. The fading moon still finds its pale reflection on the mirror-ocean.

Dad's little boat drones steadily onward out the harbour toward the light of a new day. I watch him sitting there in utter contentment, his hand resting easily on the steering arm of the motor. I know he's only completely happy when he's on the water.

We get to the fishing grounds just as the sun is poking its nose over the distant hills. Father has his line in the water almost before I have the piece of squid-bait reeved onto my hook. He makes a few exploratory jigs.

"They're down there, my son," he says in a low voice, "they're down there."

I don't know why he's almost whispering. The fish aren't likely to hear him.

I stop thinking about that in a hurry because something is tugging like mad at my line and I begin to haul up the twenty fathom or so of monofilament hand over hand. Not so hard that the hook tears out, but not so easy that the fish shakes it out. It's a fine line, so to speak.

A fat codfish flops in over the gunnel, and as I'm taking it off the hook I see Father from the corner of my eye pulling steadily at what must be a really large one. The fish bite like crazy for a while, and when they finally slack off the fish box is almost full.

Time for breakfast. Out comes the homemade bread drenched with molasses and the Mason jar of cool, clear water. No feast laid before a king ever tasted any sweeter.

"I think," Dad says, always looking to explore new grounds, "we should try out around Jamestown Head."

I haul up the small grapnel that's anchoring the boat against the tide and we head farther out the bay. The sun is up now, and the sea is catching numerous glints of light and tossing them quickly from one tiny wavelet to another. The first line of what will almost surely be my next song rises easily from the sense of wonder of creation and the nearness of the Creator.

When at dawn the sun lights up the sparkles on the sea, I listen: Someone speaks to me.

Dad speaks again over the roar of the motor.
"It's a great day," he calls, his eyes fixed on the hazy outline of Jamestown Head in the distance, "to be on the water."
I know what he means.

Gradually, I come to realize I've been in hospital for quite some time. Between the accident itself and my surgery I was several days in a special care room waiting for the doctors to get on with it.

My days in special care will be referred to by future biographers as The Lost Days. Actually, the only person they're lost to is me. Everyone else remembers them quite well. I don't have a glimmer. They tell me I spoke rationally much of the time, which was a distinct improvement over my pre-accident speech.

I'm also told that the reason I was in special care for so long before having surgery was that the doctors couldn't understand why my paralysis was so extensive. Evidently, the injury to my neck wasn't all that serious. Well, of course it was serious. I could teach those fellows who lie on a bed of nails a thing or two. I could have someone driving four-inch nails up through the soles of my feet with a five-pound hammer and laugh at it ha ha. I could walk barefoot on hot coals and not notice anything except the smell. That's serious.

The problem seems to be that my spinal canal is abnormally narrow, so the spinal cord itself has no room for movement. When the vertebrae shifted a bit, therefore, the cord was crushed. The doctors say that a person with a normal spinal canal and with injuries similar to mine would simply walk away from such an accident.

Isn't that the news of the week.

5

The closeness of my immediate family is such that I accept their being here without question. Hopefully that doesn't mean I'm taking them for granted. Perhaps I take their love for granted. Whatever, I'm supremely confident about it. So I'm not surprised that my son, Rob, has flown in from Iqaluit on Baffin Island, or that my daughters, Kathy and Michelle, who both live in the province, are here very quickly.

Marion and I are especially concerned about Jennifer. In addition to suffering the trauma of the accident, she's supposed to be beginning her second semester at Harvard Law School. How long can she wait before she's too far behind? How can she return to Cambridge and focus on demanding courses with all this on her mind? But what a tower of strength she is to us, and how we will miss her when inevitably she has to return to her studies.

I'm told Jennifer was interviewed live on the CBC evening news, and that she was eloquent and moving. My sister taped it for me, but I'm not up to seeing that just now. Jenny has also given several interviews to newspapers and radio stations. Marion seems to be leaving the PR bit to her and that's a wise decision. Not only is Jennifer more experienced with that sort of thing, but also it takes such a load off Marion's shoulders. Frankly, I'm a little flattered and a lot surprised by all the media interest.

My parents, now in their eighties, have driven the more than two hundred kilometres from their home. Their anguish is in their eyes. My sister, Pat, who lives in St. John's, is here almost every waking hour, as is her husband, Bill, when he gets off work.

Marion's sister, Jennette, has flown in from Nova Scotia, and her brother, Fred, a physician on the West Coast, is here to help with the medical and logistical red tape. Marion tells me that the number of people who have already called or visited is simply incredible. Indeed, my family and friends seem to have taken over the family room of the ICU. Too bad they aren't allowed to barbecue out there. They could have one hell of a family reunion.

Rob and Gavin have constructed an alphabet board to speed up communications. The letters of the alphabet are divided into six separate groups and numbered accordingly. The other person simply moves her finger down the numbers until I click my tongue, and then moves her finger across the letters until again I click. It sounds awkward, but it's much faster than having nothing. My words are confined to the basic and the simple.

Swearing is a problem with the alphabet board. By the time I get it spelled out, I don't feel like swearing anymore. Hopefully, I'll be finished with the board the next time I ask Marion if she wants to go to bed now or what.

I signal I want to say something via the board. Kathy picks it up and begins moving her finger down the numbers as I click appropriately. A... C... E... T

"Dad, what are you trying to say? These letters aren't making any sense."

I signal to carry on. But now she's lost her place and has to begin over. A... C... E... T... A...

"Dad, you've already got an A. Are you beginning over again?"

I signal in the positive.

"Okay, let's go." Despite the condition of her poor crippled father, I sense just a little bit of impatience in daughter's voice. A... C... E... T... A... M... Y...

"Look, this is ridiculous! You're not spelling anything. Are you sure...?"

I signal I'm sure.

Kathy is a very bright girl (my side of the family). Suddenly she drops the alphabet board and stares me straight in the eye.

"Dad, are you trying to spell acetaminophen?"

I signal yes, and try to make my face show delight. Daughter turns to the others in exasperation. "Do you see what he's trying to spell? Acetaminophen! Acetaminophen, for God's sake!" And then turning to me again, "Why couldn't you spell 'pain' like you always do when you need—?" Then the light dawns. "Why, you've been leading me on, you sleeveen! You're not nearly as sick as we think you are!"

I don't know how sick they think I am. I know how sick I think I am and that's sick enough. But I'm not too sick to enjoy putting one over on an offspring. You've still got it, I say to myself with great satisfaction, you've still got it.

After a few days in ICU, I see things a little more clearly. My frequent visits down to hellfire, for example, were nothing more than having the head of my bed lowered for washing. It's amazing how strong and powerful those dark inferno images were. My dreams, too, are in dramatic living colour. Everything is larger-than-life. My dream-scenes are like enormous comic strip characters in comic book situations. Usually I'm the good guy with a host of larger-than-life bad guys stacked up against me. The interesting thing is that I always win. Must remember to ask the psychologists about that.

In one memorable dream sequence my friend, Mel, and I save our country from nuclear attack. It was frighteningly real and had something to do with hiding everybody in large ditches filled with water. If I ever recall exactly how we did it, I'll pass it on to the Defense Department.

About this time, too, they fix my neck and shoulders into an obscenely uncomfortable brace called a Minerva jacket which they tell me I must wear for two to three months. The future does not look bright.

One day, Kathy leans over to whisper something.
"Dad, do you know who your nurse for today is?"
I signal that I don't. But I know when one of my offspring is full of mischief, and this one has it shining in her

eyes. I wait with some interest to see where this is leading.
I don't have to wait long.

"She's Andy Wells's wife," she says gleefully.

Really? The colourful mayor of St. John's is one of
my favourite targets for the occasional hit-and-run line in
my column. Let's hope Nurse Wells is not the vindictive
type.

"God just isn't on your side these days, is he?"
Daughter is enjoying herself.

I didn't even know Andy was married. But I decide to be
especially pleasant to his spouse. No point in taking
chances.

They say I have pneumonia. That doesn't sound good.
In my childhood pneumonia was almost a death sentence. I
don't know what it is now, but no one seems especially worried. I don't have the willpower to worry. I can feel the gurgling in my lungs, or at least I think I can, but it doesn't
bother me that much. When it gets too bad, meaning the
lungs get too full of whatever, they hook something up to
something else and suction out my lungs. I feel better for a
while but then the cycle of gurgling and suctioning begins
again. Actually I think the suctioning may have been for
purposes other than pneumonia but perhaps including that
as well.

I don't mind the suctioning, in fact I look forward to
it. The gadget is like a small hand pump that's held by a
technician or nurse who hooks it up to the trach and
pumps out my lungs in a hurry. The relief is so great that
I keep asking for suctioning several times an hour and
always get it.

Guess they didn't have suction pumps in the days of my
childhood.

The man in the next bed is separated from me by two
curtains, his and mine. There is no separating the sound of
his voice, however. Sometime in the night he begins to yell
and scream and shout.

"Mary! Where's Mary? I wants Mary!"

Brief silence. Then his voice comes even louder.

"Fuck Mary! I'm getting out of here. You can't keep me in this goddamn place. Fuck all of you!"

The sound of a female voice.

"You've got to get back into bed, sir."

"Fuck the bed. Fuck you. You can't stop me."

The sound of a male voice.

"If you do not calm down, sir, I will have you restrained. Do you understand? You will be tied to this bed if I hear anything else out of you."

The man mumbles something, but I can't hear what it is. Then there is silence and I breathe relief. He won't be getting out of bed and running amuck through the ICU as I feared. I'm safe for the time being.

"He's a pretty hard case," someone says.

"It's his reaction to the medication," Marion says from her chair by the bedside. "He's probably the nicest kind of man. Besides," and she chuckles at the memory, "he reminds me of that man on the *Caribou*. You remember him?"

That I do. Marion, Rob and I were sitting at a table on the big ferry on our way to North Sydney. A middle-aged man lurched down the deck, obviously a recent patron of the vessel's bar, and half fell into the seat next to ours. He was talking to himself quietly for some time, but then his voice grew stronger and we could hear what he was saying in normal conversational tones.

"The little birds, the beautiful little birds. God made all the beautiful little birds. Fuck the little birds.

"The lovely little children. God made all the little children. Fuck the little children.

"The beautiful stars that come out at night. All the stars that shine in the sky. God made all the beautiful stars. Fuck the beautiful stars."

By now, we were suffocating in laughter and trying hard not to let him see. Lord knows what effect people laughing at him might have. He continued the monologue for about twenty minutes or so, never raising his voice above conversation level, and never repeating himself. Then he got up and wandered off, still talking to himself and leaving us weak with laughter.

A psychiatrist might have understood the significance of what the man was saying. All we knew was that he probably wasn't preparing his Sunday sermon. The man in the next bed is quiet now.

It is late afternoon and Rob comes in. "You know what that old fellow in the next bed just did? He flashed me! He exposed himself to me!"

Then in typical Rob fashion he grins and says, "I think he likes me."

"Don't get too excited," his mother replies. "He's been flashing me all day."

6

Waiting strong and merciless beneath the lesser and post-accident fears of being left alone, caught in a fire or attacked while I lie helpless, is the old enemy that has dominated my life for more than thirty years. This tyrant has intruded itself into life decisions, caused me countless embarrassments and prevented me from choosing paths that otherwise I might have taken. It's one of the more common phobias, the fear of being caught in a small confined space and not being able to get out—claustrophobia.

I developed the fear that would have such a grip on the rest of my life sometime in my late twenties. Claustrophobia forces me to avoid elevators like the black plague, makes using windowless restrooms and washrooms all but impossible, and allows me to fly only with the combined support of the modern pharmacy and the modern liquor store.

Strangely, this fear didn't exist when I was a younger man, and I can think of no incident at the time or in my childhood that might have caused it. I did date an elevator girl in Simpson's Department Store in Halifax for some time, but I don't remember that as being an entirely negative experience.

I might have run for public office except I was always afraid I'd win and thus be required to use elevators and aircraft. Whenever I make reservations at a hotel, I go to great lengths to make sure my room is on the first floor. Sometimes the first floor for guests is three or four flights up and accessible by stairs only through administration offices. Embarrassing though it is, I allow myself to be escorted through these areas and up staff-only staircases while Marion takes the elevator and the luggage.

The president of the provincial teachers' association and I once had a meeting with then-premier Joseph Smallwood in the middle of a controversial and difficult strike. This meeting was so urgent that I tried to push my fear of elevators to the back of my mind, and got aboard a car in the lobby of Confederation Building for the ten-floor ride up to the premier's office. I made it up two floors before I ran out of the elevator, retching all the way. The history of education in Newfoundland was thus changed forever.

My most inglorious moment, however, was when I went to visit Marion in hospital after she had had operations on both her feet. Her room was on the fifth floor, but that was no problem. I would simply walk up the stairs. Unfortunately, the third floor stairwell was temporarily barred off and I couldn't get past it. I was sitting in the lobby in abject misery and frustration when I looked up and saw Marion hobbling across the lobby to visit *me*.

Despite these and many other embarrassing episodes neither Marion nor any other member of my family has ever put me down, made me feel weak or inadequate, or been anything but totally supportive. My life has been so dominated by this phobia, however, that I've often asked one or more of my offspring to hold the washroom doors on the Gulf ferries ajar while I was inside. The amazing thing is that they did it. My wife, for some reason, refused.

Many times in my life I've been tempted to look for professional help, but I could never take that first step towards finding it. The fear has been so strong that I've remained convinced there's no way on God's good, green earth I can ever conquer it.

But now my old, familiar enemy and I are face to face once more. They tell me that after ten days in ICU, I'm about to be transferred to a room on another floor. There's no avoiding it this time. The fact that two nurses, Jennifer, Kathy and Marion will be with me does nothing to stifle the fear rising higher and higher in my throat the closer we get to doing it.

Again, my family rises to the occasion. As we approach the bank of elevators, I close my eyes and try to pretend this isn't happening. But there's nothing more unmistakable than the sound of elevator doors sliding shut, especially when the mere idea of it sets off a panic reaction. And then, before the doors have closed and panic completely engulfs me, my offspring begin singing at the top of their lungs.

You are my sunshine, my only sunshine;
You make me happy, when skies are gray.

It's the first song I remember learning to sing as a child, and my emotional reaction to hearing it in this situation is such that almost before I know it, we are out of the elevator and wheeling down the corridor. I am pathetically grateful that it's over, at least for the time being. But at the back of my mind, waiting to pounce at the first opportunity, is the old fear feeding greedily on the knowledge that at some point I'll have to take that elevator back down.

It's unlikely that I'll walk it.

Marion

Several days after moving to the fifth floor Ed still hadn't been out of bed. When we asked why it was taking so long to get him up, the staff always had a reason Ed couldn't get up that day. There was no wheelchair available, or certain tests or procedures hadn't been carried out, or it was a long weekend and the appropriate personnel weren't working. I was getting more and more frustrated, and more than a little concerned.

Finally, after ten days in bed, Ed was told that he'd be getting up in a wheelchair sometime that day. I was so relieved, although Ed didn't seem to be fully aware of what was happening. But he seemed quite willing and I was content with that.

Sure enough, at the appointed time three nurses appeared with the wheelchair and I was told we could wheel up and down the corridors until Ed got tired. That didn't take very long, and despite my best efforts to keep him up as long as possible, Ed was soon demanding to be taken back to the room.

The three nurses came in to get him out of the chair. As they removed the footrests and lifted his leg to reach the lift sling, the chair became unbalanced. A friend was visiting from Springdale, and I had turned to speak to her when we heard a collective gasp and turned to see Ed's wheelchair falling over backwards with Ed still in it.

Our reaction was purely instinctive. Both of us dived towards the chair and got our hands in under Ed's head just as he hit the floor. Our friend injured her shoulder in the process and had to take some time off work.

The potential consequences from bouncing Ed's head off the floor within days of having his neck broken are too terrible to contemplate. The doctor was furious, and so concerned that he immediately ordered X-rays to make sure no further damage had been done.

When Kathy came in shortly after and learned what had happened she pointed to the bottom of the chair.

"Make no wonder he went over backwards!" she exclaimed. "The little anti-tip thingies that keep the chair from falling over are turned up instead of down as they should be."

Kathy was an extremely unhappy camper and took no pains to hide it. All of us, especially the doctor, were most upset but we made no formal complaint.

Not long after that, one of the nurses attending Ed noticed he was acting strangely. A doctor was called and he ordered two cultures to see if Ed was suffering from a suspected infection. The second culture was to follow the first a day or so later so that if a problem were indicated, they wouldn't have to wait as long to have it confirmed. Cultures normally take several days to grow.

In the meantime, the doctor called the infectious diseases department and asked an intern to tell the specialist that he needed help. This worthy made a note, put it in his pocket and, incredible as it seems, left for the day with the note still in his lab coat. The infectious diseases specialist who later told us about that was more than a little upset.

No one knew that the nurse concerned had made a decision on her own not to bother with the second culture because it was a waste of money. When that was discovered, an irate doctor immediately reordered the second culture but the results from that would take another three or four days. In the meantime, Ed went septic.

The only thing I knew about being septic was that it was extremely serious and potentially fatal. One of the nurses on duty made a frantic call and no fewer than three doctors appeared obviously quite concerned. ICU personnel were alerted that Ed might be returning at any moment, and a saline solution was pumped into him to try and neutralize the infection.

Perhaps it was Ed's physical conditioning before the accident that helped. Whatever, the treatment worked and he rallied out of danger.

When Ed was feeling well enough, we made several excursions around the corridors with me pushing him in a wheelchair. But he seemed to tire very quickly and want to return to his room. I always tried to delay the inevitable, believing that the longer he was up the better it would be for him.

One day a nurse we knew stopped to say hello. She looked at Ed closely.

"You'd better get him back to his bed," she said. "I think his blood pressure has gone through the floor."

And so it had, but I was blissfully unaware that I should be on the lookout for that, or that I should take him back to his room when he seemed tired and sluggish.

7

My recovery in the fifth floor room of the Health Sciences Centre is slow. After ten days in intensive care, I can find no consistency in what's happening around me up here. Sometimes everything is clear and lucid. I know who's in my room and react normally to them. I know what's happening and what's happened, and I make a conscious effort to cope. Then at other times I feel as though I'm drowning, as though I'm being smothered, as though I'm lost. I don't want to see anyone or have anyone see me.

The nights are the worst. The fear of being left alone hasn't lessened and I need to have someone with me every hour. My family makes up a schedule which includes our friends as well as family, and I'm never alone for a moment. Marion never stays through the night so that during the day when doctors and nurses and therapists are doing their thing she can be here and know what's happening. She stays as late as she can and returns early in the morning.

I'm told that staying up all night with me is a bit of a challenge. I'm constantly demanding drink and/or conversation and/or singing and/or reciting. My sleep is punctuated with shouts and yells that would wake the dead, although no instances of resurrection have actually been recorded. On top of that, my 'sitters' have to sleep coiled up in chairs, and two or three maintain they don't sleep at all.

Some nurses are especially patient "through the long night watches." One stays in my room for hours on end, singing old songs with me and reciting Shakespeare and a few of the lesser poets, like me. She has a special place in my will; too bad there's no money in it.

Marion

Perhaps because of the many drugs he was on, Ed's mind often wandered and he would say totally nonsensical things. One day our daughter, Michelle, and her family were in the room and we were talking, as the saying goes, about everything in general and nothing in particular. Ed had been participating in the conversation when suddenly he looked at Sean and said, "Don't let them get you, Sean!"

Sean said he wouldn't and for Ed not to worry about it. But Ed wasn't finished.

"Don't let the fuckers get Alex!" he exclaimed.

The swear word surprised me because Ed only swore when he was really provoked, and the F-word was one he never used, at least for me to hear. Michelle looked positively shocked. Certainly she had never heard her father use such language before. His perception that something was threatening our grandson, Alex, was upsetting him, but we never knew what it was. A few moments later Ed was talking normally again.

Although he tried valiantly to be brave, he wasn't always successful in controlling his emotions.

"I'm not afraid, honey," he'd sometimes say out of the blue, "I'm not afraid."

It was then that I knew he was most afraid of all. I'd place my hand on his head and touch his face with mine, trying to comfort him. Occasionally he'd cry softly and my own heart would almost break. But I never let him see me cry because I had resolved that he never would. That was one burden I would not lay on him.

They say one trouble never strikes alone.

As if black ice hadn't dealt severely enough with us, nature through another form of ice decided to deal us yet another blow. Two weeks after the accident, and just three days after Ed was released from ICU, a pipe in our house froze solid one bitterly cold night and burst.

Since Kathy was in St. John's with us at the time, our good friend, Mel, had been checking on the house every day just to make sure everything was okay. No one asked him to do it. He simply realized it should be done and did it. He was feeling so helpless, he said later, and that made him feel he was doing something to help. That had to be an understatement, as Ed would say, right up there with General Custer's comment when he saw all the Indians: "I think we might be in a little trouble here."

It was on one of these checks that Mel heard a noise that sounded like running water. The floor covering in the kitchen was what's known in the trade as a floating floor, that is, it isn't glued to the plywood underneath. When Mel stepped on it he realized it was floating in a much more literal sense. There was water everywhere. But where was it coming from? He discovered the basement was literally drowning in several inches of water, but Mel couldn't find any breaks to explain it. He did find the main cut-off valve on the water line coming into the house and shut it off. Eventually he discovered that a cold water pipe going to the washer in the laundry room just off our porch had ruptured and had been pouring water into the house for several hours.

The damage was severe, especially in the basement. Ed's study was at the foot of the basement stairs, as was Rob's bedroom. The closets contained, among other things, several boxes of cassette tapes which Ed had made with our friend, Pat Melindy, and which were now ruined. Ed had just had a new order come in for his last two books, several cases of which had been stacked on the floor. Many of them were waterlogged. The carpets were soaked. The old-style panel board had absorbed water two or three feet up the wall. The furnace room, which also contained Ed's workbench, a storage area large enough to take over two cords of wood and tons of boxes and miscellaneous stuff lying on the floor, was likewise inundated.

What would have happened had Mel not been "looking out for us," as we say in Newfoundland, is difficult to say. As it was, the damage was devastating.

Even more upsetting for me was knowing that strangers would be in my house cleaning up the mess and putting all our belongings into boxes. Much of our personal lives would now be opened up to others. The insurance company would be hiring people to assess the situation and take everything that wasn't damaged to a storage area. Ed writes a great deal about our lives and our family, but he makes sure everything in his column is okayed by me and any family member who happens to be mentioned. Now we had no control at all over who entered our house or what they did while in there. It wasn't a matter of not trusting people. It was simply not wanting other people peering into our lives on such an intimate basis.

But there was nothing I could do about it. I wasn't comfortable with leaving Ed so soon, even for a couple of days. I told him about the flood but I wasn't at all sure he was in any condition to appreciate how serious it was.

Kathy volunteered to return to Springdale and try to get a handle on what was happening with the house and the insurance. She didn't want to leave, but like the rest of us she had little choice but do what had to be done. Her experience as a social worker and her good common sense was invaluable in this and several other situations in which we found ourselves over the next seventeen months. Indeed, I don't know what we would have done without her.

Jennifer comes in pushing a trolley with a television monitor on it.

"Look Dad, we can watch some television tonight."

Television. I'd forgotten all about television. As Jennifer plugs it in, I begin to remember some of my favourite shows: "Biography," "Law and Order," natural disasters on the Discovery channel, our own "Land and Sea."

As Jennifer tunes in a channel, it's as though she's opening a small window through which I have a glimpse of a world I'd forgotten completely. I become aware that there's something else outside this hospital room. It's where Marion and the others go when they leave. It's where people come from when they come in. This room isn't the beginning and the ending. This room is in the middle of people coming and going. This room is in the middle of *my* coming and going. This isn't the ending any more than it's the beginning. The revelation is a sunrise that opens up a whole new day.

I try to convey to the others the wonder of what I feel, but the trach keeps me from speaking, and waving my arms about makes them think I'm agitated. I can only fasten my eyes on that dancing screen and hope there are other wonderful realizations yet to come.

I don't hear the nurse come in until she speaks. Her tone is flat and hard, breaking through and into the wonderful thoughts swirling around in my head.

"You people aren't allowed to have a television in here!"

Marion reacts first.

"Why on earth not?"

"It's hospital policy. Television sets aren't allowed in these rooms."

"That's strange," Marion says. "We asked about that and were told that it's okay."

"Who told you that? Are you sure that's what they told you?"

The tone says very clearly that she doesn't believe us.

"Of course I'm sure. How do you think we got it in the first place? We didn't just walk into the audiovisual place and take it. The man said to bring it back on Monday. He didn't say anything about charging us, but we'll be happy to pay any rental."

"It's not a matter of rental." The nurse's tone hasn't changed. "You're just not allowed to have it in here."

"Look." Marion is trying very hard to be patient. "We think this is important for Ed. We borrowed the television legitimately and it's unreasonable and unnecessary to take it back."

This isn't good at all. I don't want to get on the bad side of the nurses.

Wait, I try to call out despite the trach in my throat, I have to stay here with these people. Please don't get them upset!

"I have to take the television now," the nurse says again, her voice cold and uncompromising.

"I see no earthly reason that you should," Marion returns.

The nurse decides she's not getting anywhere with Marion, and turns to meet Jennifer's steady gaze.

"Do you have a problem?"

"Yes I do. We have permission to use that television and you have no right to take it from us."

This whole thing is escalating quickly and I'm helpless to intervene. I don't want to watch television that bad. I try to catch Jennifer's eye, to make her understand I don't want to be part of this conflict. My fear is that no one in the hospital will treat me as well from now on if this isn't resolved.

The nurse puts an end to the argument by walking out and taking the television set with her. Marion and Jennifer are really angry, but they pursue the issue no further because they believe it's upsetting for me.

It is, and apart from that I seem to have lost something wonderful that I had just a few moments ago. But now I can't remember what it was. Probably wasn't important.

Jennifer

I don't really know if there's such a thing as fate, but there was certainly lots of foreshadowing over that last Christmas. God, Christmas seems eons ago. I remember wondering what would happen to Mom or Dad if the other should die. Perhaps it wasn't foreshadowing. Perhaps it's only that they're getting to the age where bad things start happening to people. But I was considering the mortality of each of my parents for the first time, and wondering what their lives would be like without each other.

Foreshadowing?

We also had a conversation about Dad's cholesterol and how difficult it was to keep down. He talked about helplessness as a fate worse than death. He'd never want to live that way.

"Just don't let me have a stroke and not die." Those were his words.

Foreshadowing?

Dad dealt with his bad back with incredibly poor humour. At one point I opened my mouth to tell him that I hadn't heard Mom complain about her rheumatoid arthritis in ten years as much as he had complained about that back in ten days. Mom kept joking about how Dad, who hadn't spent a night in hospital since he was six, didn't know how to cope with being sick. I teased him that the only thing wrong with his writing is that he's never really suffered so he can't do drama. Every creative genius, I said, needs a great tragedy in his life.

Foreshadowing.

We had a wonderful Christmas, the images of which are with me still. Dad and the rest of us hauling the Christmas tree out of the woods with Samantha riding on top. The traditional Trivial Pursuit game which the women won yet again. The Christmas Eve singsong which our family had been hosting for more than twenty-six years, and which this year saw some new families attending.

One picture that particularly stands out in my mind is Dad crushing blueberries with a rum bottle to make blueberry wine. He told me as he worked that he finally felt like he was retired and had time to do the things he really liked to do. I laughed, and replied that it was about time—he'd been retired for two years!

"*Carpe diem*, Dad," I said. "Seize the day."

Foreshadowing.

The Undiscovered Country. That's what's keeping Ed Smith awake nights. I'm sitting here next to his bed, staffing the night shift, watching him sleep. He hasn't gotten much sleep, though. This last fifteen minutes is the longest stint so far.

I can see his eyes move under his eyelids and I can tell he's dreaming. In a minute or two he'll start to shake. If I touch his cheek as the shaking begins he'll calm down and his eyes will stop moving. If I'm vigilant, I can thwart the cycle several times before the shaking wakes him up.

The last time he woke up shaking, he mouthed to me, "I'm afraid." I asked of what. He replied, still shaking, "I don't know." I thought for a few moments, then asked, "The Undiscovered Country?" He immediately stopped shaking. I stroked his brow with my hand and translated for no one in particular, "The Unknown Future."

"No one knows what the future will hold for us," I said, "but at least we'll be together so it can't be that bad. Different, maybe, but not that bad."

He closed his eyes and went back to sleep.

As I become more aware of my surroundings, the staff begins to reveal their personalities. The physiotherapist assigned to me has an effervescent personality that makes you feel better by just being near her. Another nurse with striking good looks wears a shocking pink lipstick and I christen her Hot Lips, although not to her face. I have the feeling, however, she wouldn't mind at all.

One of the nurses looks as tough as nails. I don't like her on sight, but as the days wear on, I realize she makes me feel comfortable and secure and she becomes one of my favourites.

Today is the day my trach comes out, and I'll be able to speak again. The nurses are warning me that if my swallowing reflex isn't working properly, it'll have to go back in. But I know I can swallow so that doesn't bother me.

Finally, two specialists come in to do their bit. I wonder why there are two. Is removing this thing such a complicated procedure, or does one of them have nothing else to do? Unlikely in the latter instance, unlikely in the former, too. I don't care much either way.

"Okay," one of them says. "This will feel a little strange as we pull it out, but you shouldn't feel any pain."

He's right on both counts. Almost before I know it, he's straightening up and saying, "That's it." The thing is out! I can talk again. I can eat again. Is there anything in this world I can't do again?! I look around and everyone is waiting for me to say something. Here it comes, Smith's first words in an eternity of time. Bring in the reporters. Bring on the scribes. Let it flow.

My eyes find Marion. Marion who spends every waking moment with me. Marion who keeps telling me nothing really important about me has changed. Marion who keeps telling me she loves me, and that we'll still have good lives together. Marion without whom I am lost.

"I love you."

I look around the room and see Jennifer.

"I love Jennifer."

And my sister.

"I love Pat."

There is nothing more important to say with my first words. But they bear no similarity whatever to my next statement which is directed at everyone in the room. This is something I've been wanting to say for as long as I can remember.

"When I ask you to scratch a spot on my face or head, and I begin to turn said head one way or the other, I am trying to direct your fingers to the spot that needs scratching. If you turn your hand as I'm turning my head, you stay in the same place—the wrong place!"

Everyone thinks this is quite funny. Perhaps for one of my first sentences in more than three weeks it is. But for me it reveals one of the great frustrations of not being able to talk. I tell them that if I'm rendered speechless again, to please bear this in mind. Between chuckles, they all say that they will.

I don't take much thought for my family and how they're coping. The centre of my troubled little universe is me, and the possibility that they, especially Marion, are suffering agonies doesn't enter my mind. I just know that they are here and I need them to be here.

Marion never lets me see her cry. I have a suspicion that none of my family will shed a tear in my presence. Few visitors do, either, although I'm told many give into their emotions in the hallway after they leave.

I try hard not to lose control when anyone is in my room. I don't know how well I succeed. An old boyhood friend, Gord, comes by, and for one of the few times of which I am aware, I come close to breaking down, as does he. The memory of carefree days spent climbing rocks and fishing in the ponds is too much of a contrast with where and what I am now, and will always be.

For some reason, it's important to me that everyone knows I'm not afraid, so I say it over and over, especially to Marion.

"I'm not afraid."

It's true. Whether it's the numbing effect of the drugs or the fact that reality hasn't sunk in yet, I don't know. But I'm not afraid for the future. I do know my walking days are over, although I still think my hands are functioning. No reason to think otherwise. Marion says my hands were gripping the nurse's hand on the flight in, and the doctor assured her the operation would result in no further paralysis.

So I try to take a positive approach to my future. There's got to be lots of things I can do. I can take over the house paperwork such as paying bills and writing letters. On the other hand, given the mess I made of bill paying before, I'm not at all sure Marion will let me. But she'll let me peel vegetables for dinner, and she loves to hear me play guitar. And there's another thought. I'll get more serious about playing and singing. Perhaps I'll even make up a little pamphlet promoting my entertainment talents and distribute it across the province. I could combine that with book-selling and readings, and Marion and I could do a little tour once or twice a year. It won't be that bad. I'm not afraid.

Before too long, however, I discover the sad truth about my hands. Despite the doctor's assurance that I would suffer no further paralysis as a result of the surgery, I realize that my hands have no feeling and are now totally paralyzed. My illusions of being semi-useful around the house are shattered. Now I don't know if I'll ever say or think again, "I'm not afraid," because I can't think of any way I can be useful. I don't think I can stand being alive without being useful.

One day Marion says almost venomously, "I'm bitter about nothing else except your hands. That I can never forgive." I want to know who it is she can't forgive, but I can't hold the question in my mind long enough to ask her. The doctor? God? I don't know.

Whatever, I feel much the same way. The paralysis of my hands and fingers is the most devastating loss of all. Without them, I can't grasp, or touch or feel. Without them I am useless. Without them I am nothing.

My mother refuses to believe that I'll never have hands and fingers again.

"Don't you worry, my dear," she says over and over, "you'll have fingers again."

Her tone is so convincing and I so desperately need to believe it that for a few moments I'm almost hopeful. But then the utter finality of my injuries comes down on me again like a dark cloud and I try to make her understand.

"No, Mom, they're gone forever. The nerves are destroyed and they won't grow back."

But she refuses to accept it. Perhaps hers is the mustard seed of faith I need to move my own personal mountain. Perhaps that's what mothers do. When the night is darkest and the odds against you heaviest they keep alive that little spark of hope, no matter how unreasonable or dim.

Keep the faith, Mother, even if I can't.

Today, February 1, is Kathy's birthday. I remember her birth so well. She announced her imminent arrival in the middle of a snowstorm, through which we had to drive two hours to the hospital in Gander. A doctor friend met us halfway there and gave his opinion that Marion might make it to the hospital and might not. Three days of labour and a world of worry later Kathy reluctantly entered this world. Now she's thirty-two years old, married with two children, and I still think of her as my little girl. I fear I often treat her that way, too. This can't be one of her better birthdays but her mother makes sure that we celebrate it anyway.

There's a cake and some candles, but we aren't allowed to have open flame where there's oxygen. (They still give me a whiff now and then.) Two kindly nurses resolve that problem by disconnecting the oxygen and wheeling the tank out of the room. We light the candles on Kathy's birthday cake and all is merry as a wedding bell. Well, almost.

The time has come to talk about my continuing rehabilitation. Rehabilitation is a beautiful word for me. It means learning to do things I can't do now. How to make use of the limited movement in my arms, how to do things with paralyzed hands, how to get around and make the most of what's left to me. Most important of all, it will be a major step in my long journey towards home, a journey that will take several months. I should be home in Springdale by the summer.

Jennifer and Robbie reconnoitre the Hewitt Centre, located here in St. John's, which caters to stroke and brain-injured patients as well as spinal injuries and diseases. When they return I'm concerned about only one thing.

"Are the therapy areas on a different floor from my room?"

They have even better news. Although the rehabilitation gymnasium is on the floor above my room, the physiotherapist will come down to work with me.

I'm ecstatic. I won't have to use an elevator!

At about this time, Marion tells me about the sign that's been hanging on the wall above my bed.

DO NOT SAY THE WORD "ELEVATOR" IN FRONT OF ED.

Evidently it was displayed over my bed in ICU from the beginning. Marion's goal was to keep my stress level down as much as possible. She knows nothing strikes panic and terror into me as quickly and totally as even the idea of elevators. A couple of people who started to read the sign aloud were silenced by hard looks, furious shaking of the heads and, if necessary, a dig in the ribs. I, of course, was blissfully unaware.

Robbie leaves to go back to Iqaluit today. He's been here for three weeks and has to get back to his job as aquatics director for the town. We've always been close and both of us find his leaving especially difficult.

"You only have to say you need me, Dad," he says over and over, "and I'll be here. Just call and say you need me."

I know he means it.

Today Jennifer returns to law school. She's been so much a part of this terrible time from the beginning that having to be here without her seems wildly impossible. But I know she has no choice. She's lost a month of classes and study already. I don't know how she can ever make it up.

"I'll be back next month, Dad," she promises.

She talked about dropping the whole semester and remaining here. But she's already paid too large a price to be with us and despite the fact we lean on her so much, we can't encourage her to do that.

It is so very hard to see her go.

Early in February I'm transferred from the Health Sciences Centre across the city to the Hewitt Centre. I survive the ride down from the fifth floor in the elevator by keeping my eyes tightly shut and assuring myself that with two large St. John Ambulance men escorting me, as well as Marion and Kathy, nothing much can go wrong.

Nothing much does.

8

I'm given a private room at the Hewitt. I'm not sure why. We certainly didn't ask for it. Perhaps it has something to do with the nature of my injury. Perhaps it has something to do with the wonder of me. Whatever, I'll take it.

The day after we arrive Kathy has to return home. Each time one of my children leaves after being here several days I am much distressed. On those days I keep my eyes closed until they leave to try and shut out the pain. I don't know if they understand or not.

The first meeting with the staff is most encouraging. The doctor and the nurse supervisor, the physiotherapist and occupational therapist are all there, as is the psychologist who obviously got the short straw. Nice people every one.

They tell us what we already know. My injury is *complete*, which means there's no hope of any recovery. The crushing of the spinal cord is irreversible. Some people have similar injuries to mine which are *incomplete*. That often means the person might actually learn to walk again. Sometimes visitors and friends don't understand the difference and try to be encouraging.

"My friend's brother-in-law had his neck broken in the same place as you two years ago and was totally paralyzed. Today he can walk without even a cane, so you can do it, too, if you really try."

I find such comments to be really distressing. Deep down inside is still the faint hope that I might regain some use of my limbs, but I know it's a false hope and I shouldn't allow it to surface. Each time someone says anything like that I have to go through the pain of burying the hope all over again.

The doctor stresses that they have a team approach to rehabilitation, and I'm the central figure on that team. I'll be consulted about any action or decision regarding my treatment, and nothing will be done without my input and approval. When the meeting is over, I don't know if I'm Donald Trump or the King of Siam. One thing is sure: I'm the man; I'm in charge of me. And on top of that, no elevators to worry about. Great stuff.

The therapy for me is twofold: physiotherapy will help improve the range and strength of my arms; and occupational therapy will help me learn to use what little movement I have in my arms to pick up and hold small objects, such as a cup of tea or a piece of bread. In addition, there are exercises to keep my legs and fingers from stiffening up and my neck flexible.

Marion wants me to start getting back into life as soon as possible. To that end, she decides there should be some way I can use the telephone, and some kind of accessible ON/OFF switch for the television. She speaks to the OT department about headphones and such, but draws a complete blank. Our friends Robin and Kathy come by this evening and Marion tells them the problem.

"Not to worry," says Robin. "I can take care of that."

Next day he's back with a set of headphones and the proper phone to use with it. Before I know it, I'm talking back and forth to friends and family, and the various groups to which I belonged prior to the accident. I can even sit in on meetings. It's hard to exaggerate how important this is for me and my rehabilitation. One wonders why, in a rehabilitation centre, this stuff isn't standard issue.

No one seems to have any idea how I can read when I can't hold papers and books in my hands. Marion thinks about this for a while and then rigs up an ingenious contraption utilizing clothespins and coat hangers. It isn't pretty, but just as long as someone will clip the pages to the contraption I can read them quite well. Staff and visitors alike are amazed with this thing, and so they should be.

To resolve the book problem, she contacts the CNIB and they direct her to where she can purchase a book holder that sits on my chest and allows me to turn pages. It doesn't work all that well but it's certainly better than nothing.

The nurses tell me I have to have sweatpants. They're easier to get on and off, they explain. Right. I've never worn sweatpants in my life. I've worn dress pants and casual pants, jeans and oilskins, Ski-doo pants and Bermuda shorts, even briggs. But never sweatpants. I don't like sweatpants.

Marion leaves no doubt about how she feels.

"You're not wearing sweatpants, Ed," she says, "and that's all there is to it. I've seen too many older men who've been fishermen and loggers all their lives hauled into seniors' homes and made to wear these things because they're easier to get off and on. They wouldn't have been caught dead in sweatpants at home or at their work because they feel silly in them. Then they get in some institution and think they have no choice. Well, you do have a choice. You were a professional. You never wore sweatpants on the job, you never wore them at home, and you certainly don't have to wear them now. I'll find something else that'll make dressing you easier."

And she does. Rip-aways, they're called, and the nurses love them. So there.

I'm wondering what I'd do if Marion weren't here. Some of the staff have been suggesting to her that perhaps she's spending too much time, with me and she should get away for a while. But she resists that pressure, saying that she and I have spent all our adult lives together and she's not about to change that just because the going gets rough.

Again, the quality of my life would be so much poorer if she were not around to support and look out for me. I know she's often frustrated with the system, upset with the medical profession and discouraged with my lack of progress. I fear, too, that I take many of my own frustrations and torments out on her. Nevertheless she's always there and I am so grateful.

They tell me I should expect to be here for many months. Okay, I say to myself, but I'll be home by early fall at the latest. No way am I missing Halloween and bonfire night with the grandkids. No way.

Jennifer

I've been lying here in bed in my room at Harvard wondering why I feel physical pain in my gut.

I do, you know. But why? We're all okay. My dad is strong. My mom is a rock. Everything I love about my father is still intact. He'll be writing again soon. Sure, I keep seeing my father's blood on my hands, and I was terrified during the taxi ride into Cambridge from Logan airport, but people have thrived through worse.

Over the past week I've kept seeing visions of my father. Dad dancing with Kathy at her wedding. Dad wandering aimlessly through a mall, hands jammed in his jacket pockets. Dad checking my back for injury when I fell in the trailer. Dad running behind my bicycle as I learned to ride without training wheels. Dad playing piano while Mr. Pike and he sang songs. Dad in my backyard building my deck.

Each time I see a vision of Dad as he was I feel pain. It's really the only thing I feel anymore. I feel nothing or I feel pain. Not overwhelming pain. Kind of like a pet scratching at the back door, asking to be let in.

Why? We're all doing great. Friends at school are being wonderful. I know that sooner or later we'll all get through this.

So why the pain?

It's loss. Loss of my father. The father I knew, and the father I thought would dance at my wedding. He's gone. I'll never see him again.

I miss my Dad. Sure, I can still talk to him on the phone. But I'll never see him again. The memories I have are just memories of a time that will never come back.

I know our lives aren't over. I don't think they are. Not even Dad's life is over. It will just be different. High maintenance but really just different. Still, the old life is gone. I will never see my big, strong, tall father again. Or feel his bear hug. Or laugh at his dancing. Or lie in bed in my room listening to him playing piano or guitar and singing. Or look up to see him stride into a room.

He won't look the same. He doesn't sound the same. Will I ever hear my father's voice again?

It's like part of him has died. I'll never see that part of him again. No warning. No chance for him to say goodbye or make one last piece of furniture or take one last photo. Just gone.

There's a new Dad to take his place. A lot like the old one and just as loved.

As I write this, tears streaming down my face, I know I'm being stupid. We're all okay.

So why can't I stop crying?

Physically I'm a bloody mess.

The paralysis is almost the least of my problems.

I go dysreflexic, for example. Going dysreflexic means my blood pressure aims for the roof and is hell-bent on going through it. That little trick can be caused by something as important as a nipped-off or blocked catheter tube, or as small as a wrinkle in the sheet I'm lying on. Not being able to feel anything, I know nothing about it until I get a severe headache which means my blood pressure is getting up into stroke territory. Then the cause of the dysreflexia has to be found and remedied before I head off into the sweet bye and bye.

The other side of the blood pressure coin is that without warning it can dip low enough that I lose consciousness. That's a problem that can be alleviated with a quick shot of sugar so we carry sweetened orange juice with us wherever we go. Not serious, I think. But what do I know?

I do have to avoid getting the flu. Most people want to avoid the flu, but if they get it they suffer for a few days and then it's over. Not me. I don't have a strong enough cough to get mucus up off my lungs so pneumonia rears its ugly head.

Skin ulcers, commonly known as bedsores, usually occur in pressure areas, those places on which you sit and lie. Your circulation is weak so the ulcers take a long time to heal. If they don't heal quickly enough, they can eat away at your flesh until they reach bone and a plastic surgeon has to do his thing. Once you have a bedsore, the skin never fully heals. For the rest of your life that particular area remains nish and a potential problem.

People with quadriplegia and paraplegia are subject to frequent urine infections. All we know about it is that we feel lousy any and everywhere we can feel. The infection itself has to be treated with antibiotics, not all of which are effective. Just finding the right antibiotic for any particular infection can take days, during which time you just lie there and thank God the area in which you can really feel anything is relatively small.

I'm beginning to feel an affinity with the biblical character Job. Are God and Satan exercising their respective egos in a gigantic chess game with me, like Job, as one of the pawns? If so, I wouldn't want to find out about it.

Jennifer

Mom and I are sitting with Dad on this Friday evening. I've seen Dad on his worst days, and today is the worst I've seen. He isn't asking us to kill him, as he did in ICU, but he is crying, hallucinating, shaking his head and saying he can't make it through the long weeks to come, the long dark days and long dark nights. So many for him to face all alone.

Please don't leave him alone.

I didn't write much in my journal last week at Harvard, thinking I'd have plenty of time this week. But being with Dad is still a full-time job. From scratching his itches to force-feeding him liquids, every moment is filled. We haven't watched a movie since I've been here because we don't have time. Dad and I used to love watching movies together.

I arrived last Saturday and people keep acting surprised to see me. They don't seem to understand. I've always been here, even when I was physically in Boston I was here. Looking at the calendar I know I was away for three weeks, almost as long as I spent at the Health Sciences Centre to begin with. But that's just the calendar. I was always here.

Another small problem has developed over the past few weeks. I can't stay awake during the day. I have a tendency to fall asleep in the middle of a sentence, even when the sentence is mine. Day after day, I sleep through sessions with various staff and wake up just long enough to say, "I'm not asleep." Marion is acutely embarrassed, as I would be were I not off in REM territory. I'm given an EEG but I don't know if my medications have changed or not. Certainly there's no change in my problem.

Marion's sister-in-law, Marilyn, a nurse, comes in early one morning and notices something no one else has up to now.

"Ed's fingernails are blue in the morning," she tells Marion. "He's oxygen-deprived."

Marion passes this observation on to the medical powers that be and they bring in a respiratory specialist who states what I already know: I'm exhausted. But why is someone who sleeps in bed all day physically exhausted? The specialist suggests I'm not getting enough sleep. I know that, too, but what happens to the sleep I do get? Many tests are done and a conclusion reached.

I suffer from sleep apnea. Without going into anything technical, as if I could, this means that while I'm asleep I go without breathing for a few moments, then kick start the process with a mighty jerk which wakes me up, but not enough to be conscious of it. This cycle is repeated all through the night. The result is that my blood doesn't get enough oxygen, and the rest of me doesn't get enough rest. The constant gasping for breath doesn't do the heart a whole lot of good, either.

But hey, not to worry. This can be remedied, they say. Each night I'm to be hooked up to something called a CPAP machine which will channel the airflow through my nose instead of my mouth and thus allow me to breathe normally. I ask if this means I'll be normal during the day and get an emphatic shaking of the head from certain persons in the room. Perhaps the question was badly worded.

The machine is brought in and I immediately react. "That's a face mask! I can't wear a face mask! That's almost worse than an elevator. I can't do it."

The good doctor states that it's either the mask or another trach pushed down in me. The way he says it is almost threatening, to which I would react strongly were I not so upset.

Marion suggests I let her put it on my face now, just to try it out. So I do and can tolerate it as long as she's there to snatch it off me when I panic. Finally, after much discussion, I agree to try it for a few nights on the condition there's always someone near to take away the mask when I feel I'm suffocating. I say it in the same tone one would use to agree to try out the guillotine.

The friends and/or family who stay up with me these nights should be awarded Victoria Crosses—one for each night. I have no idea how many times they leap from their chairs in response to some shouted dream or urgent demand. It is more than once. One poor fellow who has innocently volunteered for night duty can't get out fast enough the next morning. He grabs his coat and cap and is out the door in no time flat. We never see him again.

But many do come back, night after terrible night, and my debt to them is more than I can say, let alone repay. And the fact is, the CPAP machine works. Despite the somewhat active nights, I feel better and more rested during the day than at any time since the accident. I get to where I don't consciously resist the mask, but it will be a very long time before I can sleep through the night without demanding at some point that it be taken off.

Marion's niece, Sian, is slated to sit with me tonight. She's such a pleasant young woman that I look forward to chatting with her a bit before sleeping.

She arrives with her golden retriever, Gryphon, and prepares to bunk down for the night.

"What are you doing with Gryphon?" I ask.

She looks a bit puzzled at the question.

"He'll stay here with us, of course," she replies.

I decide it's best to come right out and say it, although I'm not at all sure how she'll react.

"I'm not sure the staff will allow him to stay in the room overnight."

"Oh? Why on earth not?"

Good question. Dogs are roaming around in here all the time. They're on leashes, of course, and thought to be good for patient morale. Far as I know, no one complains and the dogs are welcome. None of them are as well-behaved and well-trained as Gryphon, for sure, so perhaps there'll be no problem.

"Let me ask the nurse on duty, just to be sure," I say, having convinced myself that no one will mind this large, friendly creature staying in my room. So I ring for the nurse and she arrives, as they always do here, almost immediately. I put the question to her. She looks apologetic.

"I'm sorry," she replies, "but it's out of the question."

No point in arguing and certainly no way we could hide Gryphon as we might if he were a toy poodle.

Sian takes it all in stride.

"Okay," she says, "Gryphon will just have to stay in the car."

"Are you sure?" I'm not real happy about this. "Won't he howl all night?"

"No," she replies, "he'll lie down and go to sleep. Don't worry about it."

So Sian spends the night with me and Gryphon spends the night in the car and it all works out fine.

The next weekend Michelle arrives from Clarenville with all good intentions of taking a turn at spending the night with me. With her comes hubby Sean and baby Alexander. They appear in my room at about 11:00 P.M. and prepare to settle down for the night.

"What are you doing with the baby?"

Like Sian, Michelle looks a little puzzled at the question.

"He and Sean are spending the night in the examining room next door."

"They are? The staff has agreed to this?"

"Well," Michelle replies, "we haven't actually asked them yet, but I'm sure it'll be okay."

I'm pretty sure it won't be, so I ask the nurse on duty about it.

"Oh my gosh no," she says. "We can't allow that at all." Michelle isn't happy about that because if the baby can't stay neither can she. So now we have a problem. Rather I have a problem. Finally I call brother-in-law Bill and he agrees to come down on short notice.

Next morning I'm telling Marion about it.

"Honest to God, Marion," I say. "Next weekend I'm fully expecting an Arab to turn up here with a camel."

My old school friend, Ray, drops by with some salmon. Great to see them both. Ray has had his own troubles lately. Last year he was diagnosed with cancer, but he looks pretty good now and he's a real inspiration to me. He reminds me that when we were boys we decided we'd each pick enough blueberries to buy a guitar. I managed to get enough for a genuine Palm Beach instrument with a palm leaf on the top straight out of Eaton's catalogue for the grand price of $12.95. I don't remember what kind of guitar Ray got back then, but tonight he takes out a beautiful old Gibson that he certainly didn't buy with blueberries, unless he's been picking them ever since. We have a great singsong that attracts several patients and visitors. I think Ray and I are good for each other.

Marion tells me today that this is as long as we can expect our family and friends to take turns staying with me during the night. They have their own families and jobs and it's just too much. I understand, but I'm filled with dread. Granted nurses are on the floor all night and although they are amazingly quick to respond to the call bell, they can't be with me continuously. On the other hand, my situation is a medical problem and thus a medical responsibility. Something has to give here.

We meet with the team. The good doctor states again that if I can't stay alone at night with the mask in place, it's another trach for me. And again, I don't like the way he says it. It's the same tone my father used to use when I tried to avoid chores.

"Now my son, you get those splits cut up and put in the woodbox or you won't be going to any movie tonight."

My father's admonition was acceptable then because I was twelve years old. The doctor's admonition today isn't because I'm not.

The doctor has a plan. They don't have enough money to keep a nurse with me on a continuing basis, he says (as if the fiscal problems of the Hewitt Centre are *my* fault), but they will attempt to wean me off my problem with the CPAP mask. A nurse will be assigned to my room all night every night for one week. The second week she will sit in a chair just outside my door where I can see her. The third week she will move the chair halfway down the corridor between my room and the nursing station. And after that, she won't be there at all.

To say I'm skeptical is the same as saying Methuselah was getting on in years.

"It'll never work," I tell Marion. "Someone has to be in the room all night or I'll never keep that mask on."

A month later I'm managing to get through the nights with no permanent sitter in my room and the mask in place most of the time. So I'm wrong again. And the doctor is right. So what. But it's not easy for me or anyone else. I know I'm sorely trying the patience of the nurses on night shift. Last night, one of them tells me, I rang the nursing station forty-two times. She smiles as she says it, perhaps to hide the murderous feelings in her heart. Another night one of them comes in and talks with me for two hours straight when I can't sleep. Beautiful people.

Marion, who would have made a great occupational therapist, rigs up an ingenious system of cords and pulleys which enables me to haul the mask off my face when I can no longer tolerate it at night. A piece of string is attached to the mask, passes through a makeshift pulley system over my head, comes down under the railing on my left side and is then attached to my left wrist. About the only function I have in that arm is to bend it at the elbow towards my head. I just have to bend the arm, therefore, and the string tightens and hauls the mask up off my face. The string-and-pulley system gives me a great deal more comfort as far as the claustrophobia is concerned because I can alleviate it at any time. The mask has to be put back on, of course, but that's a lesser problem. The major problem is resolved.

What would I do without Marion?

It's a lovely day.

The skies are blue, the seas are calm. Marion and I are somewhere out in the middle of Clode Sound in Terra Nova National Park with our jiggers overboard looking for codfish.

We've been married less than a year. Each little excursion into something different is the first time we've done that together, and everything is new and exciting. Although Marion is a townie we've both been cod-jigging many times before, but it's our first time fishing as a couple and that makes all the difference.

We're not having much luck. I think we're on the spot that the old fellow who owns the boat told us about, but I can't be sure. Marion is certain that I know exactly what I'm doing, something she'll get over before too many years have passed. That's what my mother says.

At the same time, she seems to be a bit nervous, which is much unlike my Marion. Perhaps it's because the boat is so small. Or it may have something to do with whatever is jumping out of the water a few hundred feet from us. One thing is sure, it's big. The sharp slap against the water as whatever it is falls back into the sea is easily heard, and the spray is thrown many feet into the air.

"What is that?" she asks.

"I'm not sure," I reply. "Could be big tuna or pothead whales or perhaps even humpbacks."

"Will they come this way?"

I could tell she wasn't happy about this.

"Oh no," I reply, sounding more certain than I was, "they'll stay well away from us."

"I don't know," she says doubtfully, but she keeps on jigging.

A few moments later, Marion gives a shout.

"I've got one on, Ed! I've got one on!" And she begins hauling in the line as fast as she can.

The water isn't very deep here.

"Be careful when you get your fish up close to the gunnel," I advise, "or the jigger could fly in too fast and hook in your legs or something."

"Okay."

The monsters that are a little farther off in the sound are really jumping around now, and I know she's keenly aware of that. Still, a little thing like fear won't stop Marion from getting this fish into the boat. When the jigger is right up to the gunnel, she reaches over with her bare hand to grab the prize.

She has this puzzled look on her face, as though she's not sure what's happening. Then her hand comes into view over the side of the boat and latched onto it is a beautiful big squid, the tentacles stuck fiercely to her fingers.

A scream, the likes of which hasn't been heard in this area for more than two hundred years, splits the air like a bolt of lightning. It bounces off the hills around Charlottetown and Bunyan's Cove and reaches up into Port Blandford.

"Get this thing off me!" she's screaming. "Get it off me!"

Like the good protector that I am, I manage to disengage the tentacles from her hand and throw the squid back into the sea from whence it came. Then I comfort my young wife, who really isn't the nervous type, and begin rowing back to shore as she wishes.

I will always, I promise myself, be around to take care of her.

Marion

One day not long after we came to the Hewitt Centre, a young woman named Celeste appeared out of the blue and announced she was there to do breathing exercises with Ed. I had no idea what her official role was on the Hewitt staff but she seemed to be one of the many specialists who were sent to work with him. Perhaps the psychology staff thought she might help him relax. I took one look at her and knew we had problems. Celeste was not of this world. She looked like a lost flower child left over from the '60s who found herself wandering around in the '90s and couldn't find her way back. For some reason she reminded me of Mia Farrow back when.

Celeste wanted to do Buddhist meditation exercises with Ed. Since no one had ever been able to hypnotize him, even when he was trying to cooperate, I knew Ed was going to be one of the bigger challenges in her young career. Celeste wanted to be in control. Ed was never real good at being controlled, and there was no reason to think he'd be any different now just because he had broken his neck.

The first thing she did without asking permission or approval was to walk over and turn off the TV. Ed had been watching some program or other and the look on his face suggested Celeste was not off to a good start. But to my surprise he said nothing and listened carefully as she described what they were to do and why.

"I want you to relax," she said. "Think of pleasant things."

I fully expected Ed to tell her rather forcefully that there weren't all that many pleasant things in his life right now, but again he was surprisingly silent.

At one point, Celeste thought he wasn't listening and tried to jar him into some response.

"Mr. Smith," she said somewhat severely, "I just asked you a question!"

Here it comes, I thought, and felt a momentary pang of pity for this young woman who was, after all, doing her level best to work with Ed. But again I was wrong.

"If you had been listening," he said, as sweetly as he ever said anything in his life, "you'd know that I answered it."

That first session ended in stalemate.

Next day Celeste asked him to relax the circles under his eyes, and as far as I could tell Ed was actually trying to do just that. It was when she asked him to describe the wind that he gave in to his feelings about the whole process. He said nothing discourteous to Celeste, but he went into a very long-winded description of wind in general and in specifics. Science has not yet discovered the things about wind that Ed now stated in florid detail for Celeste's benefit. He described what wind was and why it was. He talked about vicious northern blizzards, and about the warm chinooks that come with an Alberta spring. He described the doldrums of the equatorial regions and even spent some time on Coleridge's *Ancient Mariner.*

Celeste tried to stop him. My, how she tried. But Ed wouldn't even slow down. I soon realized that this was his way of telling Celeste exactly how he felt about her meditation exercises. He paused in his monologue only when she began edging toward the door. Then he stopped and said a pleasant "Goodbye" and Celeste responded with a rather hurried "See you" and was gone. When the door had closed, Ed was silent for a few moments.

"That dear little child has good intentions," he said thoughtfully, "but you know, I think she's nuts."

Celeste never came back to complete the meditation exercises that would help Ed to relax. My feeling was that she found the sessions too stressful.

9

We should have guessed it. We should have foreseen it. And we would have, too, had money not been the furthest thing from our minds right now.

We're told some of our friends back in Springdale want to set up a trust fund for us.

They say you find out who your true friends are when you get in trouble. I really didn't need trouble to know that, which is why I shouldn't be surprised. But this goes above and beyond the bounds of ordinary friendship, and that shouldn't surprise me, either. These are the same friends, incidentally, who would skin me alive at a poker game, and frequently have.

They want to know how I feel about this. I don't know. On the one hand, bless your hearts. On the other—what are you trying to do to me, b'ys? Can you know how it feels to be a charity case? You all know me well, as I know you, so why do you want to do this?

Marion has an answer.

"What," she says, "would you want to do if this had happened to one of them?"

I don't have to think very long. I'd do anything for them, unless it were on a poker night. Okay, they're my friends. That's why they're doing it. They've thought about the financial pressures we'll be under and determined that the money I make off them in poker games won't quite cover the expenses. Now that we think of it, they're right. Our expenses will be horrific. Wheelchairs, van, house renovations, drugs, attendant care and a host of other things we don't even know about now, will certainly be far above our present ability to pay. But I still don't like the idea of being a charity case, or even thought of as a charity case. I don't mind playing on my face when I've lost the limit in poker, but I don't want to be seen as a public charity case. That's just me. I inherit my father's streak of stubborn independence.

Marion used to get angry with me for taking all afternoon to do some task that with help from a couple of friends would take only ten minutes. They'd help me with a heart and a half, as I would them, but that's not the point. And I really don't know how to explain what the point is. It's just that I've always had difficulty asking people for help. I feel as though I'm imposing on their good nature. Or perhaps I don't like to admit that I need help with anything.

Marion understands how I feel, and shares much of that feeling with me. But she gives another perspective to the situation.

"If one of your friends were hurt as you are, you'd be among the first to want to do the same for him. How would you feel if that friend refused your offer of help?"

I have nothing to say to this. What is there to say?

"It's a long, hard road that lies ahead of us," she goes on, "and you're going to have to learn to accept help whether you want to or not. So don't be so proud, Ed. We're going to need lots of support from our friends and not all of it will be money."

I know she's right, and in the end we accept what "the b'ys" are offering with a shipload of gratitude. But Lord, I have mixed feelings about this.

The fund-raising effort takes off immediately. To our absolute amazement Friends of Ed Smith committees spring up all over the island. The acronym FOES is a great oxymoron.

Benefit concerts take place in Springdale, Gander, Musgravetown, St. John's and other places. Special services are held in churches in Springdale, Bonavista and several other communities. People we don't even know are working hard to raise money for the trust. The FOES committee in St. John's puts off a benefit that draws hundreds of people. I wanted to attend that one, but just couldn't bring myself to be the focus of all that attention. My parents and Pat and her husband attend, and my father speaks on my behalf. In

Grand Falls-Windsor two good friends organize a benefit dinner with guest speaker John Crosbie and it draws hundreds from the whole central Newfoundland area. The wonderful Otto Kelland, who wrote that most beautiful of all Newfoundland folk songs, *Let Me Fish off Cape St. Mary's*, donates one of his classic dories to be auctioned at the St. John's concert where it raises several hundred dollars. He gives me one for myself and I am absolutely delighted. Broadcaster Harry Brown makes several appeals over VOWR radio, and while hearing these things makes me feel uncomfortable, I marvel at the willingness of people like Harry to get involved, and again I am grateful.

I am touched especially by little things.

A school in Whitbourne holds a special Ed Smith Day, and students from kindergarten to grade eight undertake fund-raising projects. Even more, each student writes me a letter wishing me well and telling me a little bit about themselves. Some of these are priceless.

"I know we are helping you buy a special computer so that you can keep on writing," wrote one little girl, "but I think you'd be better off first buying a wheelchair."

No better illustration than that of the practicality of the female mind.

"We are selling hot dogs to raise money for your computer," said a small boy. "I don't like hot dogs but I bought one for you because I know you'd do the same for me."

I hope he's right.

I am totally overcome by the sentiments expressed in these and other letters. Cards and notes are coming in by the hundreds from people all over Newfoundland and beyond. Within a month, we lose count somewhere after two thousand. Many of them contain money and we pass that on to the prime movers of the trust in Springdale. Again, it's the expressions of love and support that we treasure most.

"We have never met you," is the most common beginning, "but we feel as if we know you and your family."

Most of those cards and letters are signed "with love."

I am overwhelmed. Without being in the least bit coy, I can say in complete honesty I had no idea of the number of people who read my column and are now reaching out to me. Many of them give specific instances where "The View" helped them or one of their family over rough times. All of them encourage me to hang tough and get back to the column as quickly as possible.

"I've read all your columns and I have all your books," one lady from Central Newfoundland writes. "Right now I'm knitting an afghan to put up on tickets for your trust fund. I'm really looking forward to reading more as soon as you begin writing again. By the way, I am one hundred and four years old."

I tell my lawyer about that last wonderful lady and he can't believe it.

"She's my aunt!" he exclaims. Small world.

A lovely woman who was one of my high-school students thirty years ago, and whom I've seen only a few times since, sends me cards on a regular basis, and never lets me forget she's thinking of me.

Another friend, who with her husband moved away from Springdale many years ago, finds time to write me a letter every single Sunday, and on top of that frequently telephones.

The list is almost endless. The support and comfort they bring us is.

We are the beneficiaries of hundreds of special considerations from professional people and businesses. The amount of voluntary labour on our house renovations is just incredible. When the work is labour-intensive such as shingling the roof or pouring cement or replacing the siding there are always several men to help out. Our basement was almost destroyed by the flood. Some of our closer friends put in many hours of work laying down a new floor, replacing the walls of the bedroom and installing a bathroom in case we need accommodations for a live-in attendant. These people are no longer friends, they are family.

Marion and I and our three girls moved to Springdale in 1971. Our plan was to stay there for two or three years while I gained experience as a high-school principal, and then move back east at first opportunity. Before our first year had ended, we knew we had discovered something special. In just a few months we found ourselves part of an amazing network of friends and acquaintances, and at the end of our second year we knew this would be our home and here we would raise our family. That was twenty-eight years ago and we have never regretted the decision. Although many of the original group have moved away or passed on, that support is still there and still very real.

We have received notes and cards from people representing almost every denomination in our town. The friends to whom we have been closest over the years and who remain part of our extended family continue to provide support of every kind. Often they visit us here in the Hewitt, even though they're many hours away by car.

What can we say of those numerous people who continue to show their love and support for us in so many ways? What can we say that can illustrate the depth of our gratitude to them? Most of them, if we tried to say anything, would look a little embarrassed and find something to gaze at off in the distance before responding in typical Newfoundland fashion.

"Don't be so foolish, my son, we didn't do anything."

Right.

10

The Hewitt staff lives up to its word.

Each day the physiotherapist takes what she needs from the rehab room on the next floor and brings it down to a classroom on the first floor where I do my exercises. Most days Marion is there, too, but sometimes it's just the two of us. I notice the PT always brings a phone and plugs it into a jack on the wall. That, I presume, is to call for help in case I attack her.

Most of the therapy is on my arms, since I have no feeling below what they like to call the "nipple line." That's what they call it on men, anyway.

I'm grateful for the consideration, and the accommodating of my claustrophobia. They take that affliction seriously here. But there are rumblings in our team meetings from the PT and the OT that the situation is anything but desirable. It is stated that I'm getting less than half the therapy I'd be getting upstairs. More than that, I'm not part of the patient rehabilitation group where I could see how others are progressing and govern myself accordingly.

It's frustrating for me, too, because I fully intend to be home for Christmas. That would make it almost one year from the accident on January 3rd, 1998. One year is enough to be travelling on this road. But if I'm not progressing according to the norm, this rehab stuff could take a lot longer and already we're into spring. Still, there's no way I can ever visualize getting aboard an elevator, even for one floor. It just ain't going to happen.

Finally, my psychologist mentions at our regular weekly session that she has a colleague who specializes in curing phobias.

"Not mine," I say shortly. "Nothing will ever cure me. I've had it too long and it's too deeply embedded."

"Perhaps," she replies, "but what have you got to lose? She won't ask you to do anything you don't want to do."

"I don't ever intend to a get aboard another elevator in my entire life."

"You won't have to unless you feel ready."

I think about this for a while. I know I'll never feel ready, but I'm not going anywhere soon so perhaps we should give this person an exercise in failure. Do her good.

"Okay," I say grudgingly, "but I want you to understand right at the beginning that this isn't going to work."

"You'll certainly be a challenge," is all she says.

The phobia psychologist, Carol, sets up a meeting without delay. She's eager to get to work and brimming with confidence. We'll see how long that lasts, I say to myself with grim satisfaction.

We get down to brass tacks immediately.

"What do you fear most about being in an elevator?"

I have to think about this. It's not a question I've asked myself. The titanic fear has been there for so long and yet I've never tried to analyze it. I know it's irrational, so there doesn't seem much point in thinking about it rationally. It's something like being afraid of the dark when you're a child. You don't know why you're afraid, you just are. But the question requires an answer.

"Because it's a small, confined space and small confined spaces make me panic."

"Why?"

Now there's a stupid question.

"They just do, that's all."

I realize that there's a stupid answer, so I try again.

"It's not elevators as such, it's the possibility of getting stuck in one."

"And why does that bother you?"

"Because I can't get out if it gets stuck."

Doesn't this woman understand anything? Evidently not, because she keeps right on plugging.

"And why are you worried about that? You know you'll get out eventually."

"I suppose so."

"Then why are you so afraid of getting stuck?"

This one requires an admission that I've never made to anyone except Marion, and I say it slowly.

"Because I'll panic and make a fool of myself."

"And what's wrong with that? People do it all the time."

"Do what?"

"Lose control of themselves. They become emotional with grief, or lose their tempers or become frustrated."

I'm beginning to understand what she's saying, since I'm getting pretty frustrated myself with this process.

"Wouldn't you avoid situations in which you know you'll go to pieces in front of other people?"

She remains calm and unruffled.

"First of all, the elevator is unlikely to get stuck."

"Really?" I can't wait to interrupt. "You know how often the elevators in this place get stuck? Just yesterday three men were trapped for over twenty minutes, and one of them lost it. I was outside in the corridor and heard it all."

She continues as though she hadn't heard me.

"If it does, you simply wait for someone to free it. If you panic, which I don't think you would, it doesn't matter."

And so it goes, session after session.

"You're not afraid of panicking, you're afraid of the idea of panic. It's the same as a person being in love with the idea of being in love rather than in love with another person."

And then one day she takes an entirely different tack.

"Is your father a very strong man?"

"Yes, but what's he got to do with this?"

"Is he the type who stays calm in dangerous situations? Is he capable of handling himself in most circumstances?"

Instantly, I remember our family being ferried across Twillingate Bight one night in a storm of wind and snow in an open boat. A couple of other passengers became so frightened they wanted to jump overboard, although I couldn't see the point of that. Another was kneeling, praying to beat the band. A child of nine reacts to such panic strongly. I joined the prayer group.

I can still see my father standing tall and strong, and telling the others not to be so foolish. I can see him throwing rowdies out of church suppers and simply being unafraid in any situation.

Okay, you don't have to hit me over the head with a hammer. I know exactly what she's getting at, and, dear God above, she might be right. It's a revelation right up there with John's on the Island of Patmos. I was never as physically strong as my father, and in my mind at least, never as courageous. Is my fear of panicking a fear of not living up to what he is, and what I think he expected of me? Could be. I know I always wanted both my parents, especially my father, to think of me as strong and fearless. Am I afraid of being afraid for that reason?

Bright lady that she is, Carol knows I know what she's getting at, and says nothing else. Next meeting she suggests we go out in front of the elevators for a few minutes, and she even asks if I would go inside if she holds the doors open. But I'm not ready for that yet. Besides, if and when I decide to do that I want Marion to be there.

The elevators at the Hewitt open on both sides so that one can walk straight through from one corridor into another. I hope no one is watching the day I screw up all my courage and drive my chair at top speed in through one side and out the other. Back and forth, back and forth with the doors on each side being held open for me. It never occurs to me to wonder what will happen if one set of doors suddenly closes.

We progress from there to staying in the car with the doors on one side closed, and then with both doors shut tight for a second or two.

Then comes that miraculous day when I agree to get into the elevator, let both doors close, and say through the hurricane of my fear, "Take it up."

Jennifer has been watching my progress from a chair in the lobby. Suddenly, she sees the elevator doors close and begin to ascend. It's only one floor but Jenny has raced up the stairs and is waiting when the doors open, throwing her arms around me in wild excitement.

"Dad! You did it! You actually did it!"

I suppose after twenty-seven years of watching her father pull every stunt in the book to avoid even going near an elevator, she could be forgiven for being somewhat delighted. And so am I, and so is Marion, and so is Carol.

It's only one floor, but it's the equivalent of riding the elevators in the Empire State Building for me. Now I can go to the physiotherapy sessions in the gym with everyone else, and take advantage of all the equipment as I can and need to. That's one giant leap for Eddie Smith.

But there's one more step. Carol wants me to remain in the elevator for a minimum of thirty minutes without getting out before she calls the treatment a success. I'm really apprehensive about this, but I have to try. So Carol, Marion and I get aboard, the doors close and we begin the trip. Also with us is a young woman student from Africa who wants to see how Carol and I relate and communicate as we proceed.

It is torment from hell. I know even as we begin that I'll never last thirty minutes. But I'm determined to hold out as long as I can. Every moment I'm expecting the thing to shudder to a stop and the doors remain firmly shut, while I go completely to pieces in front of my wife, my psychologist and a stranger. I call myself all kinds of coward and weakling. I turn my eyes from Marion to Carol to the student. They are all smiling confidently. But I'm very near the end of my rope.

Finally, in desperation I say hoarsely to Marion, "This is it. I have to get out."

"Good," says Carol, as the elevator slows to a stop.

"Congratulations," says Marion, as the doors slowly open.

"Just great!" enthuses the student, as we emerge into the lobby.

Good? Congratulations? Just great? I've only been in the thing for a few minutes. Exactly how long did I last?

"Thirty-five minutes, honey!"

Thirty-five minutes? I can't believe it! The dragon is slain. The tyrant is dead. I'm free, thank God, I'm free!

As I wheel across the lobby, the student leans over me. I'm astonished to see tears in her eyes.

"In my country," she says softly, "you would be a warrior. May I kiss you?"

And as she does, and as I'm thinking, now there's a country I have to visit some day, one other thought vibrates throughout my entire being.

Today I am a warrior!

11

Samantha is regarding me gravely.

She's just arrived with her father and mother and sister, Robyn. Robyn, like our grandson, Alex, is too young to remember or understand what's happened to me. She toddles off to explore the room while Sam stays close to her mother, her gaze steady on my face. It's the first time she's seen me since the accident.

"Hi, sweetheart. I'm so glad to see you."

She doesn't answer. What's going on in that little mind? Her mother has tried to explain the accident and that I'm paralyzed. She understands that I can't walk anymore but this is the first time she's seen me like this. She's still watching me intently. Is she remembering our times together hunting and fishing, when I used to carry her squealing across the brooks and through the deep snow? Probably not. She's only four years old. She'd be doing well to remember me at all.

Then Sam leaves her mother's side and walks slowly toward the bed. I'm too high for her to reach and hug. She stretches one small hand up until it touches my arm, then she lays her head against the covers and closes her eyes.

She remembers.

"Will we catch any fish, Skipper?"

She has always called me Skipper. When she was born I strenuously objected to Poppy, Granddad and Gramps. Don't ask me why. I don't know who came up with Skipper, but it seemed to me to be the lesser of all the evils.

We are several miles in over an old woods road, headed for my favourite fishing hole. The truck bounces over ruts and potholes to Sam's endless delight.

"Sure we will, honey. The fish are just waiting for us to get there."

Almost immediately I regret this rather impetuous forecast. As my mother used to say, fish have fins. Can't take a chance on destroying a child's faith in her grandfather. I wait a decent interval and then try to undo what I've done.

"Sometimes, Sam, the fish take a nap in the afternoon. They may all be asleep by the time we get there."

"That's okay, Skipper, I know you'll wake them up."

Her tone has all the confidence of a novice nun in the Mother Superior.

I curse myself for being so flippant. How do I explain to her if there are no trout that I can't wake them up? It's not often that I go to this pool and catch nothing, but it has happened. Don't let it happen today.

"Skipper, you remember you told me that Rudolph and all Santa's reindeer live up here?"

Another of my little pronouncements coming back to haunt me. I've seen caribou on this road and no doubt embellished the story a bit for Sam's benefit. Now she's calling me on it.

"Santa's reindeer only come out in winter," I say, marvelling how quickly the little white lie comes to my lips. "It's unlikely we'll see Rudolph today."

"But you said he was here, so I'm sure he'll be watching for us."

You must have committed some terrible sins in your past, Smith, for this to be laid on you now. How will you ever redeem this day and this child's trust in you?

We're almost at the pond, thank God! But I haven't suffered enough yet.

"Skipper, remember you said there were little ducks up here? I want to see some baby ducks, Skipper."

I know it's stupid, but as we drive around the end of the pond, I cast my eyes out over the water desperately, hoping against reason that there might be a duck and several little ducklings swimming along by the shore. But I

*know they aren't there and I'm right. I haul the truck over
to the side of the road and stop.*

*"Okay, little love, time to go look for some fish! You
bring the basket and Skipper will bring the fishing rod.
Here we go!"*

*Her eyes are shining with excitement as we scramble
down over the hill to the spot where the brook empties into
the pond. There's a small pool surrounded by lily pads, and
trout are almost always lying in the cool water. Today, the
sun is hot and bright and the trout may have gone to deeper
parts of the pond.*

I pick Sam up and lift her across another small brook.

"Hang on, Sam. You don't want to fall in the water."

"I'm hanging on tight, Skipper. I won't fall."

*The place we fish from is a muddy little bank almost in
the mouth of the larger brook. Sam is too small to cast the
line. My plan, God willing, is to hook the trout myself and
let her reel them in. One of the peculiar things about the
trout here is that while they don't go for worms or spinners,
they rise like the devil for flies. I snap the line back over my
head and cast the fly out over the pool with the fervent
prayer that some stupid fish will think it's food. I even try
to remind God that this is for Sam and not me, but it's not
likely he'll believe it.*

*The fly hasn't quite settled on the water before I see the
ripples of the trout curling about it. I give a quick jerk with
the rod and, perhaps because I'm trying so hard and perhaps because the trout is small, it comes clean out of the
water and hits Sam square in the face.*

*She gives a gasp of surprise and fright as her hands fly
to her face and the trout drops to the ground. I check briefly
to see that the fly hasn't caught her or the trout hit her in
the eye. Her mouth opens and I'm sure she's going to cry
and beg to be taken home.*

"Skipper!" She cries. "Skipper! He's getting away!"

*I'm so surprised that for the moment I'm unable to
move. Sam is in a frenzy pointing to the trout that's wrig-
gling its way over the mud and back into the water. It almost
makes it before Sam, taking matters into her own hands,
moves quickly and cuts off escape by simply sitting on it.*

I can't believe it. Here's this little three-year-old child after being slapped in the face by a live trout and concerned only about the thing getting away. Talk about your chip off the old block.

I help Sam up and retrieve the fish. Her little bottom is nothing but mud. We'll have fun explaining that one to her mother.

It's one of those wonderful days. In an hour we've caught our limit. Despite the clouds of mosquitoes, Sam never complains and reels in every trout that I hook. The only thing dirtier than her pants are her hands and face.

Once back in the truck, Samantha smiles happily.

"We got a lot of trout, didn't we, Skipper?"

That we did, thank God. That should take her mind off ducks and reindeer. We've just made the turn onto the woods road from the pond when Sam speaks again.

"Where are the ducks, Skipper?"

I should have known. Nothing escapes that little mind. I'm desperately casting around in my own mind for an appropriate answer when about thirty feet in front of us I see a miracle. Sedately making their way across the road in single file are a spruce grouse and a half-dozen little grouselings, or whatever they're called. Sam sees them and cries out.

"Look, Skipper, look at the little ducks!"

It's far more important that a little child retain her faith in her grandfather than that she know the difference between grouse and ducks.

"How about that! Aren't they beautiful!"

Sam is enthralled. After the last little bird has disappeared off the road, she settles back against the seat and closes her eyes. She'll be asleep in a minute.

We are about halfway out over the woods road and all my attention is given to avoiding the deeper potholes and manoeuvring around sticks and rocks. I don't hear the first part of Sam's question, but the last few words penetrate my consciousness in a hurry.

"... see Rudolph, Skipper?"

Oh Lord! I forgot all about stupid Rudolph. The kid thinks she's going to see Rudolph the Red-Nosed Reindeer. So what do we do about that? I've dodged the bullet twice this day already with trout and ducks. There's not a chance in Hades that a caribou is going to walk out in front of us this time of day and this far out over the road. Now, what would a three-year-old child understand in terms of an explanation?

"*The reindeer are all asleep this time of day, Sam. This is their nap time.*"

"*But you said the trout would be asleep, too, and you woke them up. Can you wake up reindeer?*"

"*I don't think so, honey. They're way back in the woods. They wouldn't hear us if we tried to wake them up. Besides, they don't listen to anyone except Santa Claus.*"

"*Oh.*"

It's a small "oh," but coated with a thick layer of disappointment. I curse myself for having created such an expectation. It might be nice, Smith, if you think before you talk.

Sam says nothing as we slowly make our way out over the road. Look, honey, I feel like saying, we've got our trout and we saw the ducks. Isn't two out of three enough? Of course it isn't. She's three years old and her mind doesn't work that way yet. She'll be okay when we get home and she starts telling everyone about the trout and the ducks.

We are making our way around a sharp bend in the road when the day's third miracle appears. Standing smack in the middle of the road is one of the handsomest bucks I've ever seen. I blink my eyes but he doesn't disappear. In fact, he seems downright friendly, standing looking at us and obviously unafraid.

Sam hasn't seen it yet, and when I glance over at her I see that her eyes are closed, although I'm fairly sure she isn't asleep.

"*Sam! Sam! Look, look at the road!*"

"*What, Skipper? Where... Skipper! It's Rudolph! It's Rudolph!*" *Her little-girl voice is almost a shriek.* "*It's Rudolph, Skipper! It's Rudolph!*"

Of course it's Rudolph. There's no doubt about it in her mind, and absolutely none in mine, which makes it a consensus. There in the road ahead of us in all his splendour is Rudolph, The Red-Nosed Reindeer. He stays there for several minutes before deciding Sam has seen enough of him and meanders off into the woods.

Sam can't believe it. She *can't believe it! I'm in shock. There's no way all of this can be happening in one short afternoon. I must be living right after all.*

But Sam has one remaining niggling little problem.

"Skipper," she says, her eyes still dancing, "Rudolph's nose isn't all red and lit up."

I'm ready for that one.

"Of course it isn't, Sam. Rudolph's nose only lights up for Christmas, same as people's houses get all lit up for Christmas, right?"

"Right, Skipper," she replies, totally satisfied, and goes on to talk about how much she has to tell Mommy and Daddy and Nanny when she gets home.

"Do me one favour, Sam," I say quite seriously. "Don't turn back-on to Mommy while Skipper is still there. Okay?"

She promises, laughing as she remembers why, and we in our truck with our trout and our memories of ducks and reindeer drive slowly out of one of those beautiful afternoons around which my life and hers will revolve forever.

Samantha opens her eyes and lifts her head from the bed.

"Hi, Skipper," she says shyly. "I'm sorry you can't walk."

12

It's probably the drugs as much as anything else, but it takes me some time each morning to crawl out from under the blanket of fog that passes for sleep. Apart from the drugs, during the night I've summoned nurses at least once every hour, torn the CPAP off my face a few times, argued with the nurses about putting it back on, and been catheterized twice. That's not counting nightmares. Make no wonder I'm sleepy. The wonder is that I wake up at all.

I know the doctor and nurse have been in but I haven't a clue what they or I might have said. They might have told me I was having major surgery for a neck transplant later today, and I might have said, "Sure, whatever." Heck, I'd say okay to that wide awake.

I hate being washed and shaved. The skin on those few parts of me that do have feeling is all pins and needles, and very tender and not at all ready for rough cloths and towels. When the nurses drop down to where I can't feel I close my eyes and pretend they're not there. Works most of the time.

Marion usually feeds me breakfast and I'm happy enough to let her. Perhaps I should be learning to feed myself, but I just don't have the initiative to make the effort. That would mean crawling out of the mental cocoon I've spun around myself. No way am I ready to think about flying.

Sometimes we talk after breakfast. Sometimes I doze while she reads or tidies up the room. She's fast becoming a lay expert on quadriplegia and the attendant complications. She thinks I should know what they are and she's right. But

I'm not ready. I don't want to know what else can happen to me. Keep that out of my cocoon for now.

I want Marion to be inside the cocoon with me. Just the two of us, cozy and secure. I know she was there during my days in ICU and for some time after. But now she's increasingly on the outside and becoming more and more impatient with my refusal to try getting out, too. She says I should be working harder at it, and I guess she can't help me do that if she's in there with me. Marion is part of the real world that at some point I have to rejoin. That I know, but I still can't begin the struggle that will see me emerge from the chrysalis, even to be with her. If that's not incentive enough nothing else can be, and she knows that. That's what's so disturbing to her.

Audrey arrives to do the range of motion exercises. Poor Audrey. She has to know I'm never ready for her, that I never want to begin the exercises, that I resent her because of that. She must see the door to my room as the door to her own little hell. But she doggedly keeps at it and rarely lets me beg off. I'm rather foggy on what the point of these exercises is, but I don't ask her to explain. Every morning as I'm lying in bed she extends my arms in different directions as far as they can go and then some, and exercises each joint in my fingers. It takes almost an hour. I grow to be quite fond of Audrey, but I doubt the feeling is reciprocated. There's no reason it should be.

Shortly after Audrey leaves, the nurses get me up for physiotherapy. Now that I can use the elevator, Marion takes me up to the exercise room on the second floor for my daily routine with Stella. Several therapists and helpers work with patients in this room. Stella and Irene, Stella's lovable assistant, get me out of the chair and onto the gym mat on a raised platform. The exercises are designed to keep my legs from stiffening up and atrophying, and make my arms and neck stronger. Worthy objectives, to be sure, but all I know is that I have to endure this for an hour.

Stella has a great personality and she's fun to be around, but having my arms twisted out of shape is no fun at all. Truth is, it hurts like hell. Frequently I cry out with pain and then I'm thoroughly embarrassed. I think Stella has some empathy for me, but she keeps at it. Similar activities are going on all around us but I don't hear anyone else moaning. That does nothing at all for my self-esteem. I'm the only person with quadriplegia around and I use that, at least to myself, to excuse my weakness. The others are mostly older people who have had strokes and are trying to regain some use of their limbs. A couple are amputees. One or two have paraplegia.

The room is not an unpleasant place to be. People are calling out to each other, the therapists sometimes tease each other and the patients, and one or two of the therapists usually have a joke, not always of the Sunday School variety, thank God. That may seem like a strange thing to be thanking God for, but I think he probably says, "You're welcome, Eddie." I like to think God knows me as Eddie. Don't ask me why. God may not know me at all these days.

Marion usually stays with me the whole time, watching carefully and learning the routines. I have a strange passion for oranges in these sessions so she'll go and get one for me. If she's not there when the session is finished, Stella or Irene will take me down in the elevator. I can get in the elevator with Marion or one of the therapists, but I won't get into one by myself. Not yet.

I'm anxious to get back into bed by now. My bed is my home and I gravitate to it at all times. That's where I usually have lunch, again being fed by Marion or one of the nurses. Sometimes when I'm feeling better I stay in my chair for lunch. That doesn't happen a lot.

Now it's poor Audrey's turn again. We ride up to the third floor to the Occupational Therapy department. There they have all kinds of weird and wonderful activities designed to make you more ready for the outside world.

Everyone in OT tries hard to be helpful, but there's a peculiar insensitivity to the mental state of the patient. They sit me down to a table on which lie several children's blocks.

"What are the little blocks for?" I ask innocently.

"We want you to pick them up and place them on top of each other."

I'm to play with children's blocks? No way. They wouldn't do this to me. I look over to Marion for help but she's staring mesmerized at the blocks, the children's blocks I'm being asked to stack, one on top of the other. I try to pick up one between my thumb and forefinger with the pincer movement caused by flexing the wrist. But my heart isn't in it and I give up after a few tries.

Perhaps the kind of blocks they're using shouldn't matter. Perhaps for many patients it doesn't. But for someone who's been almost completely destroyed physically and stripped of everything that makes him an adult it does matter. I'm as helpless as an infant. I am of necessity often treated as an infant. Even so, I'm struggling hard to try and regain some small sense of my adult identity. Kiddies' blocks don't do a lot to help rebuild adult self-esteem. Neither does batting coloured balloons around the room. The purpose of the exercise is obvious, but again one equates coloured balloons with childhood. Black might be more appropriate.

Marion thinks about this for a while and comes up with another suggestion. Instead of children's blocks, why not use something like the little creamer cups one finds in restaurants? Fill them with sand to make them heavier and have patients learn to pick them up. It's a useful skill, the cups are roughly the same size as the blocks and they're part of an adult world.

One of the OT workers gives me a small drinking cup to try lifting to my mouth. Then she says with every intent to be helpful, "My little boy is only two years old and he has one just like this and *he* can use it."

When you're as fragile as I am that kind of thing can pretty well destroy you.

Marion glares at her. The worker sees the look and understands something is wrong but she's not sure what. So she repeats what she's just said. Marion increases the intensity of the glare and the worker, really a very nice person, suddenly twigs to what's happening.

"Of course," she adds hastily, "I like to use it myself, too."

If I weren't feeling so sorry for myself, I might spare a feeling or two for her.

In a related incident at one of our family meetings, I suggest that some physical symptoms I've been experiencing of late might be due to baclafin, the drug they've started using to control muscle spasms in my legs. The good doctor doesn't buy it. But he doesn't say, "No, Ed, I don't think so," or "I don't think you're taking enough of that drug to cause those symptoms." His reaction is much more pointed.

"I've had little old ladies on larger doses of baclafin than you and it hasn't affected them at all."

Thank you, doctor. Perhaps you should try your hand at OT.

I don't seem to be making much progress at the OT sessions. No doubt this has something to do with my attitude that most of this is a waste of time. It may have something to do with the fact that some of it is. Still, if I were giving my all to these sessions no doubt I'd be getting much more out of them. But I'm not and I don't.

No one's fault but mine.

13

So, God, where've you been this last little while?

You'll have to speak up, God, because I can't hear you. Don't you have anything to say? Or do you have nothing to say because you're not there? If there's no you, then I'm talking to myself. If I'm talking to myself at least someone's listening.

Back to question one. Where've you been?

It isn't as though you haven't been needed. So if you were around at all, why did you let this happen? Life was going along pretty good for me, you know. I was grateful for what I had and took nothing for granted.

And then this happens. Why? People keep telling me it's all part of a plan, your plan I assume. But tell me. What grand purpose is served by me being in a wheelchair for the rest of my life? Do you really plan this sort of thing? I'm told you love me. You would do this to someone you love? I wouldn't do it to my worst enemy. Does that make me better than you who are supposed to be "perfect love"? I would almost rather you didn't exist if you're the kind of Being who treats its creation like this.

So why did it happen, God? Could you have stopped it? And if you could have, why didn't you? Which is it? Either you could have and didn't, or you couldn't and I'm talking to myself.

If you were to speak, perhaps you'd have an explanation. "Why not you?" you might say with a shrug of your almighty shoulders. "What's so special about you that you should never be hurt?"

You might even chastise me for asking the question.

"Look around you. How many others are hurting worse than you? Look around the world. How many are suffering and dying through disease, famine, war? You might well ask, why them? So does your question, 'why me?' have any meaning in that context?"

I don't know.

In any case, God, you answer my questions with my words. If you choose not to speak, someone else has to put words in your mouth. How valid are these words when they're only mine?

Do you make miracles, God? Do you the Creator interfere with the laws of your own creation when it suits you? Do you reach down or up or out, whichever it is, and hold a car on the highway when the laws of velocity and gravity are dictating that it crash? Or lay your hand on a spine and keep it from twisting and crippling?

I know many who believe you do just that. But where are you when little children are starving to death? When women are raped and killed? When men are executed? When men, women and children are tortured and slaughtered? If you perform miracles, God, perhaps it isn't with me you should start after all. Someone has told me they believe in guardian angels who watch over and protect us. Where are these angels when the human monsters of this earth decide to wipe out whole races of peoples because it suits their perverted and twisted minds? Or are angels responsible for protecting white Christian North Americans only?

And where are you?

Still silent, God? Because you have no answer? Because there is no answer? Because you choose not to answer?

I have friends who say we're not supposed to understand these things. Is that it? You give us intelligent minds designed to probe and investigate and find answers. And then you deliberately block those minds from seeking the answers to the most fundamental questions of life and death. Through a glass darkly and all that? It seems to me to be a cheap shot at getting you off the hook.

Do I blame you, God, for the state I'm in?

Of course not. I don't believe you had anything to do with it. Whether because you couldn't save me or wouldn't

I don't know. Why do you let children starve and people be put to death by the millions in gas chambers if you have the power to stop it? Please don't tell me it's all part of a plan. If so, the plan is as monstrous as their deaths.

The plan, the miracle, are a total contradiction of my free will, my freedom to choose, to make decisions. If you have a plan which overrides anything I choose to do, then I do not have freedom of choice. If you perform miracles that undo the negative consequences of my actions, I have no freedom of will to make decisions. If you give me free will but then state that unless I do what you want you will punish me, the concept of free will is a mockery.

So which is it, God? Do I have the dignity of a free will, or am I a puppet on a string, manipulated by you through your miracles, by the imposition of your plan?

Now I'm talking as though I believe you exist without understanding what or who you are. I always seem to fall into that trap, no matter how skeptical I am at the beginning. But there it is.

The seventeenth century philosopher, Pascal, wrote that there's no good reason to believe in God, and no good reason not to. It's a matter of choice. So I guess I believe in you because I choose to believe. It's not so much a matter of faith as a matter of choice. I know all the arguments—philosophical, spiritual, practical—pro and con, and I could argue and debate them all from either side for the rest of my life without ever reaching any logical conclusion. I believe, therefore, not because I'm *persuaded* to believe or because of the faith of my fathers or some Damascus Road experience, but because I *choose* to believe. That choice has no meaning unless I'm free to choose otherwise. Belief in you is my chosen way. Not that it makes any difference. No matter what I believe or what I choose, you are you, or you are not you. It's already a done deal.

I find myself in spite of myself waiting for some word, some act, some sign to show I've made the right choice. But when all the signs seem to point in another direction, you can understand my frustration and uncertainty, no matter how I've chosen.

God, are you listening?

14

Physiotherapists, all of them female in the Hewitt, are athletic nymphs who look as though they've been through a crash course in starvation. No one of them looks older than fifteen. In splendid contradiction to their physical appearance, some are married and others engaged. The rest need parental consent to be out after ten. Occupational therapists tend to follow the same pattern, although not always.

Physiotherapists are hugely intimidating in their youth and vitality. Spread out beneath them, legs splayed apart like a frog in a dissecting pan, we are as vulnerable as a tadpole in a pool of hungry trout. In magnificent and unfeigned unawareness of their power over us, they twist our muscles and limbs into shapes and positions they were never designed to go.

I am acutely aware that in the presence of these clean and pure young goddesses I currently have no control over some of my bodily functions. Without warning my body emits gases, noises and smells not generally acceptable in polite society or churches. Not much I can do about it, except hope that it never happens when someone is invoking a moment of silence in memory of the dearly departed.

The PT, ever the soul of discretion, always pretends not to hear the sounds emitted by my posterior. By the sheerest of coincidences she acquires great interest in what's happening on the other side of the room immediately after, and sometimes during, these foghorn eruptions. Sometimes she even has to run over there to confer with one of her colleagues. Meanwhile, I close my eyes tightly, like an ostrich burying its head in the sand, in the vain hope that when they reopen, the pungent scent will have disappeared and all evidence of it drained forever from the earth, or at least the physio's olfactory nerves.

Marion often reminds me that I'm not responsible for what happens from my shoulders down. Perhaps not, but it's me who's there when the unthinkable does happen, however rarely, and the lack of responsibility does nothing to ease my extreme embarrassment.

The lingering stink (things don't smell, they stink; people smell, and sometimes stink as well) now assailing my nostrils tells me in large capital letters that this time the cause of the aroma is more than simply air. As nonchalantly as I can, I say to the goddess-physiotherapist who's lifting my leg over my head and bending it around my neck that I have to go back to my room. She pauses and looks at me in wide-eyed innocence.

"Why?"

"Because... because... I just have to, that's all." I feel like a five-year-old trying to cover up the fact that he's just dropped a load in his pants. The only difference between him and me is fifty-three years.

There is an obvious desperation in my voice and the PT is suddenly aware of a tragedy in the making. Her eyes widen in understanding and she says, "Right!"

With the speed born of an urgency I feel and she now shares, she springs lightly up off the mat and sprints out of my line of vision. She returns almost immediately with the electric lift, two other young nymphs to help and the adult equivalent of a diaper spread over the seat of my wheelchair.

I have no words to describe the humiliation of that moment, or all the moments like it that will follow. As I'm being hoisted from the mat by the power lift, the lift sheet squeezes my body together like an accordion or, perhaps more accurately, a tube of toothpaste. What hasn't come out already would have to be strongly attached to my bowels not to follow suit.

By now, everyone within smelling range is aware of the disaster, and a few with weaker stomachs have already left the building. No one speaks, including me. I've already made a strong, non-verbal statement, and it might be better for all if I said nothing else. Of course, I can't guarantee that.

The three wonder women whisk me off to the elevator in nothing flat, but only one volunteers to get in there with me, or they draw straws—I don't know which. But as the doors close, it's hard to say which one of us is most terrified of the elevator getting stuck between floors. Even goddess-physiotherapists have their mortal limits.

Somehow we survive the trip, although my attendant is a little pale around the gills as we emerge onto the main floor and into relatively fresh air. She pushes me into my room, says a hurried "Bye," and leaves me to assault the physical senses of a new set of victims.

Now the real horror begins. I am lifted from the chair, swung out over the bed and dropped lightly on it. I can't feel anything swishing under my backside, but I'm firmly convinced I can hear it. By this time, there are three nurses competently and quickly hauling off my pants. I reflect briefly on how this process might have felt before the accident, but my traitorous mind refuses to linger on that pleasant little picture and returns to the present with a jolt.

Neither of the nurses is wearing a surgical mask and I wonder why. Perhaps they all have bad colds and can't smell anything. Whatever, they seem incredibly undaunted by the task before them. They're making pleasant small talk among themselves and seem to have forgotten all about the top half of me lying there in abject misery. I'm grateful for at least that.

They have just peeled off my underwear and revealed my backside in all its gory glory. I can take no more, and again squeeze my eyes shut on the premise that if I don't see it, it's not happening. I wonder what I could possibly have done to a loving God for him to allow this inhuman treatment of one of his creation to continue, especially when the one of his creation is me. And then I hear the voice of one of the nurses speaking matter-of-factly into one of the little silences of their conversation.

"Well look at that! Some dirty little fucker just shit in his pants."

There is shocked silence. I cannot believe what I've just heard. Of all the offensive, demeaning, unprofessional... I struggle to find words to express my outrage. Why, this... this is... this is the... this is really kind of funny.

I begin to laugh. The other nurses, I realize, are biting their lips and trying hard to hide shaking shoulders. And then they, too, begin to chuckle. In a moment we are all laughing like demented hyenas. My embarrassment is lost in the general merriment, and when it's over I'm beginning to feel more like a human being again. I realize the comment was made quite deliberately and with an obvious purpose in mind. And I'm convinced that angels are sometimes disguised as nurses who can swear like troopers.

I remember, too, something Marion has said repeatedly, "When you're laughing at yourself, no one else can laugh at you."

The banter begins again, but now I'm included in it. I say something pitiful about the loss of dignity in situations like this and get an immediate response.

"You don't know anything about the loss of dignity," one of the nurses states flatly, "until you've had a baby."

The others nod vigorous agreement, and while I can't empathize too much with the birth process, I know now that they understand exactly how I feel. That makes me feel worlds better.

I decide to return to the gym immediately. Something about getting back on the horse after you fall off. But I'm not looking forward to it. The physios will probably act professionally and pretend nothing happened, but what about all the other patients who will still be there?

The gym is as busy as when I left a half-hour ago. I enter cautiously and tentatively. No one pays me the least attention. I don't know if I'm relieved or disappointed. The PT is waiting by my mat. And I was right. She's acting perfectly normal. But as she's fixing the sling to lift me out of the chair, she leans over and whispers confidentially.

"This is the first time that's happened to you in all the time you've been here." She says it as though it were the achievement of the decade. I almost expect an award.

Angels, angels everywhere.

15

Debra Collins wants to interview me.

CBC television's Debra Collins, no less. She wants to do a short documentary on A-day-in-the-life-of-patient-Ed-Smith sort of thing. A very short day. A very short documentary. Three to five minutes. But she says their viewers will be interested in seeing how I'm doing, and who am I to contradict her (that's not a question).

God, the things a person has to do to get on television. If I were still labouring away at the keyboard out in Springdale writing The Great Canadian Novel, would Ms. Collins be wanting to interview me on "Here and Now"? Decidedly unlikely. Or if I had tripped over a tree on my rabbit trail and broken a leg, or even two legs, would her viewers want to see a day in my life, even a short day?

A friend of mine broke his two arms and had them up in splints for weeks. We all thought it was quite interesting, especially some of the details of how he was managing, but CBC didn't call him and put him on Here and Now, at least as far as I know. If they did, it didn't get aired. But break your neck and the media are all over you.

Perhaps I'm being too flippant. Perhaps there's a serious side to all this. People who have similar or other difficulties in their lives may watch this program and be affected by the manner in which I'm coping. If I'm obviously depressed and sick and not doing too well, some could be discouraged accordingly. But if I'm up and grinning and on top of it, the reaction could be quite different.

"Who the hell does Ed Smith think he is?" they might say. "If he can do that, so can I."

That's a big responsibility. If I agree to do this (you know I've already agreed), I'd better make sure it's a good day. If it isn't a good day, I should tell Debra (I already know her by her first name, you see) to come back some other time. But then she mightn't come back at all and I'd have to do something else equally dramatic to attract her interest again. Thing is, I've already broken the only neck I have.

Only one thing to do. If I wake up unwell on the morning in question, assuming I go to sleep at all the night before, I'll get them to shove enough pills down my throat to make me think I'm a cross between Peter Pan and Arnold Schwarzenegger. If I think I'm great, the viewing audience will think so, too. Then I have an even better idea. I'll have them push the pills into me, anyway, no matter how I feel. That way, if I'm feeling great, I'll look even greater. Perfect.

Debra Collins is a really nice person. I don't know what I expected: anything this side of Lizzie Borden, I guess. She knows how to make me comfortable with a little chit-chat beforehand, and then we're away.

First, we talk a little while I'm still in bed. I won't let them film me being lifted from the bed to the chair. They put you into this sling affair, which is something like a parachute harness, and then they hoist you out of the bed with an electric lift which looks like a cherry-picker for lifting motors out of cars, and deposit you in your chair. Dignified it isn't. Hard to say whether you feel more like a yaffle of fish or a sack of potatoes. Whatever, it isn't something I want Debra's viewers to see.

Then we go down to the classroom where the physio and I do our thing. Marion is there, too, as is Jennifer who is here on one of her regular visits from Boston. The cameraman takes shots from all angles, and Debra talks to me again, then to Marion and finally to Jennifer. They are both complimentary toward me, as one might expect. Certainly as I would expect.

A few more words back on the bed and it's all over.

I wonder how many other relationships have ended exactly the same way.

16

I have a little phrase which accurately describes the food in the Hewitt Centre. Regrettably, I know neither Marion nor the publisher will allow me to use it. That's unfortunate because it's most descriptive and would give you a fair idea of what passes for meals.

Fishermen's brewis is one of my favourite dishes. For those of you not favoured to live on The Rock, brewis is a hard biscuit ("hardbread" in the Newfoundland parlance) made only in Newfoundland and soaked overnight so that it becomes soft (the brewis). Then watered salt cod, or fresh cod depending on your taste (I use half and half) is boiled, drained and mixed loosely with the steamed brewis (usually steamed on top of the boiling fish until hot) and small cubes of fatback pork fried crisp and brown (scrunchions) and the resultant rendered fat. People with cholesterol problems, of whom I'm one, use Becel margarine and small pieces of onion fried brown and crisp instead of fatback pork. Regular fish and brewis, as opposed to fishermen's brewis, leaves the fish and the brewis separate, and uses the scrunchions and fat as a sauce to be poured over it. Some people, of whom I'm one, add a small amount of boiled potato to both dishes.

I'm overjoyed to see fishermen's brewis on the menu and can't wait for supper to come. When the cover is lifted from the plate, I can't believe my eyes. What greets me is a visual obscenity: a fine helping of fishermen's brewis and on the side another fine helping of steamed broccoli.

Fishermen's brewis and broccoli. Now there's a pairing to delight the palate. Show me the Newfoundlander who created this dish and I'll show you a mainlander. Marion suggests that the nutritionist wanted some green on the plate. If I look at this any longer, she's going to get it. So get rid of the broccoli. Flush it down the toilet, throw it out the window, send it up to the Confederation Building cafeteria. I don't care.

Okay, now let's get to the fishermen's brewis. I know before the stuff ever gets to my lips that I should send it scurrying after the broccoli. It's no sooner past my lips than I realize I should have thrown out the fish and brewis and kept the broccoli. The stuff is a gelatinous mass in which the prime ingredients of fish and brewis are indistinguishable from each other or anything else edible. If they used fat of any kind, it was rancid a month ago. Starving dogs would retreat from this stuff like a vampire from the sign of the cross.

I pass the plate to my father to show him how bad it is. Between wolfish bites and swollen mouthfuls, he agrees that it's terrible. It occurs to me that I've never seen my father turn down food of any nature or persuasion. If he ate a whole bottle of botulism, the little poisonous spores would curl up in his stomach and die. Cast iron gut.

What's actually edible in the Hewitt Centre tastes awful. Meals are prepared in a central location, bused out to the various institutions and served to unsuspecting patients disguised as food. It is poorly disguised at best.

Marion is getting desperate to have me eat something. I know I'm continuing to lose weight, and if the food problem continues there won't be enough of me left for the insurance company to swear on.

It's my sister, Pat, who comes to the culinary rescue. She begins bringing supper for Marion and me on those nights when the hospital meal fails to have us clapping our hands and making a joyful noise. Since the institutional meals are consistently awful, and since Pat spends every night she isn't working in my room, it becomes a routine. She or her husband, Bill, will call down just before supper and tell us what they're having and do we want any. Does Bill Clinton have carnal knowledge of What's-Her-Face? Within the hour, she or Bill (not Clinton) will be down with something which, when compared with the Centre meals, is cordon bleu.

In this way, not only am I kept alive, but also I can look forward to at least one meal in the day.

Pat, my only sibling, spends several hours of every single day with us. She could have chosen to exact revenge for the way I treated her when we were children, but she wouldn't have done that if I'd burned her at the stake once a week. She could give lessons in caring to Mother Teresa. Bill, too, spends many hours in my room, day after day. His sacrifice is especially keen because he has to sit there while the rest of us play Trivial Pursuit all night. Bill refuses to play Trivial Pursuit just as I refuse to play Scrabble, and probably for the same reason.

Usually the players are Marion, Pat, my parents and me. If one or more of my children are in town they are enthusiastic participants. Visitors and friends are often pressed into service. Some of them love it, some of them don't. We play until we're in danger of being shut down by the nurses, or we *are* shut down by the nurses, whichever comes first. The games are not without conflicts, some of them good-natured, some of them not. They're not when there are several of us and the men face off against the women.

"The answer is Joey Smallwood. Right, boys? We all agreed?" The male side unanimously agrees. "Okay. That's our answer. Joey Smallwood."

The answer is greeted with hoots and jeers from the opposition.

"Sorree! That's wrong! You lose your turn. Pass the die."

The men are incredulous.

"What?! It can't be wrong! The question was, 'What premier negotiated the Churchill Falls power agreement with Quebec?' That was Joseph Smallwood! That's what we said. So pass back the die."

"The answer *is* Joseph R. Smallwood," says Marion with a gleam in her eye, "but that's not what you said." For some reason, Marion enjoys being in the middle of those intense little arguments. "You said *Joey* Smallwood. Keep the die, girls!"

"Oh for the love and honour... You can't possibly be serious! This is absolutely stupid!" And other such and less savoury statements from across the house.

"Look, we agreed at the beginning that the answer would have to be the same as it is on the card. Your answer is not the same as it is on the card. Therefore it is wrong, right girls?"

The girls unanimously agree that this is right.

No one gives in until a nurse, or some other neutral person unfortunate enough to walk in at the wrong moment, is called upon to declare judgment. The sex of the arbitrator invariably decides the verdict.

Ray comes in once a week and we spend the night singing and playing. It doesn't take long for the room to fill up and overflow into the corridor. Jim is a young stroke victim who can't speak, but he can sing like a trooper. His favourite song is, "You are my Sunshine" and he's called upon once or twice every evening to perform, which he does without hesitation.

"Sing 'Blue Eyes Crying in the Rain.'"

Ann is a sweetheart of eighty years whose eyes are as blue as when she was sixteen. We'll sing that one for her several times before the night is through. Often, too, visitors to other patients drop by and we have one heck of a singsong before it winds down.

My father gave me a little mouth organ when I was ten. He was a half-decent player himself when he was younger, and could still play a mean jig. I'd lie in bed at night after the lamp had been blown out trying to play songs I knew. The first melody I had any success with was "Now the Day is Over" and I'd play it over and over. The harmonica didn't have the raw sex appeal of the guitar, so shortly afterward I bought a twelve-dollar guitar with a green palm leaf on it. All my musical attention focused on learning to play guitar chords and the little mouth organ was soon forgotten.

Marion, of course, is always thinking. As soon as the back-neck brace came off she had a little gift for me, designed to help build up strength in my lungs, but also intended to get me playing an instrument that didn't need fingers, like the guitar and the piano. I played neither really well but I enjoyed both immensely, especially for my own relaxation. Marion's gift is a harmonica.

To my surprise, the notes come easy and after only a couple of hours I am fairly proficient, or think I am. Father still carries an old harmonica around with him and it doesn't take long for the two of us to be playing duets. Father, I discover, although into his eighties, can play "I'se the B'y" much better than I.

Then another surprise: sister Pat has been learning to play, too, and suddenly we're the family von Trapp laying it down in my little room in the Hewitt Centre. We can play and we can sing, although no one of us is much good in the dance department. But it doesn't take long to attract attention, and soon our singsongs have the added element of a harmonica trio.

These are good times, despite our several and varied physical conditions. Truth is, we lose sight of them in these lovely hours.

The Centre's recreation department regularly provides entertainment of one kind or another. Everyone's favourite is a band called Joy. With two guitars, a keyboard and a piano accordion, they play country and western, older pop music and a liberal sprinkling of gospel. With personalities perfectly designed for live performance with this kind of audience—the Centre patients and people from the Veteran's Pavilion—the boys (actually they're all getting a bit long in the tooth) put off a great show.

Many of the crowd get up and dance, including at one point my father and Jennifer. It was one of those rare, great life moments when your camera is ninety thousand miles away. Sometimes someone who's ambulatory will take someone else in a chair and push them around the floor in time with the music. Never liked that idea myself, but to each his own. Everyone has a ball.

One night, for the first time in my life, I see my father and mother dancing together in public. The old Methodist attitude towards dancing being a sin deserving of hell's flames was still strong in many of the United Church pastorates in which my father served. The minister and his wife dancing would have been unthinkable, and the reaction from the parishioners most unpleasant. But now, here they are at the age of eighty-one coming out, so to speak, and we are all so pleased. Jennifer, who is twenty-eight years old today, is tickled pink.

"Look at them!" she says in a delighted whisper. "Look at them! They're dancing!" And so they are. I see them now, and I see them as they were long years ago when they were young and I was even younger.

"That," says my father as they come off the floor, "is the first dance we've had together since our wedding night sixty years ago."

It is July 13, 1970. I'm in St. John's for university summer sessions completing my B.Ed. There's no plausible explanation for why I leave Marion alone in Gander, four hours' drive from St. John's, with two small children and about to deliver a third. I get home for weekends, but still...

Then late one night I get a call from her. She's going into labour and has to get to the hospital at once. I am immediately more flustered than she.

"How are you getting to the hospital?"

I have visions of the baby being born in a taxi or something.

"Kevin is here," she says, "and Father Kane."

Kevin and Joan are our next-door neighbours and good friends. We've met Father Kane on various occasions, probably through Kevin.

"Okay, let me speak to Kevin."

It seems to me to be a long moment before Kevin comes on the line.

"Hello, Ed? Don't worry about a thing, my son. We got 'er all under control."

That's when I really start to worry. Kevin has obviously taken a few drinks over the course of the evening and a little thing like an imminent birth won't faze him at all no matter where it happens. Then I remember Father Kane. All is not lost.

"That's great, Kevin. Let me speak to Father Kane."

Another long moment.

"Hello there, Ed my son, and how are you doing this fine night?"

Oh my God. The boys have been together all night with similar consequences.

"Fine, Father Kane, just fine. Can I speak to Marion, please?"

"Okay my son. Don't worry about a thing."

I'm so worried my teeth are chattering.

"Marion, how are you getting to the hospital?"

"It's okay, Ed. They've had a few drinks but they're both such good fellows that I still have every confidence in them. Don't worry, I'll be okay."

How many times have I been told not to worry in the last ten minutes? I know only that every time someone says it my state of worry increases exponentially. But there doesn't seem to be much I can do two hundred miles away except sit and worry, and regret my decision to attend summer sessions at the university in St. John's.

"I'll be out first thing in the morning," I tell Marion, "and let me know immediately if anything happens."

I am lying on my bed, eyes wide open, when the phone rings about 3:00 A.M.

"Hello?"

"Ed?"

My heart leaps. It is Marion.

"Ed, you're outnumbered."

Another girl? I am delighted beyond words.

"Is she okay? Are you okay?"

"She's marvellous. I'm fine."

And in that manner my youngest daughter comes into the world. It is an auspicious beginning.

The first night I attend a Joy concert, one of the boys recognizes me and after the performance suggests I should do a song or two with them. We have a great jam session that night, and I agree that next time out I'll do something for the audience. But I'm not at all sure I will or even can.

At the next concert I'm given no choice. The boys use the audience as a lever, and I'm compelled to respond. I sing a couple of songs and the effect on me is overwhelming. I can actually get up in front of people again and sing. It's marvellous. It's fantastic. It's a whole drugstore full of uppers. It's difficult to describe the sense of euphoria that lingers with me all night and into the next few days.

It's Marion who puts the icing on the cake.

"I was so proud of you tonight," she tells me after that first performance. I give her so few reasons to be proud of me these days that I hold on to that simple little comment like the drowning man holds on to the log.

From then on I sing whenever Joy plays and it is medicine for the soul. Father, Pat and I are slated to do our harmonica rendition of "Ode to Joy," dedicated to the boys in the band, of course, but at the last minute Pat chickens out. The effect was similar to Diana Ross leaving the Supremes. But Father and I carry on, and we sing a little and play a little and the evening is magic. There are others who feel the same, I'm sure, because anyone who wants to is encouraged to do their thing. A couple will sing, someone else does a recitation or tells a story. It is karaoke night at the Centre with live music.

Joy doesn't charge any fee for performing, but they're worth more than anyone could afford to pay them. They do more to assist in the rehabilitation process than they'll ever know. For me especially, the evenings spent with them make that long, long journey towards home a little less painful, and perhaps even a little less long. I return to my room positive that I can accomplish anything and that I will be home before the winter comes.

I have always hated being patted on the head.

It started, as most of these things do, when I was a child. My grandmother was walking me down the road in our small Newfoundland outport when she spied the local merchant coming toward us. Merchants at that time completely dominated and controlled the lives of fishermen, and my grandmother, being a fisherman's wife, was conscious of the deference owed such superior beings.

"Now, Eddie," she said, "be sure to tip your cap to Mr. Parker."

At the ripe old age of five, I resented having to take off my cap to anyone. But I did it anyway, because my grandmother asked me to. Then the old man stopped, said hello to my grandmother and patted me on the head. I didn't know the word 'patronize' at that age, but I knew the feeling and I loathed it. So I stuck out my tongue as far as I could at the venerable Mr. Parker. I don't think my grandmother ever recovered from the embarrassment. I was awhile myself recovering from the punishment.

For a minister's son, of course, head patting was an occupational hazard. I learned early to duck under the hands of beaming old ladies at church. But Mohammed Ali couldn't have ducked them all, and the hands of those condescending old women were often faster than my neck. Remembering the Mr. Parker episode, I learned to suffer in silence.

Thankfully, by the time I was sixteen I was six-foot two and most people couldn't reach the top of my head with a stick. Things remained that way for most of my adult life. Obviously a kindly God was making up to me for the sufferings of my youth.

Then came the accident and I haven't been six-foot two since. Now that my waking hours are spent either in bed or in a wheelchair and thus within easy reach of everyone, the patting of Ed Smith's head has reached new dimensions.

It's difficult to overstate how much I resent this. No one has the right to pat me on the head as though I were a dog. The exceptions are my parents. Theirs was the sacrifice—and I use the word advisedly—*sacrifice* of raising me, and consequently they can do what they blessed well like.

For everyone else, patting or rubbing my head is not only the supreme condescension, but also a reminder of my lost physical stature and my current physical state. In short, it's patronizing and pitying and I react by desperately trying to avoid it. When Marion sees that someone is about to lay hands on me, she will do whatever is necessary to stop it, even to the extent of grabbing the offending hand as it descends toward my head. When despite everything it does happen, I have never been able to give full voice to my frustration.

Today an old friend of my father's comes to visit. My parents are also here and thoroughly delighted he has come to see me. This friend is very much a touchy-feely person, and as he enters the room I know exactly what he's going to do. I'm still in the process of trying to redefine myself as an adult human being, and my self-esteem and sense of worth are consequently very fragile. So when I see him coming at me, hands outstretched and face wrinkled in an expression of sympathy and concern, I lose it. All my previous bottled up resentments seem to erupt into this one solitary moment.

"Do not touch me," I say, in what I hope is a warning tone.

When he keeps coming, I raise my voice and almost shout, putting my arms up as much as I can to ward him off. And when despite my protests his hand does make contact with my head, I do shout, and what I shout at him is not "God bless you."

He draws back as though his hand has touched hot coals.

His face shows a mixture of bewilderment and hurt. Clearly, he has no idea what he's done wrong. And then I see the expression on my father's face. His head is bowed, and he's looking down at the floor in a way that suggests he might never look up again. I know at that moment he is hurting in the extreme both for me and for his friend.

When the friend leaves a few moments later, he speaks quietly.

"He was trying to be kind, you know, the only way he knows how."

It's like being hit over the head with a piece of 2x4. Through my father's eyes, I suddenly see myself as offensive and rude, and I know I have turned what was intended to be an act of kindness into a cruel and ugly reaction.

He was reaching out to me, my father said. And so were all the others up through the years, reaching out in their own way, trying to show they cared. But I fought them off like that arrogant little boy, who, more than fifty years ago, reacted to an old man who was just trying to be kind.

I will never want to be patted on the head. I believe it's an inappropriate way to treat any person, whatever their situation. But being quadriplegic is no license to treat others differently from how I wish to be treated myself—with respect and love. It's no excuse for reacting with anger to an act of intended kindness. The act itself can be gently rebuked, but the intent to reach out should be accepted and responded to.

No doubt before long someone else will again attempt to place their hands on my head. I won't like it, but my reaction isn't likely to be as extreme. Perhaps I'll try responding to that effort to reach out to me with my own effort at reaching back.

Being quadriplegic has forced me to begin building a new life, but even more I might be learning to grow up all over again.

17

I am in a strange place. I'm here but I'm not supposed to be here. The sky is a kaleidoscope of shades and confusion and the earth keeps moving back and forth in tormented rhythms. A thick, blue mist lies in front of me, like a great coloured fog bank, and I can't see beyond it. Rushing, black clouds roll through the sky and over the twisting earth. Nothing is familiar.

Other shapes and figures half-appear out of the mist and as quickly disappear. I call to them but they have nothing to do with me. They are alone. I am alone.

I am afraid. There is nothing to tell me which way I should go or what I should do. There are no paths or roads and yet I'm compelled to move forward through the blue mist which keeps me from seeing.

Then from behind me I hear someone calling my name. The voice is clear and I recognize it immediately. I turn and look back, and from a short distance behind me I see him. He's standing and running and jumping all at the same time, as if he were demented. He's near a river and then the river is a forest path and the forest path is the street where I live. Everything is changing but everything is the same.

He's calling to me.

"Ed. Come back, Ed."

I want to go back. That's where I belong. That's where I should be. With him.

"I'm coming," I call. "Don't go away."

But he is going away. Even as I watch, the distance between us is growing. I try desperately to leap to my feet

and run back towards him. But nothing happens. The voice
is growing fainter.

"Come back, Ed. Come back, come back!"

"I'm coming, I'm coming!" I scream. "Wait for me. You
must wait for me!"

But he doesn't wait. He's almost gone, and still I
struggle desperately to free myself and run back to where he
is. And then I see it.

Between him and me is a deep canyon. I'm on the edge
and I look down into a place where there is no bottom. I
look up and see that the far edge is moving steadily farther
away. He's only a small figure on the other side now, and all
I hear of his voice are the echoes from the canyon walls.

"Ed. Come back, Ed. Come back."

He doesn't seem to understand that I can't go back.
The distance is too far. The canyon is too deep. I can
never go back.

I can never go back.

18

Marion

I felt as though I had all the responsibility for Ed's rehabilitation but none of the control. The sense of responsibility
was my own doing, not just because I naturally wanted what
was best for Ed, but also because I was driving the vehicle
at the time of the accident. Ed keeps telling me that once a
car hits black ice it's game over. There's nothing the driver
can do except hold on and hope for the best. I know no one
blames me for the accident, but I'll never shake the nagging
and persistent voice that says perhaps there was something
I could have done.

I'd lie awake in my bed at night trying to prepare strate-
gies for the next day in my efforts to make sure he was getting the best treatment possible. But the world of health
care was a world I didn't know or fully understand. I didn't
know what the rules were or what my role should be relative
to Ed's care. On the one hand the staff seemed quite happy
to have me help with the daily details of that care. On the
other if I questioned something or offered an opinion, I was
made to feel as if I were interfering. Then I'd feel as if I was
in conflict with some of the health care providers and the
stress and strain of that was beginning to tell on me.
Sometimes I felt as though I couldn't hold out another day.

The rehabilitation process wasn't working at all the way
I expected. After more than three months, Ed was making no
significant progress. In fact, there was no doubt in my mind
that in range of motion especially, he had actually regressed.
The movement of his right arm was more restricted than

when we left the Health Sciences Centre and his left arm had certainly not improved any that I could see. I watched a tape of his first interview with CBC television, and it seemed to me that his arm movements were much looser and had greater range even then. His sister, Pat, agreed. His arms were all he had left and if he were to lose what little control he had over them he would lose everything.

The problem seemed to be his right shoulder. Jennifer says that she and her father used to arm-wrestle during the first few days after surgery, so it seemed fine then. A month or so after arriving at the Hewitt, Ed complained one morning that his right shoulder had been hurt while he was being turned the night before. The subsequent pain never did go away and the shoulder caused him considerable distress from then on, especially during physiotherapy.

Dr. Conifer said the shoulder might be frozen. Without getting into too much technical detail, this means that muscle fibre had grown onto the shoulder joint making movement more painful and restricted. The condition can be remedied through surgery or by continued physiotherapy. The doctor didn't recommend the surgical process and felt that therapy should alleviate the problem. That particular therapy is quite painful and Stella suggested that it seemed too much for Ed to tolerate. Nevertheless, the therapy continued.

It seemed to me, too, that the Minerva jacket which was supposed to hold his neck and spine immobile was pulling his head forward and down and to the left. My fear was that this would leave his head permanently skewed. I kept pointing this out but no one seemed to think it was a problem. Keeping the jacket straight was a challenge in itself. It tended to ride up on his body and become quite uncomfortable. To their endless frustration, every time the nurses turned Ed the jacket would have to be readjusted.

Then one day the surgeon who had operated on Ed and fitted him with the brace, Dr. Goodwin, came by to see him for the second time in three months. When I pointed out my concern, his reaction just about floored me.

"Of course it's pulling his head forward," he agreed. "Common sense will tell you it shouldn't be like that."

Common sense? This is simply a matter of everyday, common sense?

"How am I to know what common sense is in treating broken necks?" I asked.

I'm in a very strange world here, Doctor. I don't know what the rules are. I don't know where I stand or where I fit in. Sometimes I feel I'm always complaining and agitating without getting anywhere. The nurses and doctors must see me as a continuing thorn in their sides and in one way I can't blame them. But there's just this one constant in my life and that's my husband and what's best for him. That's the rationale for everything I do and the standard to which I hold myself. When I apply my common sense to his care, I'm often told I'm wrong but I'm not always convinced, even when it's in specialized care. Then someone has to show me I'm wrong before I give up on it. So don't tell me it's simply common sense. You're the doctor, you're the specialist. You tell me what's common sense this time.

"Besides," I go on aloud, "I've been asking people about that brace for weeks and can't get anyone interested."

"Okay, tell the people in prosthetics to adjust the brace a little at a time until his head is upright."

The surgeon was gone before I fully realized what he had said.

I was supposed to tell prosthetics that the specialist said to adjust the brace on Ed's neck? That was it? No note from him specifying exactly what should be done. No suggestion that he should meet with the doctor at the Hewitt to discuss the problem. No concern that perhaps the brace had been on too long in that position and some kind of therapy might be necessary to correct the problem. No desire to see Ed after so many days to see if the condition was being corrected. He was leaving it to the patient's wife to pass on a message to the prosthetics department from the neurosurgeon that the brace should be adjusted, and that was it. If it worked, fine; if it didn't, tough. When months later my worst fears were realized and Ed's head was bent down and to the left, I felt like suing that surgeon right out of his surgical gown.

Despite my concern over Ed's lack of progress physically, it was his attitude that bothered me most. When visitors or family were around he talked the talk very well. Most of the time he wasn't acting, although he was very good at that when he wanted to be. In the interview with CBC, for example, he came across as being in good shape physically and mentally, and in control of it all. Numerous letters arrived after, saying how good he looked and what an inspiration he was. No one knew except us that it was one of his worst days and he was putting on the act of his life. He had to do that, he said, because people with all kinds of problems could be watching and would need him to be positive and strong.

He could get into intense discussions about religion or politics, and his sense of humour bubbled to the surface at the most unexpected times. He enjoyed playing board games, especially Trivial Pursuit. Often visitors and friends would be pressed into the game and we'd play until everyone had to go home. But Ed would never take an active part such as trying to roll the dice or read the cards. As long as he could lie there without having to move a muscle he was content.

The Health Care Association provided him with a secretary once a week to help him write letters, and this he did right up until we left the Centre, but all Ed had to do was dictate and Danette did the work.

It wasn't the Ed I knew at all. All his life he had been an activist and a "doer." Physically he was going all the time, whether it was to one of his numerous meetings or following his hunting trails through the woods or out on the ocean in his boat or working around the house. He just never stopped. Lethargy was totally foreign to his makeup. Yet here he was now using every excuse in the book to avoid therapies, and when he couldn't avoid them he wouldn't actively cooperate. Making Ed do what he doesn't want to do has never been easy, and the young people on the staff found him more than a challenge. He wasn't difficult or cantankerous, or even moody. He just wasn't interested in doing anything physical. Consequently, he was motoring along in neutral and going nowhere, or even worse was actually regressing. I could see all of this clearly, and it was killing me because no one else seemed concerned.

I also felt that nursing policy, at least I assume it was policy, was responsible in part for Ed remaining as lethargic as he was.

Not that the nurses weren't caring. They were caring to a fault and Ed loved every one of them. Every detail of his physical needs was attended to and he was treated with dignity and respect. No matter what time of the day or night he pressed the call buzzer, someone was there in less than a minute, and they never seemed to run out of patience with him.

At this stage, for example, he should have been learning to feed himself, but since someone was always there to feed him, he never bothered to try. If an exercise hurt he didn't have to do it. If he didn't want to get up, he didn't have to. If he wanted to lie there in the dark with his eyes shut at three o'clock on a sunny afternoon, too often no one bothered him. His every spoken need brought immediate response, but he was never required to take even a small step into what was for him the unknown. If I opposed that approach, I always lost.

Even Ed's sister, Pat, who is one of the most caring people I know, saw what was happening but was unable to stop being a part of it. If I refused to do something for him that he could very well do for himself, he would comment pointedly that Pat would do it for him when she came down after supper. And invariably she would.

"I know we shouldn't be doing everything for him," she said to me one day, "but none of us seem able to refuse him anything."

On Saturday mornings Pat and I often went what Ed called "yardsaling." We both loved following the sales around the city, and Ed could sleep in because there were no therapy sessions. I used to hate driving up to the Hewitt entrance after lunch because I knew what I'd inevitably find. Ed's window was near the doors and even in the early afternoon the curtains would be closed against the light of day. Each time I'd hope against hope that it wouldn't be so, but it always was.

The room would be dark when I opened the door. Ed, groggy and half-asleep, would be unwashed and unshaven and upset at being disturbed. It's hard to describe how devastating this was for me. Sometimes I'd rush to the window and throw open the curtains. Ed would protest and try to turn his head from the light. After pleading with him at least to get washed, I'd try getting angry and demand to know why he was sleeping the day away, dirty and unkempt.

Nothing worked. And always the nurses' sympathies were with Ed.

"He just didn't want to be disturbed today, did you my love? Didn't want to hear anything about washing, either. You're just too tired, aren't you?"

Always Ed would agree that he was tired or not feeling well and wanted to be left alone for just another little while. The nurse would look from him to me as if to say, "See? I know what he wants better than you."

I don't believe there was any deliberate attempt to belittle me or put me down, but that was the result. Ed would look from them to me as if to say, "You see? They don't want to make me get up."

There were exceptions to this, of course, one of which happened in the middle of one such afternoon. After several attempts to get Ed interested in being washed, one of the LPNs, Dona, appeared with cloths and water and a determined look on her face.

"This time," she declared, "you're getting washed!"

I could have hugged her.

Most of the time I felt completely alone in my efforts to draw him back into active life, step by painful step, yet I knew that if he didn't snap out of this lethargy soon, it might well be too late. Whatever was making him this way, catering to his every wish was not the way to help him want and achieve some measure of independence.

Ed wasn't above using that situation to his own advantage in his efforts to remain physically inactive. To him I was the bitchy wife and the nurses were the loving caregivers. Often he'd say something like, "The nurses don't make me do that," meaning what I wanted from him was totally unreasonable. Sometimes I'd go into his room and hear one of the staff say, "She's here. You won't get away with anything now," and I'd feel like running as far and as long as I could.

And sometimes when I was too tired to fight yet another battle with anyone, especially Ed, I would just sit in that darkened room in utter despair and loneliness and cry.

19

It's time to take stock of the new me.

I'll do it first with mathematics. A complete one of me from tip of toe to top of head is, let us say, four-fourths, since four-fourths is a complete one of anything. Since I seem to have lost that portion of me which extends from the nipple line down, according to the doctors, we can subtract that from the total me. For arguments sake, we'll estimate that particular portion of me to be roughly four and a half feet, leaving approximately eighteen inches of perfectly good body from the nipple line to the top of my head.

For those of you perverse enough to be interested, the nipple line is an imaginary line running across the upper body from one nipple (as in breast) to the other, and presumably extending around the back until it returns to the first nipple and completely encircles the body. Any practical use of this line is likewise imaginary. Neurologists, however, have found it to be a convenient demarcation line for separating the useless parts of a paralyzed body from the rest of that body. Even then it's often inaccurate. In my own case, for example, the paralyzed part of me begins a couple of inches above the nipple line in front. I can't swear that the same is true of the back because I can't see behind me without the use of mirrors and I can't hold a mirror and measuring tape at the same time. In fact, I can't hold either of them at all so it's a moot point.

Those of you with a mathematics background will see immediately that the working or operative part of me is limited to one quarter. One quarter of me works; three quarters of me do not.

It's frustrating to feel something wrong in the three quarters of your body that feels nothing. That just isn't fair. I feel things in the other one quarter, too, but that's legitimate. The "something wrong" I'm referring to now is the very devil both to experience and explain. The closest I can come to describing the symptoms is the way my mother describes a bad flu.

"The flesh is coming off my bones."

In this case, the flesh is reacting strongly against being torn off my bones and I'm caught in the middle.

Having no appropriate medical term to fall back on, I call it The Feeling. The medical people say they haven't much training in dealing with The Feeling, so despite the best efforts of the nurses I'm left to deal with it myself.

The problem is aggravated by the fact that The Feeling torments me all over, from toe of foot to crown of head. I know this isn't reasonable, but I also know what I feel, and what I feel is The Feeling all bloody over. I wish I could state it more strongly but I can't. The torment (which, come to think of it, is a far better label than The Feeling) can last for a few hours or all night.

Sometimes The Feeling gets so intense that I can't bear to have anyone else in the room with me. Actually, I get so irritable that no one else can stand to be near me, so it works out. After much trial and error I find two treatments that seem to work. Both have to do with the cold. When The Feeling is on me, having my forehead bathed with cold water is pure heaven. Different members of my family have kept cold cloths to my head for as much as two hours and more. That gives me immeasurable relief, although it doesn't seem to do much for them.

The second step of the cold treatment is to have my windows wide open and the fan next to my head on top speed. Again, this is great for me during a spell of The Feeling, and it wouldn't be bad for anyone else in July and August. In February and March, however, the treatment is not all that popular with family and staff. Nurses put on sweaters to enter my room during these cold spells, and some are reluctant to come in at all unless they have to. Even then they complain like you wouldn't believe.

My father has always maintained that it can't get too cold to please him. He refuses to put on his outside coat and sits stoically, if somewhat stiffly, in a short-sleeved, cotton shirt. My mother, who is quite open about never being able to get enough heat, sits in the armchair that a friend gave us dressed in a sweater, her winter parka with the fur-lined hood up over her head, and the thickest blanket she can find wrapped over it all. She is shivering.

It says something about my family's devotion to me that, hot or cold, they don't leave until visiting hours are over or I get too obnoxious to be around. Actually, I can be obnoxious when it isn't cold. For my parents I suppose this is child's play compared to rearing me up. My sister says that six months of putting up with me now is the equivalent of one day of being my younger sibling as a child. My brother-in-law says simply that he's a saint.

From an engineering perspective it is inaccurate to state that three quarters of me isn't working. It's working as well as it ever did. The difference is that I can't feel the three quarters working, contrary to the overall torment of The Feeling. Nevertheless, that part of me is essential to the maintenance and indeed the existence of the rest of me.

It's something like the connection between my computer and the turbines at Churchill Falls. The proper maintenance of the Churchill Falls power plant is necessary to keep my computer alive and online, although computer and plant are separated by hundreds of miles. The top quarter of me is separated from the bottom three quarters of me by the nipple line, which might as well be hundreds of miles wide for all I feel of it.

Biologically, the one-quarter of me and the three-quarters of me are connected as always. Blood flows through the veins and arteries from one part to the other, carrying their little cargoes of oxygen and nutrients. These veins and arteries are like the high tension power lines that carry electricity from the wilds of Labrador to the great cities of Central Newfoundland. As long as they're connected, how far one is from the other is unimportant.

It is the human perspective that's most telling.

Before the accident, I lived in my whole body. I experienced the needs of that body, felt its desires and hungers and fed them accordingly. I enjoyed indulging myself with hikes in the woods, a good scoff, a great sex life, a hot shower, the exhilaration of a chilly autumn morning, the laziness of a warm summer day. I was whole and complete. Now I live from my neck up. My only desires are psychological, my only hungers mental. I exist only in my head, my brain, my mind.

I no longer have the joy, the satisfaction of experiencing physical things, and I miss them terribly. There are no substitutes. I have to let them go. But much, so very much, is gone with them. The autumn woods, the hunting trails, the trout ponds, the salmon river, the snowmobile, the boat and engine, my guitar and the sharing of physical love. I have no choice but to accept the raw reality, the inescapable fact.

Ed Smith doesn't live there anymore.

I don't know what time it is and I don't care. The closed curtains let enough light through to show that it is day, but the room is dark. Marion hasn't been down yet and the nurses haven't been in to tell me that it's time for therapy. That means it's Saturday and I can sleep as long as I want. The longer I sleep, the less time I have to think.

People are talking about my courage. What courage? I'm not facing what I am or what I will become. I'm simply not thinking about it. I don't want to think about it because I know I haven't the courage to face it head-on. So I keep my eyes shut as much as I can to bar out the world as it is for me.

My world is a very unpleasant place. There should be a law against my world. Perhaps there is and no one's enforcing it. More likely, there are no laws at all and, as the uncouth but accurate saying puts it, shit happens. It's like the world of Mad Max where only the fittest survive. So because I'm no longer among the fittest, I try to hide from that world by closing my eyes and pretending it isn't there. Works most of the time.

Marion talks about our future as though she believes there will be one, with order and structure and purpose. She says if I'd put half as much effort into working for our future as I do in avoiding therapies she'd feel so much better about it. Perhaps she really believes there's something worth working for. I don't know. I don't know anything anymore.

I used to have a future. I dreamed of retiring while I was relatively young and having time to enjoy all the things we loved doing. Jumping into the car on the spur of the moment and heading wherever we felt like going for as long as we wanted. Hunting, fishing, cod-jigging in our boat, spending time at our cabin, travelling a little, enjoying our family. Writing. Only dreams back then. Nothing more than dreams now.

As a small boy, I used to stab flatfish in the cove and feed them to my uncle's dogs. The half-starved huskies were in large pens near the water, and they were always fighting and snapping at each other. I'd throw a still-wriggling flatfish in over the high sides of the pen and watch the inevitable frenzy. The dogs would see the flatfish falling toward them and leap for the prize with bared fangs. In a matter of seconds savage jaws would tear the fish into little pieces before it hit the ground. Then for the next few moments the dogs would fight fiercely for the remains of a little fish that didn't exist anymore. That's my future, torn to shreds by the sharp teeth of a sadistic fate before it has a chance to be, and not enough of it left to worry about.

Despite myself I open my eyes momentarily. My dear God, it's true.

It's true. I'm almost totally paralyzed. My legs will never move again, and neither will I without being carried or pushed or lifted. My hands have no movement, my fingers stiff and bent like dry twigs. I'm totally dependent upon others for shelter and comfort and life. No longer will those I love depend on me for anything except, perhaps, not to make things more difficult than they already are. I'm afraid I'm not even doing that at the moment, and possibly never will.

To be or not to be. Do I ask myself that question? Daily. Anyone in this situation who says he doesn't is lying. The more fundamental question is how does one go about not being? I can't do anything for myself. Someone would have to assist. So where is Jack Kevorkian when you need him?

I don't know how serious I am about that. I guess I'm not really thinking of it from a life-or-death point of view. For me the choice is between a tolerable existence and a life that's completely miserable. I not only make that choice for me, but I make it for everyone around me. Right now I know I'm not easy to live with, and I'm not making the necessary effort, and I do want to hide away and not come out. And I'm sorry, but I didn't ask to get into this mess any more than anyone else did, so they have to cope with me the best they can, same as I have to cope with what I am the best I can.

The fact is, I'm the one with the dead legs and arms and hands. Me. I'm the one lying here totally unable to move, totally useless. So don't tell me how I should behave or what I should be doing or how I should be thinking. This isn't the flu. I don't have a broken arm. I've been barred in the cage of my own body and there's no escape. Here's where I stay for the rest of my forever. Without physical yearnings, without physical satisfactions. I am mostly dead forever.

I'm not brave. When I allow myself to see more or less clearly into my future, the terror that grips me is far beyond the things that go bump in the night. I'll do almost anything to avoid that feeling, and sometimes, perhaps often, the way to do that is to stay in the dark and keep my eyes shut. So I do. And perhaps I'll do it forever. Or perhaps tomorrow I'll feel better and open my eyes. And then we'll all feel better and won't that be just ducky?

But now like the biblical character, Job, who sat in ashes to bemoan his fate, so do I lie in ashes to bemoan mine, the ashes of my dreams.

20

I suppose I should be praying for a miracle.

Since the earliest days of my childhood I've been involved with the church one way or another, from having a clergyman father to being a student minister myself to being an active church member most of my life. Everything I've heard or read coming out of the church has affirmed and reaffirmed the certainty of miracles in our lives when we need them most. In my case, brother, the time is *now*.

So should I look for a miracle? I have to admit that I don't expect anything of the sort simply because, as I said before, I don't really believe in miracles.

Actually, what I believe makes not a particle of difference as to whether or not it happens. Reported miracles seem to happen randomly among the general population without regard for godliness or cleanliness.

When Jennifer was still a child, she developed plantar warts on her feet which got so painful she could no longer walk without limping. As we had done several times already, we took her to our family physician.

"I don't know what else to do," he said. "If we cut them out or burn them out, they'll probably come back."

He looked at us for a long moment.

"This will sound strange coming from a doctor," he said, "but I suggest you take her to see Uncle Andrew."

"Who's Uncle Andrew?"

"Uncle Andrew charms away warts."

To say we were skeptical is the same as saying Niagara Falls is water trickling over a cliff. But we were out of options and had nothing to lose by trying this one. Jennifer especially thought we were wasting our time.

Uncle Andrew and his wife turned out to be a beautiful old couple. When we told him we wanted Jennifer's warts charmed, he smiled.

"Do you believe I can make your warts go away?"

Jennifer was nothing if not honest, and obviously skeptical of this whole process. She looked him straight in the eye.

"No," she said, "I don't."

Uncle Andrew smiled again.

"Makes no difference," he said. "Take off your socks."

He touched her feet gently.

"I'll ask you not to thank me," he said. "The warts will be gone in a couple of weeks."

And they were. And never came back.

Several months later, my parents were visiting and my mother showed us a wart on her cheek that she was concerned about. We suggested she visit Uncle Andrew. She was so worried that she agreed to go, but didn't really expect anything to come of it.

My mother called a few days after they returned home.

"It's incredible." She sounded incredulous. "The thing is actually shrinking. Every day it's a little bit smaller."

Then one day she telephoned again.

"The wart was definitely going away," she said. "It's less than half as large as it was. But in the past few days it hasn't changed at all. I don't understand it."

Suddenly I did.

"Mom," I said, "Uncle Andrew died last week."

I guess we each draw our own conclusions from that.

I remember once asking him to tell me the secret of his powers.

"You have to find that for yourself," he said with a smile. "But you know your Bible, don't you? It's right there in the Bible." And that was all he'd say.

It's more than interesting to me that neither Jennifer's nor my mother's lack of faith in Uncle Andrew's ability to cure warts had any effect on the outcome. I think the same is true of miracles.

Nevertheless, a clergyman friend suggests it's all a matter of faith.

"If you have even the smallest bit of faith, Jesus said you could move mountains," he says pointedly.

This gets Marion very upset.

"That's a cop-out," she says. "It's so easy to say that if Ed doesn't get better it's because he doesn't have enough faith. How much is enough? Who knows how much he has? And if you believe that it's a matter of faith, you probably also believe that this is part of God's plan, which means God must have planned for Ed not to have enough faith. How do you explain that?"

The clergyman says nothing. I'm idly wondering why we'd want to move mountains in the first place, and where we'd put them once we'd moved them. I'm not all that inclined to take such clerical pronouncements seriously.

Another cleric, an old friend, assures Marion that God never lays on you more than you can bear. That's an old one. Probably used it myself on occasion when I didn't stop to think what it meant. Marion knows what it means.

"In that case," she replies, "we're really stupid to be strong because the stronger we are the more troubles God heaps on us. The smart thing to do is to be as weak as you can and then God will see that nothing bad ever happens to you because you're too weak to bear it."

Our friend retreats in the face of this logic.

"I've never thought of it that way," he says slowly.

"That's the problem," Marion points out. "Most of us don't."

Nothing sounds more empty to me now than those time-worn clichés. But this only fuels my need to believe in something, *anything*. Anyone with any religious background at all who comes into my room is confronted.

"Do you believe in miracles?"

The answers are almost all disappointingly similar from layperson and clergyperson alike.

"Well, it depends on what you mean by 'miracle.' For me, the birth of a child is a miracle. A person who overcomes an addiction, or makes some great change for the better in his life is experiencing a miracle."

I'm not easily put off by such evasions.

"Do you believe God can intervene in human destiny and reverse what has physically happened so that someone like me can be cured?"

"Well, that's a difficult question."

I don't think it's a difficult question. Either one believes it or one doesn't. What's so difficult about that? Perhaps I'm being simplistic.

Then one night the psychiatrist who drops in every blue moon, Dr. Holden, shows up around eleven o'clock. He's a most interesting fellow. Trained as a priest, trained as a jet pilot and trained as a doctor, he's now a psychiatrist in which area I assume he's also trained. I like to see him coming because we have such interesting chats. Unfortunately, they're much too infrequent.

Tonight I decide to nail him with my prime question. He's obviously an intelligent man and he's been knocked around a bit. I know what he's probably going to say, but what do I have to lose?

"Bill, do you believe in miracles?"

The answer just about knocks my socks off. It is immediate and concise.

"Yes."

Now I think we're probably talking different concepts.

"The kind of miracle that contradicts every known law of physics and medicine and everything else?"

"Yes."

"Why?"

"Because I've seen too many things that have absolutely no explanation otherwise."

And there it is, firm and unequivocal.

We go on to have a great conversation which cheers me immensely, although I'm still pretty sure that no miracle will ever happen to me. I don't know why the strength of his belief should make me feel better even when I don't share it. It just does.

I still don't know what I believe about God. At every opportunity I initiate conversations with people who are well educated, highly capable and have strong religious beliefs. I want to know what they believe and why. Perhaps they can show me some insight, some pathway that I've missed.

Len Williams has a doctorate and teaches at the University. He and his wife, Laura, are among the most beautiful people we know. On one of the nights he volunteers to stay with me, we get down and dirty with the idea of God. How real is God to him?

As with Dr. Holden, he has no hesitation.

"God," he says, "is a very real presence in my life, something I'm aware of every day, a presence that cares about me and what happens to me."

Why?

"It's always been there," he says, "I don't remember a time when it wasn't."

The depth of Laura's faith is revealed in the beautiful poetry she writes.

Thelma Whalen is just as strong in her convictions. She's an assistant director with one of the largest education boards in the province. She's articulate and beautiful and can tell jokes with the best. My poker buddies would love her. She'd love them. More than that, like Laura and Len she keeps bringing us marvellous food.

"For me," she says, "God is like an aura that surrounds me every day. It's there in the morning when I wake up; it's there at night when I go to sleep. I can't imagine living my life without it."

So where does this conviction come from for Thelma and Laura and Len? It's a matter of faith, they say, and an awareness of God. And though we discuss the topic for hours it all boils down to that. I can only envy them the certainty of their beliefs. I'm left with what I *choose* to believe, and left also with the strong impression that there is more passion in faith than in choice. And perhaps more conviction.

On Sunday morning, we wheel down the corridor to the chapel. A group of student chaplains is holding a series of services. I don't expect too much from the service because most of the students are untrained. Nevertheless, all of us in wheelchairs have a reason for being there. A hope, an expectation, a search.

When it's over, I'm disappointed, not so much for me but for the others who leave with the same expressionless faces as when they went in. The service is poorly conducted, the people doing it obviously unsure of themselves and the whole atmosphere uninspired. I've no doubt these people are doing their best, but their best just isn't cutting it today.

I don't really blame them, of course. Someone is teaching them; that same someone should be telling them how to conduct a service of worship. If they were to conduct a Sunday morning service in any church in the city and were that poorly prepared, the reaction from the congregation would be strong and negative. The stroke victims, the amputees, the brain-injured, all deserve the same kind of effort these people would put into a service anywhere else. Perhaps next week will be better.

The second week is a repeat of the first and I'm totally frustrated and resolve to go no more. On the third Sunday I stay in bed, angry with myself for not doing more to support the other patients, and angry with those responsible for making me feel this way. Perhaps I'm being unreasonable here, but that's the way I feel.

Fifteen minutes before the service is to begin I hear it. A beautiful and obviously highly trained woman's voice singing in the chapel. The quality of the voice is such that I know I have to get to the service and hear it up close. Desperate for spiritual inspiration of any kind, I consider for one fleeting moment racing down to the chapel wrapped in a sheet. But then one of the much older patients whose mental capacities are somewhat diminished might think I was Lazarus coming back from the dead and have a heart attack. Can't take any chances with this religion stuff.

I ring for the nurses, and as usual they appear almost immediately. I have to get to chapel, I tell them, can you get me ready in time? Well now, can they! A process that normally takes over an hour is completed in twelve minutes, and I'm at the door of the chapel before the service begins.

This Sunday the atmosphere of the service is significantly better, perhaps because I can't wait to hear the singer again, but also because the people conducting the service seem to be better prepared. Whatever, I don't speculate much about that because I'm almost completely focused on the woman who's sitting at the organ. Her voice floats above everyone else in the hymn-singing. Very few are singing in any case because, as usual, few of us know the hymn being sung. I look around and see the eyes of the other patients glued to her, and I know they're captivated, too.

Finally she sings a solo for us. Again, I don't recognize the song, but it doesn't matter. Her voice is pure gold. When it's over, there's no one in that little chapel who isn't moved.

After the service, Marion and I introduce ourselves and Victoria turns out to be as charming a personality as she is a singer. She tells us she'll be there next Sunday as well, and we assure her that we will, too.

To my dismay, I wake up the next Sunday morning feeling much too miserable to make any effort at getting up. But we can hear her voice all the way down the corridor. I tell myself it's the next best thing to being there.

The service has been over only a few moments when suddenly Victoria appears at the door with the guitarist who had accompanied her this time out.

"Since you couldn't get to the chapel," she says, "I thought I'd come sing for you here. Is that okay?"

Is that okay? Does Dolly Parton have... have... you know... hair? She sings several songs before leaving, each more entrancing than the one before. It's sometime during the singing that Marion whispers in my ear, "Perhaps she'd give you singing lessons."

Marion has been talking about this possibility for some time. I'd always wanted to take singing lessons, but had never gotten around to it. Now, Marion's interest is twofold. She believes the lessons would be good for my morale and overall rehabilitation, and she knows that learning the proper breathing techniques would be good for my lungs, since my capacity to breathe deeply has been reduced significantly. In fact, we had been actively investigating voice teachers in and around St. John's for some time and were about to make a decision. Then suddenly Victoria appears.

No chance, I say to myself. She's not going to be interested in trying to give me a singing voice. But hell, what have I got to lose? So I ask her. Hesitantly, timidly, I ask her. And almost immediately she replies.

"Yes, I think I'd like to do that."

I am floored. Before I have time to think about it, we've agreed to a time and place and the bargain is made.

"I want to pay you the going rate for this," I say hesitantly, not wanting to sound gauche.

"Let's talk about that after we've been meeting for a while," she answers.

And so it begins. Once a week we meet in the chapel or in the activity area and I begin to learn something of what it is to be a singer. Victoria is very high on attitude and approach. One must bring to the act of singing a commitment, which includes at once proper technique and genuine emotion. I learn to breathe properly and run through the scales.

I'm really enjoying my sessions with Victoria. We seem to hit it off quite well, and both of Marion's objectives, stated and unstated, are undoubtedly being met. Here is something I can do, and even improve on. Here is something over which my handicap has no effect. Lord knows, I might be useful after all.

The singing lessons give me a focus for each week. More than that, they belong to a part of me that I don't like to think much about: my future. The lessons help me to think of a future that isn't all negative, a future to believe in, a future worth living for. And Marion, bless her heart, knew exactly what effect those lessons would have on me.

We've been meeting for perhaps a month when at this one particular session Victoria points out how pleased she is with my progress to date.

"In fact," she says, "I'd like to see you begin performing in public sometime in September."

I'm astounded. I've done a fair amount of singing in public over the years, but hardly on this formal a basis. Usually it's entertaining tourists with the guitar, or giving a one-man fund-raising show for some group or other, or singing in church. A friend and I had made a few tapes and performed together under the name Pat and Ed, but again, this was something different. Is she serious? Am I doing that well already?

She says that she is and I am. Okay! Let the curtain rise! I am ready!

"One other thing," she says, "I'll be gone the first couple of weeks in July for some holidays, but I have a friend who's very good at this and she's agreed to meet with you while I'm away. When I get back we'll get started on some serious singing."

It's a high note on which to end a session. But it ends much more than a session because I never see Victoria again.

21

A nurse comes in, bright and white.

"And how are we today?"

Surely God there is no more silly question in all of healthdom. If there is, the medical community would be hard put to find it. So would the world community.

As the nurse does what she has to do and makes small talk about things in general, I try to analyze whatever it is that offends me so much. After all, it's an innocent enough little greeting. Why react so strongly to it?

Perhaps, I reason, it's because by saying 'we' she equates her feelings of well-being with mine. If she's okay, then I must be okay and vice versa. But she has no right to that presumption. She has no right to intrude her bright, happy self into my pissedoffedness. There's no room for both of us in the same room. Besides, does she really want to know how I am or does she say that to all the boys?

"And how are we today?" is probably her opening line to every patient in every condition in every room on every floor. She might as well get on the frigging PA system, say it once and get it over with. "AND HOW ARE WE TODAY!" Not a question. No response necessary.

Half of us, I mutter within myself, is having one hell of a day.

"Oh, come now," her voice is as bright as her uniform. "It can't be as bad as all that."

I hadn't realized I was speaking out loud so this time I speak even more quietly to myself. And just how in howling hell would you know how bad it can get? You're young, you're attractive, your muscles do what you tell them to do, and you probably get laid every night. You have no concept of how bad it can get.

I don't know why I'm not saying these things out loud. Perhaps because I realize none of this is her fault. Because spitting those words at her would be like throwing up over her neat, bright whiteness. Because something in that innocence and youth calls from long ago, months ago, lifetimes ago and I don't want to soil it with me. Me the crippled. Me the helpless. Me the paralyzed. I am wallowing in a tidal wave of self-pity and I don't care.

"Not feeling well today, are we?"

"No," I say in weary resignation, "we're not feeling well at all."

"That's too bad," she says. "Perhaps you'll feel better later on. What you need is a nice hot shower."

Nice hot shower? That's hardly the cure for what ails me. I'm dying inside and all she can see is the need for a shower, for God's sake. Perhaps that's all she can be expected to see. How could anyone who hasn't suffered a similar physical trauma possibly understand? It's certainly asking too much of this young woman who unconsciously glories in her health and her youth with every movement of her body.

But a shower? When will I make you people understand? The only parts of me that feel anything at all are my arms and shoulders, and they're so sensitive I can hardly bear the weight of the sheets on them. What do you think happens when you bombard me with sharp slivers of hot water? I'll tell you what happens. I go crazy. I go insane.

I look forward to showers the way cats look forward to baths. But every second morning, regular as the sunrise, in trot the staff with a strong, fair wind behind them, ready to haul me off to what I have come to regard as the Health Care Corp torture room.

The first step is being wheeled down the corridor to the shower room on a commode chair. I once saw a man about my age being pushed down the hall with only a small towel across his lap. He didn't seem to mind it much. In fact, he seemed to be enjoying himself. Probably the type who jumps in front of women with his topcoat held open. I insist on being fully draped in a sheet. There's not much dignity left to me, but what there is I will protect with my dying breath, which breath will probably be taken in the shower room.

The hallway is never as full of people as it is when I'm being wheeled out for my shower. Nurses, doctors, patients, relatives, visitors, dogs and dog handlers are all lined up just to witness my progress down the corridor. Every single one of them has exactly the same look on his face.

"I know where you're going," the faces lilt in singsong chorus, "and I know what they're going to do to you."

I swear every damn one of these people knows exactly what does go on in there. Perhaps because every one of them has had it done to them a thousand and one times.

People who've had this particular procedure have a special look to them. Those who've gone to the bottom of the Mariana Trench in a diving bell have a similar look, as does anyone who's been shot out the mouth of a circus cannon.

"I've been there, man," is what the look says "and I ain't going back."

The less said about the procedure the better. But at the Hewitt Centre in St. John's, they deliberately choose the youngest and the loveliest to do it to the oldest and the ugliest. Not that I'm either. I'm just trying to make a point here. It seems to me that at least every second time out, the nurse is a nubile young thing straight out of nursing school who's doing it for the very first time.

Today's young Nightingale is really pretty, and I'm just old enough to be sexist enough to say so and not give a Fig Newton. The supervising nurse goes out for something or other and we are left alone in the shower room. The air is loud with silence. I glance down at her as she performs her lonely ministrations and catch her looking tentatively up at me. I try hard to think of something to say which will make both of us feel less uncomfortable.

"It'll never replace holding hands."

She smiles. I don't know if she relaxes at all, but she does smile. The older nurse comes back in with an armload of towels.

"All done?"

"I'm done. I don't know about her."

"You're not funny," she says in mock severity, and to the younger nurse, "He's not nearly as funny as he thinks he is, you know."

The younger nurse smiles again as she straightens up. It strikes me that she smiles a lot. Probably a defense mechanism. When in doubt, smile. I've seen the same smile on Salvation Army officers standing by their little pots in the malls at Christmastime.

"I don't know," she says unexpectedly. "I think he's sort of funny."

"You can go now," says the other nurse. "I'll take care of his shower." She pushes me into the shower stall, and pulls away the sheet that's keeping alive the illusion of modesty.

So what's this? She wants to be alone with me in the shower? Perhaps she intends to attack me sexually. I'd be helpless to resist, wouldn't I?

A couple of nurses have been telling me about some of the older men in other institutions who sometimes proposition them. One of their favourite stories is about an old fellow in his eighties who beckoned his nurse closer to his bed one night in the wee small hours.

"How about you hauling the curtains around the bed and climbing in with me for a few minutes?"

"I certainly will not!" The nurse was indignant, although somewhat amused.

"Why not? There's no one around this hour of the night and it won't take very long."

"Because I don't do that kind of stuff."

"I'll give you twenty dollars."

"No! I told you. I don't do that." The nurse was still amused. "But if I did, I'd charge a lot more than twenty bucks."

"Oh? How much would you charge?" He was probably thinking she might be had after all, if the price were right.

"At least a hundred dollars."

"A hundred dollars!" The old fellow just about came out of his bed. "A hundred dollars! I can tell you, me dear maid, that the little thing you got there ain't worth no hundred dollars!" And he turned his back on her in total disgust.

The stinging shower spray hits me square between the shoulder blades, high up enough to feel.

"Owww! That's cold!" Could she know what I was thinking a few moments ago?

"Sorry." She does sound contrite. "How's this?"

"This" is better. After I'm washed, soaped, sprayed and towelled down, we run the gauntlet of the corridor again and I'm deposited on the bed.

"Now that feels a lot better, right?"

It feels better because it's over, something like the feeling you get when you stop hitting your head against a stone wall. I don't feel cleaner because there's not enough of me that feels to feel cleaner. I don't feel more relaxed for much the same reason. But I'll never make them understand that. The shower is supposed to make you feel better, which it does for ninety-nine percent of their customers. But I'm not in the ninety and nine. I'm the one away on the mountains wild and bare, away from the tender shepherd's care. I'm the one who's lost.

Oh God, here I go again. Enough self-pity for one day. I will drown in this stuff if I keep it up.

"Absolutely," I say with a smile. "Nothing like a good, hot shower."

Nothing.

22

A man came to visit us today, and Marion and I still don't know what to make of his visit. To say we are astounded is the same as saying mad cows are sick.

Let me backtrack to my days at the Health Sciences Centre in January. About three weeks after my surgery, I received two dozen long-stemmed red roses from a fellow named Arthur Fielding in Montreal. The roses were beautiful, but who the heck was Arthur Fielding? I cast about in my mind and remembered two men in my dim and recent past with that name. One had been the mayor of a town we lived in almost thirty years ago. Unlikely he'd be sending me flowers, especially since he's dead. The other was a fellow I knew professionally several years ago, but only for a short time. We'd had some great chats at the time, but still he was almost as unlikely a candidate as the mayor.

We were totally puzzled. Then a few days later a letter arrived from the second Fielding, and it did turn out to be the man with whom I had worked. The next time he was in the vicinity, the letter said, he'd be dropping by to see me. This was all well and good, but why was Arthur Fielding being so nice to me?

I was already getting used to the hundreds of cards and letters coming in from all corners of the province, all parts of Canada and beyond, and all faiths and persuasions. People I had never heard tell of were writing beautiful notes to Marion and me, filled with expressions of love and concern. I was beginning to believe the old fellow who confided to me a couple of years ago, "My son, you're world-famous in Newfoundland."

So Arthur's kindness wasn't so unusual, even if the expression of it was unique. To be truthful, neither of us expected to see him very soon.

Then today in he strolls. I remember him instantly: a big man, articulate and outgoing with whom I'd gotten along quite well. He'd been something of a mystery to me because he seemed to emerge out of nowhere and after a few months quietly disappear. Anyway, here he is in the flesh, and I'm still not sure why he's paying us all this attention. There's no element of cynicism in my wondering, just an active curiosity. I've certainly done nothing to merit any attention out of the ordinary from him.

Arthur is the genial person I remembered. Marion is the only other person in the room, and we enjoy a few pleasantries for a while. But I'm still in my casually curious mode when Arthur comes over to the side of my bed.

"I have a proposition for you," he says with a smile, "which I hope you will accept."

Marion and I exchange glances. We have no idea what's coming next. I'm hoping whatever it is will explain Arthur's close interest in us a little further. He wastes no more time on preliminaries.

"If you accept, you won't have to worry about money again for the rest of your life."

I'm not sure I'm hearing him correctly.

"I don't understand," I say hesitantly, looking at him closely. I see a friendly face wreathed in smiles and seemingly very sincere. "What do I have to do to accept?"

Arthur is positively beaming.

"You don't have to do anything," he says, "except take the money."

For once in my life I am utterly speechless.

"But... but I don't understand."

"Nothing to understand. I've done really well on the international markets. I can afford it and I want to repay you for what you did for me."

My mind is in absolute chaos. I look over at Marion. She's staring at Arthur, her eyes wide. I know what she's thinking. We'll need hundreds of thousands of dollars for equipment, nursing, home care and attendants, not to mention drugs and house renovations, and all the myriad expenses associated with being quadriplegic for the number of years I have left.

I'm suddenly aware of what he's saying.

"What in the world did I ever do for you that you'd be offering me this?"

"It doesn't matter. What about it? No strings attached."

I know there's something terribly wrong with the way I think. I know I have a streak of pride and independence down my back a foot wide and I know it's one of the things that will make life with quadriplegia even more challenging. But, like Popeye, I yam what I yam. There's no question what I will say.

"That's an incredibly generous offer, Arthur." I'm trying desperately to keep the emotion and hesitancy out of my voice. "I can't think of anything I've ever done to deserve anything like that. But I can't accept it. I can't take what you're offering."

What I'm really saying is that I'm too proud to spend the rest of my life, such as it is, financially dependent upon another human being. I can't tie myself to another person with such permanent bonds. But another part of me is saying "This is your way out." Another voice is strongly suggesting I should be thinking more of my family, especially Marion, and what financial independence could mean for them in caring for me, not to mention my own health and comfort. The strongest voice of all is a flat accusation rising from somewhere deep inside.

You bloody, bloody fool!

And from somewhere even deeper inside, somewhere where Ed Smith really lives, comes the final judgment on the question.

"I can't tell you how humbly grateful I am, but I can't accept what you're offering."

Humbly? Humbly my bum! What a hypocrite you are, Smith! If you weren't so damn proud, you'd be on your hands and knees (figuratively speaking, of course), kissing his feet and asking, "Where do I sign?"

So from where does this final judgment come? From the fear of being beholden to and dependent on one person for the rest of my life? The fear of my own tenuous individuality being subject to another, stronger individual? The fear of losing completely what little is left of Ed Smith? And if that happened, what would I be? What would Marion love?

Accepting Arthur's offer would destroy me more completely than any broken neck, any degree of paralysis, any physical impotence. The final judgment is irrevocable. I choose to remain my own person, because that's about all I have left.

"I can't accept your offer, Arthur."

Arthur is looking from me to Marion and back again. I don't know what he's thinking but he must be in even deeper shock than I am. I don't dare look at Marion.

"Tell me you'll at least think about it."

"Okay, I'll think about it, but I won't change my mind."

"Very good." Arthur doesn't look at all discouraged. He turns to Marion. "Have you had a busy day, Mrs. Smith?"

Somehow Marion finds her voice.

"Yes, I have. I've been phoning people all over Canada trying to find information on voice-activated computers. No one seems to know anything about them, and if he's to continue writing, that's what Ed's going to need. Besides, a lot of people have contributed to that one objective."

Arthur comes to his taps as though he's been zapped with an electric cattle prod.

"Say no more! And look no more. This is something I am doing, and you're not going to stop me." This last delivered in my direction.

"Many people have donated money to the trust fund," I protest, "believing they were helping me buy a computer to help me write. What do I say to them?"

"People gave you money to help in whatever way is best." Arthur looks extremely determined. "I know they won't mind you putting their gifts to another use, such as a proper wheelchair."

"I have to admit I'm concerned about that, too," Marion says. "But I'm certainly glad to have some help. What are you going to do?"

"I'm going to call my people in Montreal and tell them to find the best state-of-the-art voice-activated computer available. And then I'm giving it to you."

Again, we are left with our mouths open, staring at this man who is determined to be our patron. Shortly after, he picks up his coat, says good night and takes his leave. His parting comment is that we should hear from his people in about two weeks.

Marion and I look at each other, for the moment at a loss for words. I recover first.

"That man has got to be pulling on all four of our legs," I burst out.

"Perhaps," she replies, "but I could have thrown a brick at you just now! How could you possibly turn down an offer like that? Most people would kill for that kind of gift."

I know by the way she says it that she isn't serious, and she does understand and support my reaction. But when you stop and think about it... My God! Did he really offer to support us financially for the rest of our lives? And did I really refuse? I'm a nutcase.

In my heart of hearts, I don't know what to believe. He certainly seemed serious. Perhaps he's just a very nice man with an overactive imagination. After all, I don't really know him that well.

We finally conclude that we probably won't hear from his people about a computer or anything else at any time. Too bad. He's the closest thing I've ever seen to the real Santa Claus.

It is six weeks later. This morning Marion found an e-mail on the computer from a man in Montreal who identifies himself as a business associate of Arthur Fielding. He wishes to inform us that a voice-activated computer is being shipped to us today, compliments of Mr. Fielding, and that arrangements are being made with a computer company in St. John's to provide as much training as I need.

Neither of us can think of anything to say.

23

I've met some fine doctors during my time of rehabilitation.

I've also met one or two who won't remember me with kindness. The doctor-patient relationship in those cases has been one of differing views, shall we say. Naturally, in those differences I've felt that I'm consistently right. I'd be foolish to say otherwise. You'd be even more foolish to believe it if I said it.

Let me take a giant leap of non-faith here and suggest that I've been wrong fully half the time. Half the time is a lot to admit to, especially for me. That means the doctor is right half the time. But it also means he or she is wrong half the time, and half the time is too much for any doctor to be wrong. It's probably too much for any patient to be wrong as well, but I'm willing to go fifty-fifty here.

It is early morning.

Anytime before I awake is early morning. I am not a morning person. Never was. Never will be. I am not at my best at early morning. Ask Marion. When you add the effect of several nighttime medications, some of which are designed to make me sleep, I am at best one or two decimal points above comatose on first awaking.

The good doctor and his nurse are standing at the foot of my bed like sober apparitions. I have returned a mumbled "Good morning," and am still struggling to rise to the level of semi-alert. Most mornings during these rounds, I make it just as they're going out the door. God knows what they've said. God knows what I've said in return. One of my great fears is that someday I'll be held accountable for something I've said in those early morning rounds.

At one of our team meetings (the team of which I'm the central figure, remember) I try to make this point.

"Don't expect me to remember anything you've said in the morning. Don't expect me to remember anything I've said. The questions I had for you the night before are buried deep in my subconscious when I'm first awakened. Consequently, they don't get asked. Since you people make rounds in what is for me the early morning, that's a bit of a problem."

I don't really expect much sympathy from anyone. People who rise and shine bright and early understand people like me the same way doctors understand nurses.

Thing is, I need to communicate with this man. There are things I want to know, things I have to ask him. He may want to talk with me. But before I've fully awakened? Forget it. There has to be another means of communicating, and I'm sure it's just a matter of working it out.

To my great surprise, my friend the MD says he has an idea.

"Okay," says he, "write your questions on a Post-it Note the night before and stick it to your forehead so I can read it in the morning."

For once in my life I don't know what to say. It's as though my minister met me at the church door on Sunday morning and said, "Flake off, Smith." There is no hint that the doctor is anything but serious, and more than a little annoyed. Hardly a trace of sympathy.

Marion and Jennifer are staring at him wide-eyed. Most of the others are looking down at the table. Two or three are watching me for reaction.

Jennifer tries to rise above the new level to which we've sunk, and continues to speak to the issue we've been discussing. But she does respond briefly to the good doctor's idea.

"I assume your comment about the Post-it Note is a bad joke."

The doctor interrupts before she's finished speaking.

"No, it isn't," he says. "I'm not joking at all."

When the minutes of that meeting are circulated there is no mention of the "Post-it Note" comment. Marion tracks down the secretary and points out the omission.

"We would like to see that statement recorded," she says.

The secretary remembers the doctor's comments and agrees to include them. But when the minutes are read at the next meeting, there is still no mention of the offensive words.

Anyway, through half-open eyes and semi-conscious mind I see the doctor and the nurse standing at the foot of the bed.

"We have decided," the doctor is saying, "that you should move out of this room and go on the ward."

That I hear! That brings me awake like a bucket of cold water full in the face. Move to a ward? I've been in this room for months. This is my home. This is my world. Why do they suddenly want to move me to a ward?

"Because we think you need more socializing."

More socializing? I need more socializing like I need more doctors. More people pass through the doors of this room than through the doors of the West Edmonton Mall. Other patients come in for chats, my family is here every day, and visitors and friends form an almost continuous line. During the day and early evening I am never alone. Any more socialization will kill me.

"Okay." They seem to concede that point. "We think you need to be with other patients so that you can be inspired by their progress."

Right. For the most part these other patients are here for much shorter periods than I. As amputees and stroke victims they get the necessary therapy, get fitted for new limbs and are soon gone. God bless 'em. I can be happy for them, but the overall effect on my morale is anything but positive.

"Do you need the room for another patient?" I ask. Perhaps this is the real reason for wanting me out, although I'm puzzled as to why they just wouldn't say so.

"No, no," the doctor protests. "Not at all. We think it's in your best interest to go out on the ward, that's all."

Thank God. I'd have to give it up if someone else really

needed the room. So on with the battle. I state my resolve to stay where I am.

The good doctor doesn't take this well at all. The team has been talking about it, he says, and everyone feels the same way. Everyone, that is, except me, and I don't seem to be on the team anymore.

They depart the premises with the comment that we'll leave this for the time being, but there'll be a family meeting within the next few days where the issue will be decided once and for all.

It's too late to go back to sleep after they leave, even for me, so I review the situation carefully. Am I being unreasonable here? Why is it so important that I stay in my room that I'm willing to fight the establishment?

I try to answer the question as objectively as I can. This is a rehabilitation centre. And I'm here for rehabilitating. One of the most important factors in my rehabilitation is that I've retained close relationships with the health care board of which I'm still chair, the board of management of my church of which I'm still chair and a dozen other lesser responsibilities. I even attend meetings through phone hookups.

A friend comes in twice a week and does private correspondence work for me, of which there seems to be no end. And the number of people who want to visit, some of whom I don't even know, others who want to discuss business, and many who have driven for hours just to say hello, would never be permitted to disturb other patients on the ward to that extent.

We even have a little touch of home. Marion loves flowers and wanted to plant some in our window. So she asked Dad to make her a little flower box that would sit on the ledge outside the window. He did, of course, and the plants are growing well in this warmer-than-usual spring. I don't know what kind of flowers they are, but they look absolutely beautiful and not at all out of place. As Marion would say, why should they?

I didn't ask to be put in this room, but having been here for several months I've built up and continued relationships and responsibilities that are important to me and my continued progress. There is no way on God's good green earth I'm going to drop all this to go on a ward because someone thinks it's in my best interest. That's patently horse crap.

So what happens now? They can, I suppose, take me body and bones and simply lug me out to the ward, kicking and screaming all the way. Well, screaming anyway. Physically is where I'm most vulnerable and they could decide to take advantage of that, but I don't think so. We're all civilized around here, right?

It's interesting that I, as a member of this team, am being presented with this idea as a *fait accompli*. What happened to no decision being made without my input and approval? Something wrong here.

Marion is really upset when she hears what's happened.

"Don't let them do this to you, Ed," she pleads.

"If you let them move you from that room," a doctor friend states flatly, "I won't speak to you for three months." It's a tempting offer, but I decide to stick to my guns, anyway.

The family meeting is well attended. Marion and I feel something of what the early Christians must have felt in the Roman amphitheatre. Actually, most of those sitting around the table are professionals in the truest sense of the word. I wonder what position they'll take.

The issue is raised and the arguments for moving me given: socialization and inspiration. Sounds like the title of a sermon. I respond with my own arguments and repeat my position. Then they administer the *coup de grâce*. Behold, they need the room for another patient.

For a few moments my resolve wavers. If they need it for another patient... But then I remember that only a few days ago they maintained strongly they did not, repeat did *not*, need the room for anyone else. It's rather coincidental that a patient they knew nothing about earlier in the week has suddenly materialized into needing the room desperately. It's so coincidental that I don't believe it.

Then I get angry. How dare they try to take advantage of what would normally be my sympathy for such a circumstance! They're trying to lay a colossal guilt trip on me here, and it just isn't fair. No way will I give into that kind of tactic.

I repeat that I will not leave my room. No one else sitting around the table speaks. Finally, the division manager, who doesn't normally attend family meetings, states that the decision is now hers, and she will think more about it. The mood, as the meeting ends, is hardly jovial.

The next day she meets Marion in the corridor.

"I have decided," she says, "that Mr. Smith can stay in his room."

While she doesn't say so to us, we are told later that the reason she gives for her decision is that I had better arguments for staying in the room than the others had for moving me. No mention of another patient. But I do appreciate that this decision would require no little intestinal fortitude on her part.

Marion and I know we are in a no-win situation here. The team, excluding us, made a decision which they now have to reverse. That has to be hard for them to swallow. Although we know that the quality of nursing care for me will not change, neither of us feels very welcome here anymore. We wonder how long we'll be permitted to stay, how long before the wheels are put in motion to discharge me, or have us transferred to some other centre.

It's a most uncomfortable feeling.

We make friends with Ben and his wife. Ben has a good voice and can sing "The Fields of Athenrye" like a true son of the auld sod. He's had his leg amputated and he's not feeling real good about it, for some reason. I feel it incumbent on me on occasion to supply Ben with some liquid comfort and support, of which I have a copious supply. A minister friend in the city is a winemaker and he sees to it that I have enough on hand at any given time to supply the wedding at Cana where Christ turned the water into wine. The reverend's stuff is so strong that a greater miracle would be to turn the wine back into water.

Marion's brother, being a doctor and acquainted with the stresses and strains of hospitalization, keeps me supplied with port and insists I drink it regularly. I suggest to Ben one night that he might benefit from a glass of port as well, and he agrees. He's on his second glass when he decides he has to leave. I suggest he take the rest of his port with him rather than abandon the nectar of the gods to the sink. Ben is only too happy to oblige.

Early next morning the daily apparitions of doctor and nurse are standing at the foot of my bed and I can tell, even from my sleep-drugged state, that they are not happy.

"Last evening you gave Ben a glass of port," accuses the doctor, in the ringing tones of a judge reading the charges against Jack the Ripper. Actually, this doctor doesn't have ringing tones but the point remains the same. He's dead serious.

I don't see much point in denying it.

"That," says the doctor, "is an absolute no-no!"

The nurse shakes her head emphatically.

"An absolute no-no," she repeats.

Now that I think of it, I realize there's a law against having alcoholic beverages in the Centre, but I'd forgotten all about it. They've got me dead to rights on this one. I can be charged not only with possession, but also distribution.

The doctor goes into some detail with the reasons for the regulation, which are mostly legitimate. The major problem seems to be in Ben wheeling merrily down the hallway with what was left of his glass of port prominently displayed. Someone saw, disapproved and was small enough to report us both to the authorities. At the same time I do understand. If Ben can wheel down the hall with a glass of port held proudly in his hand, someone else can walk down the hall with a bottle of beer in theirs. Given the real possibility of some people abusing liquor, it's not hard to see where problems could begin. So I agree to cease and desist, thoroughly chastened. Well, perhaps not thoroughly, but certainly a little bit chastened. As chastened as I can be, anyway.

Ben comes in later that morning and tells me he's been grilled, too. They hold out an olive branch to him by saying that when he's home on weekends he can have a beer or two. In what he hopes is a strongly sarcastic tone,

Ben thanks them very much for telling him he can have a beer in his own house. He is not a happy camper. I feel bad about it because I'm the one who gave him the port in the first place, and suggested he take it back to his room in the second.

The next time Ben and I have a glass of port together I'll make sure the door is firmly shut. Sorry, Doc, but it's the best I can do.

24

It is time, or so they say, that I begin to foray out into the wide, wide world.

Truth is, I'm happiest when I'm lying in bed. That's not the way it should be, but that's the way it is. I have absolutely no desire to get up and go anywhere. Going out is a glitch on my otherwise comfortable little existence. I can tolerate getting up for therapy when I can't find any way to get out of it. I actually look forward to taking in the entertainment over in the Veterans' Pavilion some evenings and I can manage to get up for chapel on Sundays. I don't want to hear tell of anything else.

Unfortunately for me, Marion doesn't go along with this. She tries to persuade me to take the wheelchair bus for a short trip, or to visit with Pat who lives only a few minutes' drive away. The nurses, too, are encouraging me to get out of the Hewitt as much as I can. But I don't even want to take the chair out on the parking lot.

After I've had a chance to mull this over a bit, however, I begin thinking that perhaps a trip out to Pat's is not a bad idea. I can't get into her house yet (Bill is in the process of building an ambitious series of ramps and platforms leading up to their patio doors), but she and Marion are talking about a barbecue in the backyard for Father's Day.

"What happens if it rains suddenly and I can't get in out of it?" I ask.

"No problem," replies Marion, who rarely sees an unsolvable problem in anything. "We'll just throw a sheet of plastic over you and the rest of us will run for the house."

Knowing her as I do, I'm not at all sure she's joking. But finally I agree to the expedition and even begin to look forward to this little do at my sister's. It's Father's Day after all, and my father will be there. I'm a father, too, and I'll be there. I still have some misgivings but I'm willing to make the effort and see where it leads. The more I think of it the more enthusiastic I become.

It's all set for tomorrow. The necessary preparations have been made and the appropriate people in the Centre notified well in advance. No one seems to have a problem. The weather forecast gives for showers but no one worries about that except me. I seem to worry about anything involved with getting me moving. Just the same, I'm thinking I might enjoy this first trip away from the Centre. We've been over to the Health Sciences Centre a couple of times for X-rays and the like, but that was by ambulance and far from a pleasure. For some reason I don't like ambulances.

So I cut the final cord that binds me to this place and remind the nurse on duty, Cheryl, that I'm going out for a few hours tomorrow to visit my sister.

"That's great!" she enthuses. "I'll make sure everything is ready."

Now the die is cast. I'm finally going somewhere on my own. Well, perhaps not entirely on my own, but I'm going.

The morning comes, and the weather looks okay. The morning nursing routine is done, and I lie here waiting for Marion and the actual getting up and going. The others are waiting for us at Pat's. I can almost smell the steaks cooking on the hot grill as small drops of fat drop onto the burning coals and sizzle into wisps of fragrant blue smoke. Ah yes, I am ready!

That's when the bomb drops.

Cheryl comes into the room. She's one of the best nurses around, and when I see her crestfallen face I know something's wrong.

"I'm so sorry, Ed," she says, "but you can't go out to your sister's today."

"I can't? Why not?"

"The doctor says you can't go anywhere without some kind of medical escort."

"You've got to be joking!" Her face says she isn't. "Look, it's only five minutes up the street. What can happen that I couldn't get back here in time to take care of?"

"It's policy, Ed. The doctor's not going to take a chance on something happening to you while you're out unless someone's with you. You're still our responsibility."

"Okay, would a nurse or LPN satisfy the requirements?"

"Yes, either one would." Cheryl looks and sounds really upset. "But we don't have anyone we can release to go with you. I'm sorry," she says again, "I know how much you were looking forward to this."

"It's not your fault, Cheryl," I say.

"If we had been told this before," Marion says when she comes in, "we could have hired a private nurse or something."

Seems like a drastic measure to me, although I know she's ready to do anything to get me out of the Centre for a few hours. But it's too late for that now. My trip is over before it begins. Marion is especially upset because she knows what it's going to take to get me outside again.

In the end, my parents and Pat and Bill come down to the Centre and we have our supper in the kitchen.

Marion doesn't give up easily. On the next warm, sunny day, she and Pat appear with sandwiches and Kool Aid and the announcement that we're going out to the little picnic area across the parking lot to have lunch. No one asks me if I want to go so I don't get a chance to say no. Before I know it, I'm following them out the door and down the ramp to the pavement. I resent this, why I'm not sure, and any little thing that goes wrong gets blown out of proportion in my mind.

I can't get off the pavement onto the little path leading to the picnic tables. I can't get in through the gate to the picnic area. I'm sitting on half the earth's population of ants. I can't hold onto the sandwiches. Where the patience of the others comes from I don't know, but they don't react to me at all and carry on as though I were the most pleasant of men. That makes me even more upset because my feeling is that they should be upset in empathy. No way should they be enjoying this farce of a picnic when I'm having such a terrible time. Although I know I'm being more than unreason-able, I seem to have little control over my grossly negative attitude.

By the time the picnic is over, however, my natural ebul-lient self begins to rise to the surface and I realize the sun is warm, sitting beneath the trees like this is actually pleasant and it's better, at least for a little while, than lying in bed.

Having discovered that being outdoors on a warm day is rather nice, I get to taking little spins around the parking lot. I gain a whole new perspective on this activity when I find I have to compete with cars, trucks, motorcycles and vehicles of all sizes and description. All of them are larger than my chair. All of them could do me damage, and since some of the drivers of these vehicles see the parking lot as the Indianapolis Speedway, the potential for such damage is very real. So I don't go very far and I don't go very fast. There are enough fools using this parking lot already.

I resolve to make some recommendations to the admin-istration of the Health Care Corp on improving the safety of the parking lot before we leave here.

That should have them trembling in the boardrooms.

Jennifer

We were out sitting in the sun yesterday. Dad, me, Gumpy and Uncle Bill. It was a beautiful day. Looking down the street and across the city Dad spoke quietly.

"I want to get up and run."

I didn't reply. There is no reply. Just be with him in his pain.

All told, this was the first time I could say Dad seemed better. Not that anything was improved, but he seemed more even emotionally. Until now, he'd had a small grip on a tiny ledge of equilibrium and anything could unseat him: a sad news story, a Hollywood movie, Hollywood violence—any-thing.

I leave for Harvard tomorrow morning at 6:00 A.M. because I've learned that Dad can't cope with goodbyes. During my February and March visits, the day I left Dad stayed in bed with his eyes closed. He asked for sedatives and tried to stay asleep so he wouldn't have to deal with the pain of separation. Unfortunately, Dad spent most of my last visit miserable with a fever. His best two hours for the whole nine days were reserved for the CBC camera crew which came to interview him. It's funny. As much time as I've spent with Dad over the winter, I always feel as though I haven't seen him in ages. In February he hit major depression the week I was here. In March he was sick with infection. Now there are just too many people around to have much quality time.

I'm grateful he doesn't hallucinate as much at night anymore. In February he was still having horrible nightmares. The worst was the dream where he was picnicking with his family and all was lovely. Suddenly a man was attacking his family. In his dream he metamorphosed into a cripple, trapped in a wheelchair. Helpless, able only to watch the horrible assault, he'd wake up crying, saying I was the only one safe, standing by his chair.

It doesn't take Freud to figure out these dreams.

25

The series of services in the chapel lasts only a few weeks. It ends, we all assume, because the students have finished their course and no longer need us as worship service guinea pigs. That seems to be a cruel judgment when I first hear it stated by another patient, but it's probably accurate in fact if not intent.

Despite the shortcomings of those first services, the patients are obviously in need of a time to strengthen their spiritual resources. Those who grew up and spent their lives in small communities are usually closely associated with some religious denomination or other. Twelve or fifteen have been attending chapel faithfully each Sunday and no doubt feel a keen sense of loss now that it's over. The last two services from the chaplaincy class are by far the best they've done. I feel much better about their efforts, and have myself enjoyed and benefitted from them.

Marion has hinted several times that I should take responsibility for keeping the services going. She doesn't come right out and say it because she knows she doesn't have to. I know what she's thinking. I've been critical of the other services, so perhaps I should put my money where my mouth is. She does remind me that I'm a lay reader in our church, that I was three years a student minister, and that my father is a retired clergyman. I would seem to be eminently qualified, at least on the face of it.

My own confusion over any relationship I might or might not have with the Creator would have to be put aside for the time being. Does that make me a hypocrite? Probably.

Our friend, Tom Lush, volunteers to help, not just with the service itself, but also with committing the resources of his office as MHA to printing bulletins and the like. Tom and his wife, Lily, are trying to cope with having an adult son at the Hewitt Centre who was brain-damaged in a plane accident. Their suffering is etched on their faces.

"I know Ed's quadriplegia is causing you great pain," Tom once said to my parents, "but I'd give anything in this world just to have a conversation with my son."

For my parents, it is a glimpse into another broken heart, the wound as raw and aching as their own. They see their own grief from another, shared perspective and that sharing helps. No matter how great the empathy, only the Lushes, or another parent in that same situation, can truly share their mutual pain.

My father endorses the worship service idea as well and so we decide to give it a shot. Jennifer says she'll play piano for us whenever she's back from law school for a visit, so we even have music.

Our services are better planned than D-Day. Tom sees that bulletins containing the order of worship are prepared and conducts the service. Father does the prayer and sometimes sings. There is no shortage of patients and relatives to assist with reading Scriptures or leading in responsive Psalm readings. When Jennifer goes back to school, a good friend of my parents plays for us. My job is to give a brief meditation, usually based on some Bible story and applied to the challenges faced by the disabled and their families.

Our approach is decidedly ecumenical. At any given time we have members from several denominations sharing in the worship. We get our hands on hymn books from The United Church, the Roman Catholic, the Anglican, the Pentecostal and the Salvation Army. Then we search through all five to make sure the hymns are common and the liturgies familiar to everyone. That part of it is surprisingly easy. We also find that people who have never spoken in public before are eager to be involved.

The response is astonishing. At first, only the regulars at chapel services attend. Then we find we need the help of volunteers and family members in getting people down from other floors. Finally, we have to begin ferrying people a half-hour early so that we can get them all into the recreation room on time.

In addition to the patients themselves, families and friends from outside the Centre begin attending because there is such a warm feeling of fellowship. Perhaps it's because those who are presenting and conducting the service, whether patient or family, share the same fears, frustrations and pain as those who worship. That basic understanding of each other's needs and experiences creates a unique context for worship. Or it may be that we simply find solace in each other's company. If so, the degree of our comfort is far greater than the melding of our individual parts. Perhaps too great to be explained by the simple fact of our coming together.

But come together we do. I look out over the little congregation and my heart is filled. Some with missing limbs, some twisted and maimed with stroke, others paralyzed with spinal injury or disease, still others with the catastrophe of brain injury. Spouses trying desperately to cope with a new and demanding relationship, parents suffering for their children, children trying to find the parent they loved and lost in this new and different person.

The common denominators among us are pain and grief. Pain, physical and mental. Grief for the loss of the person we once were, or once knew. But somehow in this little gathering pain and grief for the moment are strangers. Drawing on our own strengths, and the strengths of those around us, we manage to rise above our personal and collective demons and are temporarily freed. Here we are understood, and accepted for who we are and not what we are. Here we can share worship with each other in perfect understanding, whatever our unique and varied perceptions of the Creator may be.

God, I hope you're listening.

When the substitute music teacher didn't appear in July, I was certain there'd been some misunderstanding among the three of us. The substitute had been given the wrong name or the wrong facility or the wrong time. I had the wrong day or the wrong time or the wrong venue. Shouldn't be a difficult problem to resolve, yet no resolution could be found.

Even when July ended with no sign of Victoria, I was convinced she had simply extended her holiday and would soon be back. But now it's been six weeks with absolutely no word from her. We make inquiries of people we think might know something, but it's as though she dropped off the edge of the world.

If Victoria is ill, no one seems to know it. If she had an accident, it must have happened in a vacuum. Each day without any explanation deepens the mystery.

Could I have offended her in some way? I trace every moment of every session in my mind and I know nothing of the sort could possibly have happened. Did she feel her time was being wasted on someone with no talent? Understandable if she did, but that last session was so positive that such a conclusion doesn't seem credible. Besides, she would surely have told me, gently but firmly, that further sessions couldn't be justified for either of us. And what about her last comment about a public appearance in September? She obviously thought I had some potential. So where is she, and what has happened?

She certainly didn't strike either Marion or me as the kind of person who would simply vanish into thin air without any explanation. She was friendly and outgoing and had me believing that perhaps I had enough talent to work with. I know I'm no Frank Sinatra, but making the most of what I do have seemed to be a worthwhile goal for her. She had no right to take me to that point, only to have the point turn into a cliff over which I have tumbled head over heels.

Any progress I had made from a rehabilitation point of view is now reversed. I'm convinced it's something about me that made her drop so completely out of sight. But what? And why so suddenly? And why no explanation? Why no word at all? It is maddening and frustrating and something I need like another Minerva jacket.

I never again want to hear of voice teachers. Marion hasn't mentioned it since, either. But right up until my last day in the Hewitt Centre, I'm half expecting to look up and see her standing in the doorway and saying, "I'm so sorry, but you'll never guess what happened to me!"

When we leave the Hewitt in late August, the mystery of Victoria is as deep and raw as ever.

The end is near.

So saith some psycho or psychic or something in Halifax. She's announced to all who'll listen that on August 1 of this year of our Lord, 1998, a great tidal wave will sweep in over the Avalon Peninsula and carry it and everything on it into the sea. That's tomorrow. She's been interviewed by all the media, and her prediction of gloom for the Avalon is now known to everyone. She admits she could be wrong on the exact date, but it'll happen within a day or two of that time.

Everyone's talking about it, and almost everyone's laughing at it. You can't find a soul within a hundred miles who gives any credence to this woman and her predictions. Interestingly enough, something else you won't find within a hundred miles is a life jacket. Sold out, every last one.

I don't think I'd have the face to walk into a sporting goods store and ask to buy a life jacket these days. Everyone would know exactly why I was doing it.

"You're afraid of the flood? You're actually taking this silly woman seriously? Come on, my son, come on. Get a life!"

Nope, I'd have to have an explanation or two or three as to why I'm purchasing a life jacket at this time.

"Yep, finally getting to go on this fishing expedition I've been planning for so long. Yes, taking the wife and kiddies with me. That's why I want two large and two small. Oh yes, and the smallest flotation device you have for the poodle. Can't take a chance on losing the poodle, you know. Could jump in the pond. Now what have you got by way of larger flotation devices? Got any cork? Rubber rafts? Inflatable mattresses?"

Many people have to be taking this thing seriously to have such a run on life jackets, and I'm wondering what they're thinking. A tidal wave that's going to pick Cabot

Tower off the top of Signal Hill and deposit it somewhere back of Come-by-Chance is not a thing to be fought with life jackets. A life jacket in the face of that would be as effective as a bikini in a high Arctic blizzard.

We're told that many in the city have developed urgent business in Central Newfoundland for the three-day window in which St. John's could take on an Atlantis complex. I think if I were to do that, I'd keep on going until I was at least on the West Coast. No point taking chances. If I had legs, I'd take to climbing Gros Morne.

One lady who has a relative here in the Hewitt says she'll be staying up all night and watching the Narrows through her window. That's going to help a lot, too. As the crest of a thousand-foot monster wave curls in over Signal Hill she at least is going to see what gets her. Personally, I'd just as soon not know until I get wet.

And that reminds me. It would be most unfair to sweep me out into the ocean along with the Avalon Peninsula. That would be double jeopardy. Springdale is far enough away from the Avalon to be safe. Were it not for the stupid broken neck I'd be in Springdale now and not wondering if some pseudo-psychic in Halifax knows what she's talking about.

Actually, I'm not much worried about that foolishness. I figure any power with enough force to wipe out the Avalon Peninsula and compassionate enough to tell someone about it in advance would at least tell someone important. Someone people would listen to, like the mayor of St. John's or the premier of the province. Or me. The power certainly isn't going to tell Halifax Harriet and depend on her to get the word to us. It's not kosher. It's not according to Hoyle. It just isn't done.

Tonight's the night. If we wake up soaking wet tomorrow morning we'll know what happened. Or we'll know nothing because we're dead. Or we'll be the same as we are now.

Whatever. It's not in my hands.

26

I wasn't exactly spry when we arrived here in February. I knew when I was coming and going but I hardly knew where or why. We are now well into summer and I'm still showing no interest in making any physical progress. I use any and every trick in the book to avoid therapy and getting out of bed. I don't mind putting my brain to work just as long as it doesn't involve physical effort. Part of the problem may be that I see no significant improvement in my condition and thus there's nothing to work towards. That's hardly the fault of the respective departments since they seem to be doing their best for me.

Marion is becoming more and more frustrated. Nothing piques my interest. I have no initiative and no drive. Even being washed in bed is an irritant I try hard to avoid. On Saturdays and Sundays when there's no scheduled therapy all I want to do is sleep. Sometimes I awake late in the morning or early in the afternoon to find Marion crying by my bed. I'm going nowhere fast and that knowledge is driving her to the end of her rope.

When I'm having a particularly bad day, I don't want to see anyone except my immediate family and a few close friends. With them I don't have to pretend. During visiting hours, Marion runs interference for me when I'm feeling like that and keeps visitors to a minimum. The staff nurses, too, will ask visitors to wait until they're sure I'm up to seeing people. Sometimes acquaintances I would really like to see at any other time are kept from entering my room. I hope they understand. On two or three occasions, friends whom I would want to see under any circumstances are also not permitted to come in, and this I deeply regret. At the same time, I do appreciate the efforts of the staff to look after me in that regard. Sometimes people I do know and like are in the room, but I can't find the will to respond to them.

Then there are those who simply walk in from off the street and directly into my room, despite the sign on the door, PLEASE CHECK WITH NURSING STATION BEFORE ENTERING. If the door is closed, as it usually is, they'll open it without knocking and no matter who else is in the room come straight to my bed and try to grab my hand. Not only is this rather rude, but also my hands are so sensitive that I can't stand to have anyone touch them. My reaction is consequently quick and sharp and sometimes uncivil. If Marion is there, she grabs the arm of the person to keep him from touching me. Sometimes they just stand in the middle of the room without speaking and stare. I'm afraid I'm not very friendly on such occasions.

The other side of that coin is that we've met many wonderful people we didn't know before. They come to visit because they want us to know we have their support and love.

Marion

Both staff and family had some difficulty with people who insisted on getting in to see Ed or getting information on his condition. These were always people we didn't know and they sometimes went to elaborate means to get in or to get information. One fellow kept calling the switchboard claiming to be a fireman and as such had the right to be kept informed.

Most people understood when told that Ed was too sick to have visitors, but others were a little more aggressive. On one occasion Ed was having a particularly bad day and I was the only one with him. I heard a noise at the door and looked up to see a strange man trying to get past a nurse outside.

"Mr. Smith is too ill to have visitors today," she was saying. "I'm sorry but you can't go in. Are you a friend?"

The man shook his head and then brushed on by her and started in through the door. I met him just as he was entering the room.

"I'm sorry, but you can't come in. If you know Ed, I'll tell him you were here. Perhaps you could come back another time when he's feeling better."

He stopped momentarily.

"I have to see him," he said, trying to look past me into the room. He began moving towards Ed's bed which was screened in.

In order to get past me he would have to push me out of the way or go through me. I didn't budge an inch.

"You're not coming in here," I said in as firm a voice as I could manage. Truth is, I was getting a little scared. Ed gets some strange letters from people who are a few bolts shy of a full bucket. Perhaps this man was one of them.

"I just want to look at him for a few minutes," he said.

That did it. No way was this man getting anywhere near Ed. I put my two hands up against his chest and pushed. I didn't stop to think what might happen then. He was much bigger and stronger than I and could easily have overpowered me. To my surprise he gave a little. I pushed again and continued to push until I had backed him right out through the door. Then I closed the door quickly, half expecting him to open it and force his way in. But nothing happened and when I looked out a few moments later he was gone.

The staff psychologist, Marilyn, and I are having an afternoon session. Usually we have a little sign on the door asking that we not be interrupted, although I'm not sure if it's there today. Whatever, the door is closed. Suddenly it pops open without a knock and a tall, thin man dressed in a black suit starts across the floor. Without even a glance at Marilyn, who is in the middle of a sentence, he interrupts and proceeds to tell me who he is. I don't wait for him to finish what he's saying.

"Excuse me. I'm in a session with my psychologist. Would you mind coming back another time?"

I hope my voice doesn't betray how angry I feel at the intrusion. He looks at me for a brief moment and then continues as though I haven't spoken. I still don't absorb his name or what he's doing here.

"Please," I say, again hoping that I'm not being as rude as he is, "this is a private session and I'm asking you to leave and come back another time."

Without another word, he turns abruptly and walks out.

"Am I that sick?" I ask Marilyn.

"What do you mean?"

"Well," I say, "if I'm not mistaken, that was an undertaker."

We have a good laugh, but such incidents aren't always funny.

The more thoughtful staff nurses will drop by whenever they know people have made it into the room without asking, and if they see I'm having a bad time they'll tell the visitors they have only two or three minutes. But on at least one occasion they themselves could have used a little help.

Two nurses are going through the morning routine with me. All of a sudden the door opens and this woman, nattily dressed, strides into the room. She pushes her way right past Marion, who isn't easily brushed aside. Marion probably thinks she's a new member of the staff. She doesn't say "Hello," "Good morning," "Kiss my bum" or anything. She comes over to the bed and watches for a few moments. The nurses say nothing to acknowledge her presence. I assume she's a new supervisor of some kind.

"You people aren't doing that properly," she says as the nurses roll me to another position. The nurses say nothing, which I think is strange. The woman continues in this vein for several minutes.

"You're going to hurt your backs. That's not the right way to do that. You're doing that all wrong."

Her voice has a sharp edge to it, indicative of a supervisor who's new at the job and determined to lord it over everyone beneath her. Well I'm not beneath her, and would never want to be. Her personality would harden jelly. I do know she shouldn't be treating anyone this way.

"Just who are you?" I ask, making no attempt to be civil.

She doesn't even look my way. The nurses look up at me questioningly, and I assume they're somewhat surprised that I'm talking to this woman in such a tone. They shouldn't be. But now her ladyship has found something else to criticize, although I can't see what it is.

"You're not doing that right, either."

This has gone far enough.

"Just what do you think you're doing? If you want to conduct a seminar on patient care you're not doing it in my room."

She still doesn't spare a glance in my direction although she does deign to answer the question.

"I'm looking for the mental health seminar."

I can't believe it! This woman doesn't even work here?

"Good," I say with all my mental resources trained on being as sarcastic as possible. "You could use a lot of help."

That's when she does turn and look me square in the eye, obviously ready to do battle. Good, I think to myself. I'd like nothing better than to exchange a few words with you. But alas, it is not to be. One of the nurses breaks in and directs her to where the seminar is being held. She turns on her heel and walks out.

The nurses visibly relax.

"Have you ever seen her before?" I ask them.

No, they say, although one thinks she might have seen her in the injured workers department upstairs. They thought at first she was someone I knew and consequently didn't tell her to get the hell out of the room.

"If she works anywhere in this building," I say, "you should lay a strong complaint against her. I'll back you up."

We were to learn later that they did, and her ladyship was disciplined.

Happily, people often drop by when I'm feeling relatively okay and not in the middle of a procedure or a session. Then I can enjoy their company whether I know them or not. And there are always those precious souls who can lift my spirits by just appearing for a few brief moments no matter how I feel. God bless 'em.

Neither Marion nor the rest of my family can understand why I seem so listless, even at the best of times. The consensus is that my attitude, as well as the frozen shoulder, plays a large part in the lack of progress in physiotherapy and occupational therapy. Despite the best efforts of the therapists, the range of motion and strength in my arms are not improving. In fact, Marion is certain I've lost ground over the last few months.

I don't know who begins talking about it first, but every so often someone will mention the idea of going to another rehab centre. When I strenuously object, as I do at the beginning, the subject is dropped. But more and more often the topic is raised and dropped again in the face of my reaction.

Then Marion and her sister, Jennette, make a fateful weekend trip to Springdale to see how renovations are coming on the house.

Early in my rehab we had decided major renovations were needed to allow me free and easy access inside the house. I mean they couldn't just stick me in the living room and leave me to travel in tight circles for the rest of my life. What really pained us was that we had spent a lot of time and money last fall making the house the way we had always wanted it to be. The living area had been drastically altered, the kitchen was fitted with new cupboards and counters and new large appliances, and we had installed new carpet throughout. Now the carpet would have to be taken up in favour of hardwood floors to make wheeling easier. We would need a much larger bedroom, a wheel-in shower and wider corridors. I would need a large study with wheel-under desk and computer station.

Sometimes I think this wheelchair business is the pits.

Obviously we needed an extension to the house to incorporate such features. We had already installed patio doors in the living room and had planned a small deck outside for barbecuing and the like. Now the deck will have to be large enough to allow me room for wheeling exercise and taking the air. A ramp has to be built from ground level to the main floor. I have to get into the house, after all, especially when it gets a bit chilly. Our flood back in January has also necessitated major rebuilding in the basement. We gave some thought to an indoor swimming pool.

We hired a local contractor to begin work in early summer. He gave us the best possible price and although he was on hourly wages, made it clear that volunteer work from friends and neighbours would be welcome at any time. Marion and I discussed the building plans at length, but she had to take responsibility for the final decisions and actually initiating and supervising the work. I wanted to be part of the decision-making process, but I had difficulty summoning the necessary mental energy. In short, I wasn't a lot of help.

When she gets back the house is almost the last thing on Marion's mind.

They ran into our pharmacist while out shopping, and like you would, he wanted to know how things were going and how I was doing. The conversation was long enough that Marion began telling him how I was behaving: no interest in anything, no initiative, no spirit.

"Hold on," Jeffrey said. "That doesn't sound like Ed at all. We've had too many debates and arguments about health care and pharmacies when he was chair of the hospital board. That's not the Ed I know."

One thing led to another and Jeffrey out of professional interest asked what drugs I was on. From the beginning, Marion could rhyme off the three or four hundred pills I'm on daily so she told him. It was Jennette who asked the fateful question. Perhaps it was the nurse in her that prompted it.

"What effect would Croterion have on him?"

Jeffrey could hardly contain his astonishment.

"Croterion? He's on Croterion?"

"Yes," Marion said. "Why do you sound so surprised?"

"Because that drug is rarely prescribed anymore due to the nasty side effects."

"What side effects?" Marion was really interested now.

"Extreme behaviour patterns, mood swings, and sometimes a lack of interest in anything. How long has he been on this?"

"I don't know," she replied, "almost from the time we've been there. Four or five months at least."

"My God, Marion!" Jeffrey burst out. "That's never prescribed for more than one or two weeks at most. It's a wonder he's conscious at all!"

"I don't doubt Jeffrey," Marion says after telling me all this. "But I've got to do a little more research to be sure."

She calls three pharmacists at random from the phone book and each one confirms Jeffrey's opinion. That drug is rarely used and then only for a short period.

I don't need to hear anymore.

"I'm off it as of now," I tell Marion, and we tell the nurse supervisor of my decision.

It takes several days but gradually I begin to feel more aware of myself and what's been happening than at any time since the accident. I take stock of where I am and where I should be, and pass my conclusions on to Marion.

"Marion, I'm not doing one damn thing here!"

"Thank God," she says fervently. "You're back!"

Her sentiments are echoed by Jennifer who later confides to her mother, "Dad is back to his old self."

Now when the subject of another rehab centre is broached, my reaction is not so negative. I still don't like the idea but I'm beginning to think about it some. In the meantime, I'm taking some flak from the good doctor about taking myself off Croterion.

"As your doctor," he intones at one of our family meetings, "I should know about any change in medication. In fact, no change in meds should be made without consulting me first."

I can't argue with that.

"You're right," I say, "but we did let the supervising nurse know about it, and I understood that would be the channel to you. Besides, I'm not happy about having been left on a drug for several months when its use is intended for only a few days."

In fact, the more I thought about having been kept on that drug so long the more unhappy I became. Surely God someone in the medical faculty should have noticed that and questioned it.

"My feeling was," the doctor chooses to ignore the last point, "that you were deliberately trying to avoid telling me at all."

"Good heavens, no," I reply truthfully. "Why would I want to do that?"

"I was wondering the same thing," he says, "but I'm glad to see it's not the case."

There is a silence. No one else speaks.

"Do I make you paranoid, Doctor?"

"No." He manages a small smile. "I've been paranoid all my life."

Not much I can do about that.

For some time, now, I've been watching a certain process with no little interest.

The process doesn't have a name but if it did it would be called The Conditioning of Ed Smith to Accept Going to Another Rehabilitation Centre on the Mainland. The conditioning begins gently but doesn't stay that way for long. At the end, there was less pressure on Vesuvius to erupt.

It started several weeks ago, perhaps longer. My awareness of what's going on around me has admittedly been sometimes dim. Whatever, Marion has begun pointing to a self-evident truth which, as most people know, is an axiom. The axiom is me. More accurately, the axiom *has to do* with me and the inescapable truth that I'm not progressing in my rehabilitation as quickly as I should. More accurately still, I'm dead in my tracks. That axiom is so self-evident that it's evident to me.

Both the occupational therapist and the physiotherapist are suggesting that I've gone as far as they can take me. By now, too, the name of a rehabilitation centre in Toronto is being openly suggested. My physician brother-in-law keeps asking by telephone and e-mail if I'm considering Scarbrae Spinal Cord Centre, and if not, why not. It's supposed to be one of the leading spinal cord centres in the world.

Marion has also been checking out Scarbrae, even to the point of asking her sister, who had been visiting Toronto, to go have a look. Jennette declares herself to be highly impressed. She does, however, put one rider on her endorsement.

"What I saw, Ed," she says to me, "I saw as an inquisitive visitor and not as a patient."

As the summer wears on the Scarbrae option grows more and more viable, and the pressure to make a decision gets heavier each day. Finally, early in August a family meeting is held at which I'm told outright by the good doctor that either I accept a referral to Scarbrae Hospital from the Hewitt Centre, or they'll begin the discharge process immediately.

There's that hint of threat again, but it isn't necessary.

"I've already decided to go to Scarbrae."

It's the first time I've said it aloud and I recognize now that the die is cast. I'm not happy about it but I see no other option. Apart from any other consideration our house is still up in slings. If they do kick me out of here we have nowhere to go.

The doctor obviously feels, and perhaps with good cause, that he has won the war. One way or another I will soon be out of his hair. But he has to take one last swipe.

"You won't be getting any private room in Scarbrae," he says with great satisfaction. "There won't be any private room for you there."

I say nothing. I have no intention of asking for a private room at Scarbrae any more than I asked for one here.

The process of being transferred has already begun. Scarbrae has agreed to admit me for a two-week observation and assessment period, during which time they will decide either to admit me for the full rehabilitation treatment, or conclude there is nothing to be done and send me home again. If the latter happens, it is made clear that the Hewitt will take me back and begin the discharge process immediately.

To be fair, the therapists at the Hewitt Centre have been more than patient. Thanks in large part to the drug Croterion, I haven't been fully cooperative with them. The nursing staff has been faultless in terms of caring for a patient who must have caused them endless frustration. The other departments such as Social Services and Psychology have been more than supportive. In short, I realize the Hewitt can't be expected to keep me here ad infinitum, especially when everyone agrees I'm going nowhere fast.

Once the process is started, little time is wasted on getting me out of the Hewitt and on to Scarbrae. Within a couple of weeks, the necessary paperwork is completed and we are awaiting a call from my doctor at Scarbrae that a bed is ready. That comes very quickly, too, and now I find myself with only a few days left before being flown to Toronto. They have to test me here for any sign of a super bug that might be immune to their antibiotics, but once I'm declared free of contamination it's onward and upward.

Truth is, while somewhat apprehensive, I'm looking forward to rehabilitation at Scarbrae. I've spoken with people who have been patients there and who have nothing but the highest of praise for it.

This summer we met a couple who know Scarbrae better than most. Ivan Gill had a car accident near Toronto five years ago, and his injuries are similar to mine. He and his wife, Karen, drive to Newfoundland every summer to visit their families in Trinity Bay. My parents met them earlier, and knew we'd want to talk with them.

We hit it off at once. Both Ivan and Karen are really friendly and supportive. They live in Oshawa, about forty-five minutes' drive from Scarbrae, and promise to be in touch as soon as we get there. Ivan had been in Scarbrae for several months and said that he found the Centre to be excellent. But they, too, had a rider to their endorsement.

"We've heard," Karen says, "that Scarbrae is not the place it used to be when Ivan was there, but that's probably only rumour."

Perhaps, but we remember a comment made by someone at the Canadian Paraplegic Association while we were still at the Health Sciences Centre and thinking about rehab centres generally.

"Scarbrae used to be one of the best rehabilitation centres in the world," she said, "however we've heard that it's changed in the last few years."

That's probably just talk and we dismiss it from our minds. We have to. Scarbrae is still the focus of all our hopes. If they admit me as a patient, there's no doubt in my mind that I'll progress far beyond anything I could have hoped for here.

Now I can't wait to go.

Marion calls Air Canada to make reservations.

"I want to book eight seats," she tells the ticket agent. "I understand there's a seat sale from St. John's to Toronto at three hundred and sixty-four dollars return."

The agent assures her that this is so.

"Fine," Marion says. "I'd like to pay for these seats now."

He's okay with that, and could she now give him the names of the people involved?

"One seat is for me, Marion Smith."

No problem. Payment made. And the next?

"Millie Ivany." Millie is the nurse who'll go on the plane with me.

Next?

"The other six seats are for my husband, Ed Smith."

Marion had already discovered that I and my stretcher would take up six seats. Her understanding was that the seats would have to be removed.

"He needs six seats?"

"Yes, he's on a stretcher."

"Oh," says the ticket agent, "I can't help you with him. You have to go through our medical desk."

So Marion gets rerouted through the medical desk. She tells the person there about me and the six seats. She's told that won't be a problem, except for one small detail.

"Your husband will have to pay full fare for his seats."

Marion just about falls off her chair.

"Are you telling me he can't have the seat sale price like anyone else?"

"Yes," she was sorry about that, but it was Air Canada policy.

Marion still can't believe her ears.

"He has to pay full price for each of his six seats?!"

"Yes."

"So how much will that come to?"

"It's nine hundred and ninety dollars a seat, which comes to five thousand, nine hundred and forty dollars."

"You mean to tell me I can fly to Toronto and back for three hundred and sixty-four dollars, and my husband, because he's quadriplegic and has to travel on a stretcher, has to pay five thousand, nine hundred and forty dollars for the same ticket?"

"Not quite," the medical desk person replies. "That's the price for one-way. His return ticket will cost him eleven thousand, eight hundred and eighty dollars."

It's incredible. It's unbelievable. But nothing can be done. It's Air Canada policy.

We spend the next few days calling people we know who might be in a position to do something about this, but without success. That's the Newfoundland way. Whenever we run up against blatant injustice or bureaucratic stupidity the course of action is clear; 'somebody' has to 'do something' about it. What the something is that somebody has to do is not always clear and definitive. But in this case it's as clear as the proverbial crystal. No one, healthy or sick, fit or unfit, rich or poor should have to pay eleven thousand, eight hundred and eighty dollars for a return ticket from St. John's to Toronto. And show me the Newfoundlander who doesn't plan to return.

As if all that weren't bad enough, they also reneged on the nurse's seat which had already been bought and paid for at the three hundred sixty-four dollar seat sale price. Since she was flying up as an attendant to me, they magnanimously agreed to sell her a seat for half the full fare to Toronto, but since she'd be returning alone, that seat would cost a full nine hundred and ninety dollars, for a grand total of one thousand four hundred and eight-five dollars.

Air Canada's policy stinks, sucks and otherwise fouls up the atmosphere. We are determined not to drop the issue when we get to Toronto. Someone has got to do something about this.

The day of departure has come. Dr. Holden has given me some happy pills to make the flight bearable, and even written me up a prescription for whiskey. God bless him.

Marion has decided to take an earlier flight in the morning so that she'll have things ready at Scarbrae when I arrive. It's interesting that the entire staff at that facility is incapable of having the place ready without Marion's help. But I know what she means and I know it's a good idea. She needs to be there and halfway settled before attending to my arrival. Four hours later I'm to follow on a direct flight.

Air Canada has said that seats will be removed in the forward section of the aircraft and there will be a privacy screen around me. I'm happy about the screen bit. The last thing I want is to have people staring at me when I feel so physically and mentally vulnerable. Translation: I don't want people seeing me throw up.

My room is full an hour or so before I leave. Several of the staff come in to say goodbye, as do some of the other patients. Many of my family are there as well.

Sometime before the ambulance comes to take me to the airport, my mother disappears and I don't see her again until we're on our way out the door. I understand why. I see her and my father standing close together on the Hewitt steps as the ambulance pulls away, and I realize again how agonizing this must be for them. Living through the accident and resulting quadriplegia has been one long nightmare, but at least they could be with me. Now they're saying goodbye for nobody knows how long.

This is their second season of suffering for their two children. The first was when my sister, while still a very young woman, was diagnosed with cancer. But she beat that. And I'll beat this.

On with the show!

27

I don't see any privacy curtain.

I'm at the rear of the aircraft, and my stretcher seems to be on top of folded-down seats. The luggage compartment is only inches from my face. The windows are below the level of my eyes so that I can't see out even if I want to. I don't like this very much at all.

Millie is seated near enough to touch me, which is very good. I have a feeling I'll need lots of touching in the next couple of hours.

The plane is roaring down the runway. If it weren't for the happy pills and the liquor I'd be really stressed out. As it is I've felt better, which is the same as saying Mt. Everest is high. I relax a little when the takeoff roar of the engines subsides to a steady, understated drone as the plane reaches cruising altitude.

We're right next to the washroom. I never knew so many people could want to pee at the same time. There's a continuous lineup for the toilet. Every mother's one of them has to pass within twelve inches of me, and every one sneaks a curious look. Their faces are carefully neutral, showing neither concern nor disgust. But I bet their minds are active.

Lord, he looks sick. Poor bugger, wonder what's wrong with him. Might be contagious. Better keep as far from him as possible. Could have AIDS. Must be serious if they're flying him to Toronto. Heart problem, most likely. He'll be lucky if he makes it alive. Oh my God, we could have a corpse on the plane. That's bad luck!

I open my eyes and look into a line of faces, some just beginning their surreptitious glancing, others just ending as they move farther up the line. I try winking at a couple, but they simply look away. No one smiles. Strange. Doesn't seem to be a Newfoundlander aboard. Why would a whole planeload of mainlanders be leaving St. John's at the same time? Mice leaving the sinking ship? Sorry, that's not nice.

The flight attendants give us a wide berth, too, although one does deign to give me a small smile when our eyes meet. Her grandmother probably came from Sop's Arm.

I close my eyes, trying to pretend I'm somewhere else. I don't care where: hell or purgatory or Toronto—makes no difference. It doesn't work, so I open my eyes again and the whole damn lot in that lineup seems to be staring straight at me. So naturally I get sick.

From my lofty perch atop the seats, and right in front of all those lovely people, I vomit all over my shirt and God knows where else. I cast a tormented glance at the washroom lineup and suddenly not one soul is looking at me. Every head is turned in the other direction. Up come the three plates of fishermen's brewis I had for lunch, which is interesting considering I had only two. Then dinner from the previous day. I throw up things I'd eaten days ago. I throw up things I never swallowed.

Millie's face is roughly equal with my chest, and I pity her even more than I pity myself. Somehow she manages to clean me up enough to remove my shirt and put on another. How she does that I'll never know, but she must be wishing she'd taken up belly dancing as a career. My mind flits back to a night several months ago when I woke in the wee small hours to see Millie and another nurse doing a fair imitation of a belly dance to the all-night music on my radio. Doesn't seem so funny now.

It's a rough flight from beginning to end which, when combined with my normal meds, the tranquilizers and the whiskey, is probably what's making me ill.

I feel a bump, then another and then Millie's voice.

"We're down, Ed, we're down!"

She sounds even happier than I feel.

We wait for the other passengers to disembark, and then the Toronto ambulance people arrive to get me off the aircraft. Which is great, the only problem being that they don't seem to know how to do it. They can't detach the stretcher from the mechanism that holds it to the seats. The most disturbing thing for me is that I'm attached to the stretcher.

They call a flight attendant, then another. They all stare gravely at the problem, ignore me completely, make a couple of half-hearted attempts to loosen this and unscrew that and then retire in helplessness. An official-looking person arrives from somewhere and attacks the problem with great gusto while the others stand back and admire his efforts. Gradually his initial enthusiasm wanes and after several minutes he, too, admits defeat.

The cleaners have now arrived and are sweeping out the plane. I'm beginning to wonder if Air Canada will leave the thing on the ground for the next several months with me in it. Or even worse, keep the plane flying on schedule with me as a permanent resident. Even the workers make a suggestion or two, none of which are worth a loonie in an American supermarket.

Finally, they all stand back and regard me with the same look one gives a dying sheep after its throat has been cut.

"This man wants to get off this plane," someone says, which statement is right up there with Noah's comment to his friends, "I sure would like to get off this ark."

The group redoubles its efforts to free the stretcher from whatever chains are binding it. They are again getting nowhere fast when one of the sweepers, a young lad about fifteen, pauses in his work, takes a quick look at the problem, and suggests they release something or other, which they do and lo and behold, I am free. That's one kid who deserves a promotion to maintenance supervisor, if not airport manager.

The two ambulance attendants grab the stretcher and proceed to lug me up the aisle. My elbows bounce off the seats on either side, but I have no feelings there, anyway, so what the hell. Then we get to the forward bulkhead where we have to take a left-handed right angle turn to get out of the aircraft. That's the place where the flight attendant stands and chirps, "We have enjoyed having you on this flight." No one there now. Guess she got tired of waiting.

The ambulance attendants pause and discuss briefly how they're going to get me around this corner. They stand me straight up. They turn me over on my side. They twist me like a pretzel. Nothing works. I can see down into the cockpit where someone in the pilot's chair, presumably the pilot, turns around to see what the commotion is about and then returns to his work.

An interesting situation has developed. The attendants are losing their grip on the stretcher handles. They say they can't hold onto the thing much longer. There's no space on the floor to put me down, and they say they can't make it back to where we were. That's their problem, I say to myself, and then immediately realize how stupid that is. Their problem is my problem, and that's a fact. By now, there are no fewer than eight people trying to get me around the bulkhead and out of this accursed airplane.

Suddenly I am struck with an inspiration. I can either throw up again or break wind. Either one should clear the area in a hurry. But try as I might, I can do neither. Guess losing the ability to do either voluntarily is one of the downsides of being quadriplegic. But now I have another inspiration. By gosh and by golly, I have discovered another Newfie joke. Normally, I hate those things with a passion, including the word "Newfie," but when I'm the creative genius who thinks it up, it's okay.

"Millie," I call out to my nurse who is standing at the rear of this motley crew, "have you heard the latest Newfie joke?"

Heads turn towards me. I don't know if they want to hear the joke, or if they're astonished that I can joke in this situation. I know I am.

"Millie," I call out again, "how many Torontonians does it take to remove one Newfoundlander from an aircraft? Answer, more than eight."

No one laughs, not even Millie, not even me. But then, I'm not telling a joke, I'm making a point. Just in case no one gets it, I volunteer the information that in St. John's the ambulance people had no problem at all getting me into this thing. No one comments.

The attendants say something has to be done immediately because they are about to lose their grip. And then someone makes the suggestion of the year. Why not simply lift me off the stretcher with the sheet that's under me, and carry me off in it? So they do. I'm lifted in the sheet, broken neck and all, and scooted off the plane as if I were in a body bag. Something tells me this is highly irregular, but at the moment I'm too pleased to be off the plane to care.

As they're loading me onto the stretcher inside the terminal, a distinguished-looking man comes over and thanks me for my patience.

"Sorry, b' y," I reply without looking at him, "but there's not enough left to thank me for."

And that was that. Welcome to Toronto and all for the low, low price of $5940.00 one way. I guess when you consider the little things, like not having a privacy curtain, being stuck on the seats for an ungodly length of time, being lugged off the plane in a sheet, to mention only a few, it all adds up.

You want the extras, you gotta pay for 'em.

The ride into Toronto is uneventful, if you don't count being frequently sick. The ambulance attendants are friendly and chatty, and Millie is no doubt ecstatic over this trip nearing its end. I'm a bit relieved myself.

As the ambulance turns into Scarbrae, I throw up one last time just for the hell of it. The thought occurs to me that I'm marking my trail with vomit, much as a dog does with urine. In which case, I should own most of Eastern Canada and much of the Atlantic Ocean.

I have a fairly good view of Scarbrae ceilings as I'm wheeled in through the lobby, but not much else. Indeed, in the last eight months I've seen more ceilings than a new bride.

Marion, accompanied by her cousin, Eleanor, is there to welcome me as she said she would be. It's hard to believe we've each travelled two thousand miles since we left St. John's earlier today. But she seems to have done a good job of getting the place ready. Nurses are on duty, there's a receptionist at the desk and a security person in position. No wheelchairs are blocking the corridor and they even have a bed all made up for me. Way to go, Marion!

"My gosh," I say as orderlies, accompanied by a nurse or two, wheel me to my bed, "this is just as good as a private room."

"It should be," someone says, "because it is."

The looks I get indicate my powers of observation haven't made much of an impression on Scarbrae staff. Gee whiz, guys, I've been gravely ill right outside your front door and I was looking at the ceiling all the way in and there were people walking alongside the stretcher blocking my view. Now that I can look up and around me, I can see that this is a private room. No other beds but mine. Definitely private.

Perhaps I'll impress them with my sense of humour or something tomorrow.

So here we are at Scarbrae, the Promised Land of the paralyzed. Marion has rented a room at a small motel where the parents of children who are being treated at Bloorview-Macmillan Children's Hospital are permitted to stay. She can remain there as long as they don't need it for more legitimate guests. They assure me it's only a couple of parking lots away and quite safe.

The reason for the private room is to keep me isolated from the rest of the patients for a week or so until they're satisfied I'm not carrying any super bug. They don't seem to have much confidence in St. John's medical people who have already declared me to be bug-free. Thing is, people up here are deathly afraid of some virus that might be immune to their antidotes and start a wild spree of contamination.

For the first few days I'm half expecting someone to come in and hose me down, and then check the bed to see if I'm carrying anything containing soil. That's what they do in Port aux Basques before they let you and your vehicle board the ferry to the mainland. Something to do with keeping potato canker confined to the Island.

It strikes me that mainlanders are somewhat paranoid about keeping little things like bugs and canker from crossing the Gulf and into their pure soil and selves. Unfortunately, we have nothing similar in North Sydney to keep unwanted elements out of Newfoundland. That's me being sardonic again. I tend to get sardonic under pressure, a state of mind that can develop into full-blown sarcasm but not often.

While I know it's only temporary, I still get a measure of satisfaction in remembering the words of the good doctor at the Hewitt who said and I quote, "You won't be getting any private room at Scarbrae." Somewhat childish, I agree, but still satisfying. I think briefly of calling him long distance to gloat, but it probably wouldn't do much for our relationship.

The team drops by to meet us. Dr. Lingworst looks like Klinger, the cross-dressing character on the TV series M*A*S*H. With him are the physiotherapist, Diane, who looks Swedish and is; Angela, the occupational therapist, who looks a really cute fifteen, weighs all of eighty-five pounds and is married; Gloria, my primary care nurse who looks tough enough to be a bouncer in a strip joint; and a couple of others whom I haven't yet placed. They are all very positive and declare themselves to be patient centred. Now where have I heard that before? Come now, Smith, this is Scarbrae so chill out.

They think they can improve my physical condition, they say, and state that I won't be leaving here until they do. Sounds as though they mean it. Sounds good to us. At the end of the session I am convinced I will leave here a new man. Why did I fight this move for so long? Because you're stun, my son.

They tell us I can go outside if we wheel through the lobby as fast as possible and don't stop to speak to anyone along the way. Honest to my Maker; that's what they tell us. So that's exactly what we do. Marion and I, and whatever super bug may be lying in wait inside me, go tearing through the lobby, avoiding people like the plague, and out into the warm late-summer air. I look back to see if any bodies are lying in our wake but no one seems to be even aware of the narrow brush with death they've just had.

Several patients are wheeling around outside or just sitting and taking the sun. A couple are on banana carts, beds on wheels for people with pressure sores or skin ulcers on their backsides. They lie face down on these things and push them around as they would a manual wheelchair. It looks extremely uncomfortable and I hope to God I never have to use one.

The people on banana carts all seem to be rabid smokers, which is probably why they're driven to using them instead of lying comfortably in bed. Inside the building there's a room reserved for smokers with a giant screen television and plenty of room. The floors look as though they've been pockmarked with one hundred thousand burning butts but that may just be the decor. At the other end of the corridor there's a much smaller no-smoking lounge area with a much smaller television. Go figure.

We take a jaunt around the beautiful grounds and then it's back into bed, following the same procedure as coming out: driving through the corridors like a bat out of Hades and desperately trying to avoid coming within ten feet of any other human being. It ain't easy.

I suppose there's sound medical reason for this foolishness, but I think they'd be as well off spraying me thoroughly with a can of Raid and letting me go. Works on television commercials.

Other than that, our first impressions of Scarbrae are entirely favourable. Nice building, lovely grounds and pleasant people. On top of that the meals are actually edible.

What more could a man ask?

28

I say I'm looking forward to beginning therapy at Scarbrae.

That's what I say. Truth is, I feel a little intimidated. Along with the glowing accounts of Marion's sister and others, their promotional literature paints a picture of an institution where patients are expected to conform to strict regimes of waking, eating, sleeping and therapies. I'm not good at following strict regimes. I wouldn't have lasted two weeks in the army. It's a wonder I've lasted this long in my marriage.

"No slackers allowed!" is what the literature in effect proclaims. People who don't measure up will be asked to depart the premises. While I'm no longer the semi-comatose figure I was for much of my time in the Hewitt, I'm not at all sure I can live up to such expectations, either by nature or design. Besides, the staff at the Hewitt was downright friendly and accommodating. The crowd up here sounds like what you imagine a woman to be when she's described as wearing sensible shoes: firm, no-nonsense types who'd as soon tell you to depart the premises as look at you.

Everyone must be up, have had breakfast and be ready for the day by nine. Meals are served strictly on time. Patients must be in the dining room unless ill unto death. The pitiful few hours during which the patient is allowed some flex time are clearly demarcated. Relaxing outside those hours is a capital offense. Patients must be in their rooms by a certain time and in their beds by another. The pool, of which they seem to be inordinately proud, is stated as being an important part of physiotherapy, and patients are expected to frolic in it on a regular basis. The word "frolic" is mine.

It all sounds a little summer campish to me. On the other hand, it might be more boot campish and they might be downright serious about this stuff. Perhaps that's the only way to get results from 'civilians. Perhaps that's why they have such a good name. And that's why I'm so apprehensive.

I guess they're taking it easy on me this first week of isolation. I'm still in the private room, they're bringing me breakfast in bed and I don't get up until nine-thirty or even later. This is the good life, brother, but I know it's not going to last. Shortly, some tough-looking nurse wearing sensible shoes is going to march in here and put a stop to all this foolishness.

"Okay, Smith. Depart the premises at once!"

The day begins with occupational therapy at eleven. I'm there a good forty minutes in advance, just in case Sensible Shoes is watching. The small rooms are crowded. If the therapists were anything other than nymphs in tight clothing they'd be forced to build an extension. But they find a place for me at a table on or near the appointed time and we begin.

Without going into the tedious details, occupational therapy basically attempts to maximize the movement in my arms and hands through range-of-motion exercises, various skill tasks and frequent massaging of the hands and fingers. Although I can't feel anything, I can imagine what it's like and so it's not at all unpleasant. Angela is an excellent conversationalist and there are enough interesting things happening around me to make the time pass quickly.

Angela herself is one of the bright lights in this institution. She's always smiling and enthusiastic and ready to try anything that might contribute to my rehabilitation. Marion mentions that a page-turner of some kind might be useful with my reading. Before long Angela comes up with a contraption that doesn't really work very well, but that's not her fault. She certainly put some effort into finding it.

Angela's efforts run the gamut from showing me how to butter bread for sandwiches, to twisting my arms and fingers in therapeutic massage, to accompanying me downtown to look for a CD player that I can operate. I've never heard her say no to any suggestion, no matter how far out. We'll try it until it's obvious that it just won't work. The world—at least my world—could use more Angelas.

We have physiotherapy in the gym after lunch. As usual, I'm there early. A dozen patients are having workouts of one kind or another on individual mats grouped together in the middle of the gym. But as I look around, I'm surprised to see how similar the exercises are to what Stella and the others are doing at the Hewitt. The place is bigger, there's lots more equipment and there are more patients and therapists, but apart from that the routines seem to be the same. I remember the doctor at the Hewitt, after returning from a fact-finding mission to Scarbrae and other hospitals in the Toronto area, telling me that the physiotherapy in both places is essentially the same. He's right. It is.

During one of my first sessions in the gym I'm intrigued by the lettering on one of the stools.

FOR THE RAPISTS ONLY.

For the rapists only? What in the world can that mean? Someone's idea of a sick joke? I don't think it's funny, and I say so rather strongly to Diane, the physiotherapist. She looks at me strangely.

"Whatever can you mean?"

"I think the lettering on your stool is in very bad taste."

She still looks confused.

"What lettering? I don't understand."

"Where it says 'For the rapists only.' Why would you leave that there?"

Diane looks as though she can't believe what she's hearing.

"Ohmigosh, Ed," she manages to say, "that's not what the lettering says. What it says is 'For therapists only.'"

I look more closely. There's a dent in the metal between the E and the R making "therapists" look like two separate words. Okay. What do I say now? Is there any way of communicating how stupid I feel, and do I want to? I decide to say nothing. Diane looks as though she's about to burst, although I can't tell if it's laughter or the desperate need to tell others about this. Should I remind her of therapist-client confidentiality? Probably not. I have a feeling it wouldn't be worth a tinker's cuss today.

I have to be back in my room by three so they can put me back to bed for a rest until supper, which up here they call dinner. Dinner they call lunch. I don't know what they call a mug-up. Perhaps they don't even have mug-ups. This is a backward province.

Lunch and dinner are served cafeteria-style in a spacious dining room. The food is excellent. Practically all patients take their meals in the dining room, so it's pretty full at meal time. It is at such a time with the dining room full that, with a little help from Marion, I make a complete fool of myself.

We're a little late getting to supper-dinner. We see a table with only one person at it, so I head for the vacant space while Marion gets our suppers. The tables are adjusted to different heights for different-sized chairs. This one isn't quite high enough for me to get the chair in under so I stop with the chair joystick next to the tabletop. The joystick controls the chair for both power and direction when it's pushed, but when it's released it drops back to a neutral position.

Marion arrives with the suppers and seeing that I'm not quite in under the table reaches out and pushes the joystick ahead to get me in closer. The joystick jams underneath the table with a predictable result. The table gives a mighty lurch and chair, table and I begin a merry ride around the dining room. The chap across the table from me finds strength in places he didn't know he had places and leaps backward in his chair with his supper on his lap. He is Scarbrae's first and only miracle cure.

I have no control whatever over the chair or the table or me. We all sweep grandly along with our direction in the hands of the gods. For once, the gods are on task and we don't strike another table or another patient or anything. Marion is running alongside crying, "Stop him! Stop him!"

I'm shouting, "Stop me! Stop me!"

Everyone in the dining room is watching with great interest. Those nearest the runaway table are making plans to evacuate should the need arise. We are headed straight for the full-length plate glass windows that front on to the lobby when a large and quick-thinking waitress runs over and lifts the table off the joystick in mid-flight. The joystick falls back into neutral and we stop a few feet from the windows.

The joyride is over, and everyone goes back to their suppers. But a general sense of merriment above the normal seems to pervade the whole dining room. While it does seem to be suppressed, short, sudden bursts of laughter do punctuate the air every few moments. And it is some time before I can wheel down the corridor without hearing, "Hi, Ed. Hijacked any tables lately?" with several variations on that theme. It took some time for me to emerge from the embarrassment and see the humorous side of it.

Marion catches a rather unfunny side effect to the incident. At the next meal she passes near Daniel's table and overhears him telling another patient the story which, if told well, would be quite funny. I have no problem with that, but then Marion hears Daniel use a term always offensive to us.

"Talk about your stupid Newf!"

Marion stops. By the uncomfortable silence they know she's heard. A response of some kind seems to be called for.

"Comments like that are never funny, Daniel," she says quietly and then moves on.

Later that evening, Daniel comes over to where we're sitting alone.

"I apologize for what I said earlier today," he says. "It was offensive and stupid and I don't know why I said it. Please forgive me."

We go on to become friends, and Daniel later becomes quite helpful to us with advice on our financial situation.

The evenings are free to do what we want as long as we're sitting in our rooms at nine, waiting to be put to bed.

That's another thing. The Scarbrae brochures say there's activity of some kind in the gym every night. There isn't, not by a long shot. And what there is is almost always only for community-based groups and not for patients.

The gym, weight rooms and exercise rooms are all closed at night and on Saturdays and Sundays, as they are at the Hewitt Centre. Back then, I looked forward to the break. Now I'm bothered by the lack of physical activity. Somewhere I read that missing one day's therapy sets one back two days. If that's true I'll be old and grey by the time I get out of here. Okay, so I'm old and grey now. You get my point.

29

No one on earth is more arrogant than a writer.

You have to assume first of all that what you're writing is worth reading. Second, you have to believe that one or two or three editors will want to pay you for that assumption. I've already made the first hurdle. I know lots of people who'll read my column: my mother and father, my sister and her husband—at least my sister—my older cousin in Kippens, and... there are probably several more.

Editors are a more tricky lot. A journalist friend assures me that they'll jump at the chance to hire me again. I'm not so sure. In fact, I'm so unsure that instead of telephoning the editors who published me in the Before Time, I send them a letter announcing my intention to begin writing "The View from Here" again. Then if they don't want me, they can write a nice little letter saying so. Words set down on the printed page don't seem to hurt nearly as much as when they're spoken in your ear.

To my great surprise, I get a most enthusiastic welcome from each one. The prodigal son didn't get a warmer reception. What do you know about that!

I intend to write every second week at first, because I don't know if I have the physical stamina or the creative juices to carry it off more often. And there's the little factor of not being able to type anymore. Marion reminds me of people who have written novels with a pencil strapped to their foreheads. My response to that is the same as when my mother used to try to get me to eat fish.

"Ed my dear, think of the starving little heathens in far-off lands."

My response?

"Name one."

It isn't as silly or shallow as it sounds. If I don't know any starving heathens, I reasoned, I can't think of them. Sounded good to me, but for some reason I always ended up eating the stupid fish.

Now that I'm an adult, I can state with virtual certainty that I will not begin writing a novel with a pencil strapped to my head. I'm not that dedicated, I'm not that disciplined and I'm not that sure I have anything to say worth saying.

As it happens, I don't have to pursue the pencil option because I have Arthur Fielding's voice-activated computer. It arrived while we were still at the Hewitt, but the time was so close to my leaving for Toronto that we didn't unpack it. We did tear off a corner of one of the boxes to see if it was real. The computer, not the box.

I still don't have a clue what I did for Arthur Fielding. One of his business associates came to see me shortly after we arrived at Scarbrae to talk about the computer.

"Do you know why our friend, Arthur, is being so very good to me?" I asked.

The other man thought for a moment.

"Not really," he replied. "I only know what he answered when I asked him the same question."

"Well?"

"He said you gave him back his dignity."

And that was it. It was an excellent thing to have given him to be sure, but for the life of me I can't think how I might have managed it. So here we are, ready to go with this marvellous system that will allow both Marion and me to write in comfort.

Marion laboriously wrote out in longhand the first few columns I did earlier in the fall, but by the time we had edited what was originally written the process for each column took several nights, several pencils, at least one eraser and most of Marion's patience. Fortunately, Arthur Fielding's people had transferred the training program from the St. John's company to a group in Toronto. After several weeks a young woman showed up one night and announced that she had been contracted to do the training.

For the first several years of her life, she must have been fed a regular diet of black coffee instead of mother's milk. She must still drink twenty or thirty cups a day and on top of that swallow a dozen uppers. I've met people who are hyperactive or wired before, but great heavenly day! Maureen takes the cake. Her voice is incredibly high-pitched and she speaks approximately three times as fast as your average Newfoundlander, and that's *fast*.

The first night of training she bursts into the room at highway speed (God knows what she does on the highway), cries "Hello," and by the time I get around to saying hello to her, she's halfway through the first lesson. After a while, Marion and I learn to take a couple of hours to prepare ourselves before she's due to arrive. This involves meditation, sedatives and prayer. By the time she leaves, we're exhausted and require several hours bedrest. But she's a sparkling and effervescent little person (why do all high-energy types seem to be so physically small?) and despite her Formula One metabolism shows lots of patience and is really very nice.

A young Mexican man named Julio is a real prize. He helps me understand the software of the NaturallySpeaking program, and puts together a gooseneck affair that will allow a microphone to be bent in almost any direction. That's really useful when I'm lying in bed. Julio and Jim, both employed by Scarbrae, are always available with help and are unfailingly pleasant.

After having a user-friendly Macintosh computer for many years, the directions for the IBM Dragon NaturallySpeaking program leave me hopelessly confused. Whatever, the lessons progress and gradually I get good enough to begin writing columns with the new program. I'm pleased. Marion is ecstatic. She has a public burning of her pencils out on the lawn. It's well attended by male patients who had heard it was a bra-burning ceremony.

I really don't know if I should continue writing the column or not. I don't know what the injury has done to my mind or my sense of humour. And most of all, I don't know if readers will still find my writing readable and entertaining. Marion says I'm as good or better than ever, but I'd expect her to say that, unless I were making a total fool of myself in which case she'd suggest I find another line of work. I hope from a therapy perspective that the column works out better than the singing lessons.

The staff psychologist who's assigned to me, John Williams, listens to my concerns gravely.

"What you need," he suggests, "is a psychological evaluation of your ability to recall, analyze and create."

"Can you measure what you find?"

"We can't tell you how you're doing relative to what you were," he replies, "but we can give you a good idea of the level at which you're operating now."

I'm not sure I want to know that, but I guess there's little choice. I'm handed over to Thea who specializes in testing and evaluation of cognitive and mental functions. For a full week I spend two hours a day in her office performing various tasks and answering various questions that will somehow magically decide whether or not I'm fit to run loose. At the end of it all I'm given a written summary of how I've done.

The results indicate that I should be able to function in polite society without undue embarrassment. That's comforting, but it still doesn't say whether or not I can write as I did before. Nothing to do but carry on and let the readers be the judges. Now there's a scary thought.

Readers have a habit of being right.

My first column covered the flight from hell.

There is no question but that Air Canada has to be investigated regarding both the cost of my ticket and my treatment aboard the aircraft. And the Toronto ambulance service has some explaining to do about the manner in which I was deplaned. This might be a busy fall.

Almost twelve thousand dollars is an obscene amount of money for a return ticket from St. John's to Toronto, even when six seats are required, and especially when seats aboard that same flight were going to "normal" passengers for three hundred sixty-four dollars return. Our position is that the seats should have been available to me at the seat sale price for a total cost of two thousand one hundred eight-four dollars return, approximately one-sixth of what Air Canada did charge. We've talked to literally dozens of people in a position to know something about this, within and without government, and we can find no one who supports Air Canada's policy. Yet it seems as though I have no choice but to pay the full amount. Something very wrong with this picture.

What's even more upsetting is that the seat sale price was not available to me because I'm quadriplegic. If a person without a disability were to purchase six seats, she'd pay only six times the seat sale price, rather than six times the full fare. In Air Canada's world having a disability can be rather expensive.

The fact that my stretcher was not screened off from the other passengers, as they promised it would be, was a nightmare for me. I was so high up on the seats that I was in full view of everyone, and couldn't even see out the window.

No one, least of all medical people, can believe that the ambulance personnel from Toronto whisked me off the plane slung in a sheet. The potential for damaging an already broken neck was high. And if the ambulance people from St. John's could get me on the plane with no problem at all, how come the Toronto personnel couldn't even get me off the seats, let alone out of the plane? I'm looking forward to the answer to that one.

So we go to work. What do we want? Apologies from all concerned and a rescinding of Air Canada's prejudicial and expensive policy towards persons with disabilities. That's a minimum. We may decide on more. In the meantime, my first column since the accident is largely about the flight from hell and the response to that is just incredible. The main sentiment expressed by readers is disbelief and indignation.

One woman is absolutely incensed, but expressing that to me is not enough for her. She wants action. She has a DJ friend in Toronto. Would I object to her calling him and getting some public reaction? She wants to write a letter to the CEO of Air Canada expressing her feelings.

I discourage her from going public at this point, given that we're currently in discussions with both Air Canada and the ambulance people. But I suggest in a telephone conversation that the letter would be timely. She agrees, and says that she'll send me a copy of her letter to Air Canada and also enclose a little something for me. I assure her that isn't necessary, but this is a lady who's obviously not easily swayed when her mind is set on something.

She declares she will never again fly Air Canada. Further, if anyone visiting her flies on that airline, she will not pick them up at the airport! I have absolutely no doubt but that she means it.

Jean, by the way, has recently moved to Newfoundland from her native Ontario. At an age when most people have retired and settled down to live their senior years in peace and comfort, she's uprooted everything, loaded up her car and driven to Newfoundland because that's where her heart is. She has no idea why. She only knows that's where she has to be. We Newfoundlanders have no trouble understanding that, of course.

A week later I get a letter from Jean. In it is a copy of her letter to the Air Canada brass. It is well-written, as I knew it would be, and gives them such a dressing-down that they shouldn't hold up their heads in public for a month. But there is something else.

Marion, who has been reading her letter to me, takes out a cheque, looks at it, and wordlessly puts it in front of me. The cheque is made out to me in the amount of six thousand dollars.

As soon as she finds her voice, Marion reads on. She's not wealthy by any means, Jean says, but the way Air Canada has treated me is so barbarous that she's not content with words. She has to do something tangible to help. What a force this woman would be in politics!

I call her that same night. After trying to find words to express my appreciation for such marvellous generosity, I tell her I cannot accept the money.

"For one thing, Jean, I won't have to pay the full amount of that fare. The Newfoundland Department of Health will pay some of it because we should have gone by air ambulance. We're hoping insurance will pay some as well. At any rate, we won't be out the full six thousand dollars."

There's not the slightest hesitation on the other end of the line.

"Makes no difference," she says. "I want you to have the money anyway. I really don't care how you spend it."

"Jean," I try again, "I can't accept such a large amount of money from you."

I sense a small trace of irritation in Jean's voice.

"Look, Ed, let me explain something to you. I can't begin to tell you how happy I am to be living in Newfoundland. It's crazy, I know, but I feel as if I'm home. I've been trying to find a way to say thank you to Newfoundland for this wonderful feeling and then I hear about you. Everyone knows you, it seems, and everyone's sharing in your pain. If I do something for you I feel it's the same as doing something for everyone in this wonderful place. Now, I'm giving you this money and you're going to take it. That's all there is to it."

I know when I'm licked. It remains for me to say thank you as graciously and sincerely as I can. Fact is, there's no end of things towards which we can put the money. Perhaps even more important, we know we have found a wonderful new friend. We can't wait to meet her in person.

We first contact Air Canada and the ambulance service by telephone. After some effort in each place, we find someone who seems to have some authority and who'll speak to us. After we explain the situation and our concerns, Air Canada asks us to put our complaint in writing, which is what one would expect. The ambulance service, on the other hand, expresses some concern over the incident, and says they will send their supervisor of operations to talk with us. An interview time is set up and the gentleman appears in my room.

We discuss what happened for more than an hour. The supervisor is polite and courteous and blames the whole thing on Air Canada. Air Canada did not tell them special equipment would be needed to get me off the plane. That equipment was easily available and would have solved the problem, he says. We point out, however, that it wasn't Air

Canada who decided to take me off the airplane in a sheet, and for that they are fully accountable. Our ambulance friend is slow to accept responsibility for that little error in judgment, and keeps insisting that Air Canada is primarily at fault. Perhaps, but we are in no hurry to let the ambulance service off the hook.

At the end of our discussion, he agrees the whole thing was most unfortunate and Air Canada should certainly be brought to task. In that we're in full agreement.

We draft a letter to the people at Air Canada, setting out in detail exactly what happened on that flight and demanding a change in policy toward both the cost and the manner of transporting people with disabilities. We also point out that the ambulance service concerned believes Air Canada is primarily at fault. We send a copy of the letter to Jean.

A couple of weeks later, we get another call from the ambulance people. The supervisor with whom we spoke before would like to talk with us again. We soon understand why. His attitude towards Air Canada's role in the whole fiasco has softened considerably. He even goes so far as to suggest that neither of them is responsible for the deplaning incident at the airport. We don't say so to him, but we suspect that the Air Canada people have been in touch with his organization and perhaps objected somewhat to being labelled the villains. We smell collusion.

Air Canada still hasn't responded to our letter. We know that the mills of the gods grind slowly, so we're prepared to wait a reasonable length of time. As of this date, however, it seems that Air Canada's definition of "reasonable" might be somewhat different from ours. We'll wait awhile longer.

30

Once having settled into Scarbrae, the temptation is to begin comparing it with the Hewitt Centre back in good old St. John's. That exercise is roughly the same as comparing apples and oranges, or grapes and kumquats or dogs and cats. Not much sense in it but having begun I might as well carry on.

Both places have comfortable beds as far as I know which isn't that far, given that I wouldn't feel the difference between a down mattress and a bed of rocks. The foregoing is an excellent example of a comparison that's neither significant nor interesting. I don't know why I'm including it.

The grounds at Scarbrae are beautiful. Huge trees hang over paved walkways and wheelways that lead around the building and down into the valley of one of the Don River tributaries. Wheelchairs don't compete with other vehicles. There's no motor traffic, just people walking their dogs or running, and almost everyone friendly enough to say hello or even stop for a chat. It's enough to make you want to select a nice green area, set up a tent, put in a fire and begin roasting wieners. That would obviously attract some like-minded people and soon you'd get out the guitars and have a great singsong: "In the Evening by the Moonlight" and all that.

The Hewitt doesn't have the luxury of the outside physical space that Scarbrae has, and it doesn't make safe or practical use of what it does have. Wheelchairs have to compete with cars, delivery vans and trucks for the same area. The bridge outside the main door is so small that only three or four chairs can use it at a time, and even then people have to move to let others in and out. I mention this because I don't think it has to be that way. Because it shouldn't be that way.

Scarbrae hospital serves food. No one has yet identified what it is the Hewitt Centre serves, but food can probably be ruled out. The meals at Scarbrae are excellent. The reason is that the food is prepared right here. Meals at the Hewitt are prepared somewhere in Outer Mongolia and reach the patients no less than a month later. I did hear of a man who once ate Hewitt food, but he died in the middle of the night in screaming agony. His death was put down to unnatural causes, which is as good a description of the food as any.

The most important and significant difference between the two Centres, however, has to do with people and personnel. The Hewitt Centre employs graduate nurses and licensed practical nurses (LPN), some of them cute, some of them not so cute. Most are friendly and caring, one or two of them not, same as in any profession.

Marion's sister, Jennette, was told when she visited Scarbrae before our arrival that they don't hire LPNs because they don't have the same level of training and knowledge as graduate nurses. They hire only graduate nurses so as to have the highest standard of care possible.

Interesting. By the time we arrive a few months later Scarbrae has nurses all right, but amazingly much of the basic care is being done by orderlies, practically all of them male. LPNs must complete a rigorous course of studies; orderlies must be able to exhale and inhale. It's disturbing to me that at Scarbrae orderlies without any training are permitted to carry out tasks and procedures that at the Hewitt only nurses may do. Before long, I feel, I'll be shouting, "Give me LPNs or give me death!"

I have nightmares about being in heart surgery and looking up to find an orderly standing over me with a scalpel.

Some orderlies have been here for years and know their routines well. Others were obviously hired yesterday and are not yet aware that they're here. One chap from Singapore stopped off in St. John's for three months on his way to Toronto and now considers himself an expert on

Newfoundland and a blood brother to all Newfoundlanders. He normally feeds me breakfast, which consists of toast, cereal and a running commentary on his adventures in Newfoundland. Periodically he laughs uproariously. I don't understand more than two words out of any sentence, although he seems to have no trouble understanding me. Why is that? Is he that much brighter than me, or does he have a particular facility with language generally? Anyway, I don't know if he considers himself a mainlander making fun of Newfoundland or a Newfoundlander making fun of everyone. Whatever, he's a royal pain in the ass even when the ass is totally paralyzed.

An orderly comes in to give the morning wash.

"You want soap on your face?" he asks.

I think of how soap gets into the eyes and nose when you're lying down and someone else is washing you.

"No, no soap."

A moment of silence.

"You want water?"

I reflect briefly on the effect of having my face washed without water and decide not to explore that option further.

"Yes, I'll have water."

Happily, the orderly has come prepared for that contingency.

Sometime in the wee small hours of the night watch, I ring the nursing station and ask for a drink. A few minutes later, an irate orderly comes in and begins berating me for ringing for water three times in ten minutes. If that's accurate, I don't blame him for being a little upset. But there's got to be a better way of making the point. I don't know I've rung that often. I only know I'm thirsty.

I don't take well to being berated by anyone, least of all this rude and ignorant man. I go back at him with as much energy as I can summon at that hour and with words appropriate to the situation. We do not part friends.

I lie awake for some time remembering the two nurses at the Hewitt Centre whom I summoned forty-five times in one night. If anyone had just reason to be angry with me, it was they. But when I apologized profusely in the morning, their smiling and good-natured comment was that at least it kept them awake.

The next night a similar thing happens and again we have words, not all of mine chosen from the Sunday school curriculum. When I tell the nurses about it next day they smile and say something about Emile having a short fuse and not to worry about it. I have no intention of worrying about Emile's fuse, long or short, but I do know that if it happens a third time I'll have an appropriate response.

The third time doesn't take long to come. A few nights later, His Royal Rudeness begins to chastise me again, this time about needing the CPAP mask adjusted in the late hours. I interrupt him.

"How do you spell your last name?"

He pauses, obviously a little perplexed.

"My name is pronounced..." He does this deliberately and slowly as one might speak to a child. His tone does nothing for our relationship.

"I don't care how you pronounce it. I just want to know how you spell it."

"Why do you wish to know how to spell my name?"

I, too, state my words slowly and deliberately.

"Because I wouldn't want to misspell your name in the book I'm writing about all this."

Emile doesn't reply. He finishes adjusting the mask in silence and walks out. But his attitude towards me from then on undergoes drastic change. He is smiling and pleasant and I reach the point where I can tolerate him for short periods of time. What he doesn't seem to know is that I would never use his proper name in my book. Emile has been properly had.

Most of the nurses at Scarbrae are pleasant and competent. Two or three are so outstanding that Marion and I talk about writing a letter of commendation to their supervisor. But they discourage us from doing that because they feel it might cause resentment among some of the staff.

The alpha male among the orderlies is a big fellow named Dick. He's arrogant and overbearing to both the patients and his peers, and I have the impression that many are afraid of him. He talks in strange, twisted sentences about Newfies and screech and fish. I think he means to be insulting, but I can never understand enough of what he's saying to get annoyed.

Dick's favourite word is "shit," and when he uses it in conversation, strangely enough, he becomes quite understandable. I don't normally mind the word that much. I've been known to use it myself when the occasion demands. What I do resent is when he says it in the context of a bowel treatment, and instead of being a mild expletive the word becomes personal and offensive.

"You got lots of shit in you today. We need to get all that shit out. You don't want your shit coming out in front of those pretty girls in the gym." And on it goes.

The closest I came to anything like that at the Hewitt Centre was with a male LPN who made a comment in the wee small hours that was meant to be funny. As the nurse drew back the sheets, he spoke from the other end of the bed.

"Well, look at old crinklebutt here."

I was so sensitive to anything concerning my physical condition at the time that I cringed under the other end of the sheet. When I told some people about it next day they felt he should be reported. But I didn't, not for one stupid remark.

I don't know why I don't report Dick's ongoing behaviour. Perhaps I feel that reporting him would only make matters worse for everyone, including me. Perhaps I see him as a pathetic human being trying to gain a measure of self-esteem by lording it over others. Perhaps that's it. I feel sorry for him. But I sure as hell don't like him.

There's just one more significant difference between Scarbrae and the Hewitt and that's how they treat skin breakdowns. Let me explain.

My parents and sister arrive today for a short visit. Although it's been less than two months since we left Newfoundland, it is so good to see them.

At the same time I'm really upset. I have on my lower back a "nish" area from a previous skin breakdown. At the Hewitt they use a dressing called Duoderm which protects the area from further damage while the patient goes on with the normal daily routine. Here in Scarbrae they don't use Duoderm, although we haven't yet been given a satisfactory reason for that. Instead they keep you in bed with your butt uncovered and open to the air until such time as the area looks to be improved. That can take a long time, and when you're in bed it can be a very long time. When your family is visiting for only a few days and you're in bed because this crowd hasn't yet caught up with modern dressing, it can be an extremely long time indeed.

We don't get to go sightseeing or shopping or any one of the thousand and one things there are to do in this city. They come in the morning, sit around my bed all day and go home at night. It's hardly an exciting time. But they maintain they came to see me and that's what they're doing so that's fine.

I admit there isn't much we can do about it, but that doesn't make me feel any better. I've already spent too long in bed when I'm convinced it isn't necessary and that's frustrating in the extreme. However, no one here is very likely to get excited about it on my account.

Some differences are important, some aren't. Some favour one institution, some the other. The jury is still out as to which one will ultimately come out on top. And perhaps that isn't very important, either.

31

We aren't long at Scarbrae before we discover the truth of something we've suspected all along. Newfoundlanders and mainlanders are different. We've totally different perspectives on things. Mainlanders, for example, are astonishingly lacking in a sense of humour. It may be that theirs is simply a different sense from ours. If so, it's so different that most of the time I'm unable to find it.

To be fair, we've met mainlanders who are so bright and intelligent that they're almost good enough to be Newfoundlanders. We've met others who, like me, seem to need help getting dressed.

Today, my physiotherapist came waltzing into the gym and asked if I would like to have my legs stretched. There isn't a red-blooded male in Newfoundland who wouldn't have something to say to that little offer. Last time I checked, and it wasn't that long ago, my blood was flaming red.

"Only if you would really *like* to stretch them," I say, forgetting for the moment where I am.

If I had said that to any physiotherapist in Newfoundland, I would have gotten a response something along the following lines.

"No, b'y, I'd rather be stretching Arnold Scwart... Swartetonz... Schawt... Big Arnie's legs."

Or... "You think I'm nuts? You think I'd be doing this if I weren't getting paid for it? Your legs aren't the greatest in the world, you know."

Or... "Naaah, forget it."

That would be in Newfoundland. But here in Toronto they're different. The physio's face looks puzzled for a moment, and then darkens.

"If I wasn't supposed to stretch your legs," she says tightly, "I would not have offered to do it."

You see? More humour in a barrel of sour apples.

The second night after we arrive, the man who collects rents for the small television sets over each bed comes by to activate the television and take the money in advance. It's eleven dollars. Feeling the need to connect in a meaningful way with the people I'll be living and dealing with over the next few months I jovially offer a light comment.

"Now don't you try to go south with all that money."

It's a line Newfoundlanders know well. It's old but will still draw a response of equal silliness. Not from this fellow, however. "Oh no, sir," he says, anxious to put this matter straight, "this is not my money. This belongs to the company. I get paid a salary."

I can only stare at him, at a total loss of how to respond.

"Do tell," is all I can muster.

This poor fellow is obviously overwhelmed by the seriousness of life. Perhaps they don't joke about money in Toronto. Perhaps people who are paralyzed in Toronto don't joke at all.

I've developed a bit of a different response to the everyday question, "How are you?" I know it's a greeting rather than a question, but the normal "Fine, thanks" is a kind of closure to any further discussion and leaves both of you staring off into space and at least one of you shuffling your feet for want of something better to do. So when people ask me how I am I often say, "Going downhill fast."

In Newfoundland, that draws all kinds of responses. "Me, too, b'y," is common. "Oh yes? I haven't even started up the hill yet," is another. "See you at the bottom!" has also been used a few times. Whatever, we usually get started on a conversation of some kind or other, however silly, which is better than leaving you both staring off into the distance and at least one of you shuffling your feet in the dirt.

It doesn't work at all in Toronto. Try that line on one of your run-of-the-mill Torontonians and you get everything from a blank stare to an immediate offer to call an ambulance.

"Oh my, are you feeling unwell? Should I call the doctor? When did this feeling start?"

Even when I answer, "When I was about twenty-two," most just don't get it.

The trouble, I think, is that Torontonians take themselves much too seriously. They actually believe that the rest of Canada depends on them for its continued existence. That's a heavy load to carry. To be fair, if we in Newfoundland felt that we were responsible for the continued existence of Saskatoon, for example, we'd be driven clean off our heads. You can imagine how being solely responsible for the heart and soul of this great country must affect your average Torontonian. They carry the weight of the nation on their stooped and narrow shoulders. Let's hope they never decide to shrug.

I present one of the workers in the gym with a little riddle, just for the hell of it.

"Antoinette, why can a man not marry his widow's sister?"

Antoinette looks at me blankly.

"Why do you want to know?"

"It's just a riddle, that's all. It's not a test or anything."

"Oh."

She furrows her brow and looks thoroughly perplexed.

"I have no idea," she says after a few moments. "Come on, tell me why he can't."

That's okay. A lot of people don't get it. So I wait a few moments and then decide not to tease her any longer.

"If a man's wife is a widow," I explain, "he must be dead and not in fit shape to marry anyone, including his sister-in-law."

Antoinette looks even more bewildered.

"I don't get it," she says, with a trace of irritation, "but I'm not thinking too well today. I'll think about it overnight and have the answer tomorrow."

"But Antoinette, I just gave you the answer."

"I'll figure it out," she says as she moves away. "I just need some time to do it."

"But I just told you..." I begin, and then realize how utterly futile the explanation is for her.

Marion has been listening to this little drama.

"That," she says, "is unreal."

Perhaps the differences between Torontonians and Newfoundlanders have more to do with our respective cultures. The dietitian has been laying down the law to me about the fat content in beef.

"No need to worry about that, my dear," I say. "When I get back to Newfoundland I'll be living off moose, anyway."

The dietitian is visibly perturbed.

"That stuff is full of calories. You shouldn't be touching it if you have a cholesterol problem."

For a dietitian, she has an abysmal ignorance of wild game.

"You should stop eating out of aluminum pots," I reply. "That's the stunnest thing I've ever heard. Moose is very low in calories and fats. The dietitian back in Newfoundland gave my wife a chart which shows moose to be one of the healthiest things you can eat."

"Really! I don't know what they do back in Newfoundland, but that stuff is chock full of things like milk and..."

"Milk?" I say unbelievingly. "Milk?! I've shot cow moose but I never saw any milk in them."

"... and chocolate," she goes on as though I hadn't said a word. "There's nothing that'll put the weight on you faster."

It is then that the light dawns. She's talking about dessert, and I'm talking about the main course. A better example of the difference in our respective cultures you'll never find.

Mainlanders like to make "stupid Newf" jokes. The trouble is that they've come to believe we're as stupid as these jokes suggest. Consequently, they really don't like it when they're outsmarted by one of their lowly cousins from the East. Which is strange, because it happens so often.

Marion and her sister were shopping in downtown TO earlier today. Sister had crammed twenty pounds of stuff into a bag designed to take five and the bag was naturally breaking open. They darted into a Sears store and asked one of the cashiers if she'd give them a larger bag. They felt quite comfortable doing that. Everyone knows Sears. Their catalogues are in every household, and most communities have at least a Sears outlet. Besides, when we renovated our house last year we bought all our major appliances from Sears. Marion buys so much from them that I figure everyone in the Sears accounting department knows her by credit card number. No problem her running into Sears and getting a large bag.

The cashier said an abrupt "No."

No? In Newfoundland they'd give you three or four large bags and ask if you needed any more. But this is Toronto. The cashier refused to give them a shopping bag because the goods in question hadn't been bought in that store.

This provoked a great deal of righteous indignation on the part of the sisters in question.

"Sputter, sputter," went the first sister.

"Sputter, sputter, sputter," added the second sister, but to no avail. The cashier was firm. You don't buy the goods, you don't get the bags. Any mainlander would understand this logic and quietly take their leave. But these girls were Newfoundlanders and that, as the poet said, made all the difference.

Marion swung into action. She grabbed a couple of little knick-knacks off a nearby shelf and brought them to the cashier. When she had paid for them the cashier put them into the appropriate small bag.

"Excuse me," said Marion sweetly, "but would you please put these things in a large bag?"

The cashier knew she'd been had and was furious. She had no choice but to place the two items in a large bag and pass them over. Without further comment Marion slipped around to the next cashier and said she wanted to return two items. The Sears crew had no choice but to comply. The sisters proceeded, in front of them all, to transfer the contents from the broken bag into the now empty large Sears bag. Then they went on their way rejoicing. Score: Newfoundlanders 2, Mainlanders 0.

Our friends Norm and Glenda are exceptions to the general rule concerning mainlanders. Glenda, who suffered similar injuries to mine in a car accident at almost the same time, loves a good joke. She couldn't wait to tell us this one.

"Wait 'til you hear what happened out in the gym today," she recounts gleefully. "I was telling this joke and the physiotherapist, Diane, looked at me for a moment and... Wait, let me tell you the joke first. A horse and a chicken live in the woods together. One day while they're out walking, the horse falls into some quicksand. The chicken runs back to their house, gets their Cadillac convertible and some rope and drives back to where the horse is sinking quickly. The chicken ties one end of the rope to the bumper and throws the other end to the horse. The chicken then hauls the horse out of the quicksand and onto dry land.

"The next day they're out walking again and the chicken falls into some quicksand. Quick as a wink, the horse straddles the quicksand and lowers his penis to where the chicken can grab it. The horse then hauls the chicken out of danger.

"The moral of the story is that you don't need a Cadillac convertible to pick up chicks if you're hung like a horse."

That's a pretty cute story, especially coming from a mainlander, and we all chuckle appropriately.

"Wait," Glenda laughs, waving us quiet, "that isn't the really funny part. Do you know what Diane said?"

Obviously, none of us do.

"She said, and I quote, 'I didn't know horses had penises.' Can you believe that? She didn't know horses had penises!"

That's more than astonishing, given the fact that Diane is twenty-five years old and engaged to be married. I don't know what she knows about husbands. She may be in for a big surprise.

I decide one day to try telling a few of the really silly jokes we used to tell each other in college. The sillier they were, the funnier we found them. As soon as I have an audience of three or four out in the gym during therapy, I go for it.

"Any of you know why elephants paint their toenails red?"

Dead silence. They look at each other, not certain how to respond to this. Finally Diane says, "That's stupid. Elephants don't paint their toenails red."

The others nod their heads acknowledging this bit of wisdom. In for a penny, in for a pound. I decide to carry on. They already think I'm nuts, anyway.

"So they can hide in cherry trees."

Now they're looking at me really strangely. One or two move back a step.

"That's even more stupid," says Mavis, a physio helper who has strange, strange thoughts. "Elephants do not climb trees."

The inherent humour in this bit of fluff is obviously lost on this lot. Since they now believe I'm in the wrong institution I may as well finish it off.

"Ever see an elephant in a cherry tree?"

They don't even bother to shake their heads.

"Works, doesn't it?"

And then I just wheel away leaving them staring at the retreating form of a person whom they believe strongly to be a few pages short of a full joke book.

Mavis is highly religious. I don't know what church she belongs to but it might be interesting to attend it sometime. One Monday morning she is so full of what happened at church the night before she can't wait to get it all out.

"The spirit was really moving among us last night," she declares, her eyes wide. "Miracles were happening all over the tabernacle."

I consider myself to be a religious man and I certainly have an abiding interest in miracles these days.

"What kind of miracles, Mavis?"

"I know this is hard to believe," she says in a low voice, looking around to see if anyone else is listening, "but God was actually melting down the gold fillings in people's teeth."

I look at her closely but see only wonder in her eyes. No question but that she believes what she's saying. I want to ask her if she saw anyone actually spitting out pieces of gold like drops of ginger ale, and if the pastor held a collection plate under their chins like the nurses do with those little kidney-shaped things when you're vomiting. But I realize that's like asking her if she knows why elephants paint their toenails red. Besides, I really don't want to put her down for her religious beliefs.

Perhaps that incident explains better than anything else why so many of these people seem to have no sense of humour. They take themselves so *seriously*. On the other hand, they aren't above making jokes at other people's expense.

I am sitting at a table with three women. One of them, Emily, leans toward me.

"You're from Newfoundland, aren't you?"

I admit to it.

"Well," she says, "have I got a great Newfie joke for you!"

When you're a long way from home I guess the immune system has difficulty tolerating anything offensive. Sometimes you let the offenses slide and sometimes you just can't.

"No, you haven't," I reply, trying to smile and staring her straight in the eye.

"Yes, I do. This Newfie was..."

"I don't do Newfie jokes, Emily," I say, smile gone but still trying hard to be polite.

"You don't? Why not?"

"Because they're reruns of old racist jokes told about polacks, wops, Swedes, Jews and a host of other nationalities, just to make them and us look stupid, and I find them offensive. Can you understand that?"

How can she understand that? She doesn't seem to be a member of any minority. How can she know what it means to be continually put down by the overwhelming majority?

Newfoundlanders tell Newfie jokes all the time, of course, but a joke told on oneself is the essence of the humour for us. The same story told by someone from outside our province becomes offensive. Mainlanders seem to have trouble understanding that one, too.

Emily hesitates for a moment, but only a moment.

"Okay, let's say this Swede was..."

Again, I interrupt her gently. I really don't want to upset her, but I've about had it with the "stupid Newfie" syndrome. Surrounded by mainlanders, it feels much more offensive than hearing it at home. And racism is racism, no matter who it's aimed at.

"I don't do racist jokes, Emily."

She looks around the table. The other two are studying their dinner plates, obviously embarrassed although I don't know if it's for Emily or me. Without another word she leaves the table and wheels away.

The first time I met Emily was at her first supper in Scarbrae. She came to our table and introduced herself. She was a large woman who had tumours on her spine that left her paralyzed. She was more than talkative, so when she said in the same conversational tone of voice with hardly a break in her words, "I'm going to be sick," I was the only one who heard it and was consequently ready, more or less, for what happened next.

The fish chowder she had been eating with great gusto left Emily's stomach with equal enthusiasm and spewed out over her front, her supper and much of the table. It was difficult to see how it could have missed any of our plates.

The other two gentlemen departed almost immediately without finishing their food, and I was left sitting alone with a much embarrassed Emily, and a floating stomach of my own which threatened to go airborne anytime. As one of the waitresses helped clean her up, I assured her that we were used to this sort of thing because it happened all the time. I can lie with the best of them when I have to. This, after all, wasn't Emily's fault.

Several days later we had the same fish chowder. I was sitting alone when she wheeled up to my table, dug into the meal with the same relish and remarked that she hoped what happened last time didn't happen again tonight. It was all I needed to explain that I wasn't really hungry and had an appointment, a really important appointment, for which I was already ten minutes late.

I guess God has decreed that Newfoundlanders and mainlanders will always have their differences, even if it's only so that he can tell us apart. Whatever, vive la difference!

I'm ready to begin travels within the Greater Toronto Metropolitan Area, wherever that is.

They have something in Toronto called a WheelTrans System which caters to people with mobility problems.

Being quadriplegic I think I qualify. No way will my chair and me fit into an ordinary taxi. It's the WheelTrans system or nothing.

We call the WheelTrans office. A pleasant voice tells us that before we can use their buses we have to apply for a WheelTrans pass. Okay, where do we get one of those? The voice gives us a street address downtown. So all we have to do is get an application, fill it out and mail it in, right?

Wrong. I have to present myself at this downtown office and fill in the application in the presence of a WheelTrans official. Okay, but given the circumstances my wife can come down and fill out the application herself in the presence of said WheelTrans official, right?

Wrong. No one else can do that for me.

"You won't accept a written statement from my doctor saying I can't walk?"

"No, you have to be here yourself."

"How about if we get a sworn statement from a judge of the Supreme Court stating that my legs don't work?"

That piece of levity goes over like a balloon full of truck batteries.

"You have to come to our office yourself, sir. That's the rule."

The voice has lost a significant degree of its pleasantness.

Wait just a small minute here. Let's review the situation.

I can't travel in Toronto without the WheelTrans system. Right. I can't use the WheelTrans system until I, as in I myself, go downtown and fill in an application. Right.

Does anyone see a problem with this picture? Like, how do I get downtown to get a pass if I can't use the system to get downtown in the first place?

"No problem," the voice on the phone says. "You simply apply for a temporary pass."

Okay. I know what comes next.

"I have to go downtown to your office and fill in the application myself for a temporary pass, right?"

"Wrong. We can mail that out to you."

The tone of voice says "Don't be stupid."

Okay, but how am I supposed to know when *they* stop being stupid and start being reasonable? I don't say this out loud. I do ask them to please mail us that temporary pass to get me downtown to apply for the permanent pass.

A few days later the temporary pass arrives and we book a WheelTrans bus for downtown.

We find the building and the office and announce ourselves.

"I am here to fill out an application for a permanent pass on the WheelTrans buses."

A young woman behind the desk looks me over carefully. She's probably trying to decide whether or not I can walk if I really try.

"Right. You're Mr. Smith? Good. Let's get started."

She picks up a thick sheaf of papers and turns to the first page.

The application form is thicker than a New York City telephone directory. I'm beginning to wonder if we've gotten into the immigration offices by mistake and they think I'm a Bosnian Serb trying to get into the country illegally.

"Now the first question." She says it clearly and enunciates each syllable as though to make sure I don't think it's the second question. "How *far* can you walk on your own?"

I glance at Marion who gives a small shrug. I mean, the woman did see me come in here in a wheelchair.

"I can't walk anywhere on my own," I reply patiently, being full of the milk of human kindness. "I'm quadriplegic."

She writes something on the application form.

"Okay, Mr. Smith. This is the second question."

I knew that.

"How many *steps* can you walk on your own?"

The milk of human kindness begins to curdle.

"I can't walk any steps on my own. *I am quadriplegic.*"

She writes something else on her papers.

"Right. Now, Mr. Smith, how many *steps* in a *staircase* can you walk on your own?"

The milk of human kindness goes sour. But still I try to give her the benefit of the doubt. Perhaps she can't spell "quadriplegic." Perhaps she doesn't even know what it means. Perhaps not knowing what it is and not being able to write it down, she forgets it from question to question.

"Look," I say, trying very hard to be patient, "the bottom line here is that I am quadriplegic. I'm paralyzed from the chest down, and not in real good shape from the chest up. I cannot walk. I cannot climb stairs or mountains. I cannot compete in the Boston Marathon. My legs are *dead*. Now, can we forget everything else in that stupid questionnaire and go directly to the last question, which I promise to attempt to answer?"

She looks at me for a moment and then reluctantly turns to the last page in the phone book.

"Okay! This is the last question. Mr. Smith, when do you expect to walk again?"

As Robert Service said in *The Cremation of Sam McGee*, "a promise made is a debt unpaid." I said I'd answer it and I will.

"Not for months," I say, "and months and months and months."

She doesn't even blink.

"Okay. Your application will be processed, Mr. Smith, and you'll be notified of our decision."

Oops. I thought this would be automatic, given the quadriplegia and all. Perhaps I could have handled the interview better.

"Don't forget to state," I say as Marion is getting up to leave and I'm turning the chair to go, "that I'm quadriplegic."

"Right," she says, not looking up, and writes something else on her papers.

No one is more surprised than I am when a few days later my permanent pass on Toronto's WheelTrans system arrives in the mail.

32

The number of ways one can break one's neck is enough to make your head spin. Most of the younger ones did it diving into shallow water.

"I don't understand it," one young fellow tells me. "I dove in that same spot at least a dozen times that day. My friends were diving in the same area. And then on the umpteenth dive, my head struck this sandbar just under the water and that was it. I felt absolutely nothing. I couldn't move my legs or arms. I was lying on the bottom totally paralyzed and I knew I couldn't hold my breath for much longer. I had taken in a couple of mouthfuls of water when someone noticed I wasn't moving. By the time they got me out I was half drowned and barely conscious."

He's twenty-six and quadriplegic for life.

Sam, a strikingly handsome young man in his early twenties, stops for a chat in the corridor. We all talk a lot to each other, especially when someone new comes in. It's to let them know they're not alone and that we're there for them.

Sam's paraplegic and can really make his chair fly. He loves to come straight at you at top speed, and just when you think a collision is inevitable, he grinds to a stop mere inches from your legs. I'm used to him by now and don't jump higher than a couple of feet when he does that to me.

It occurs to me that I've never asked Sam about his injury. "Hi Sam," I greet him, and then after a few comments about the weather, "you've never told me how you were injured."

No one here finds the question offensive because we're all intensely curious about each other's injuries or diseases.

"No, I haven't," replies Sam. "I got it jumping through a second-storey window and landing on my head."

"What in the world were you doing diving through a second-storey window? Not that smart, Sam." We kid each other a lot, too.

"No, I guess not," Sam said. "At the time I was trying to escape from the mental hospital."

Not much you can say to that. I change the subject in a hurry.

I meet a stockbroker named Stan. He broke his neck slipping on wet grass on the golf course. Stan is about my age and has similar injuries. Unfortunately, nothing in his insurance covers that kind of accident. As a highly successful broker, Stan was extremely well-to-do. He had a cottage, actually a luxurious summer home, up north that was full of guests and all-night partying every weekend, a city full of friends and a lovely home in Mississauga. Now he's in a pretty tight corner financially. He can't afford the expensive clothes anymore, he had to sell the summer home up north and now he's almost a pauper. Most of his friends have disappeared. I think of most of my friends and I'm grateful.

The strangest case we've heard of is about a young fellow who was holidaying in the Caribbean. They were in a boat miles offshore when everyone decided to take a break and go swimming. They were all having lots of fun when this fellow dived over the side of the boat and went headfirst onto the hard shell of a passing sea turtle. He ended up quadriplegic. It's enough to make you think somebody up there doesn't like you.

There's a fellow here thirty years old. He was playing in the backyard with his children when water splashed out of the little plastic pool. He slipped on the wet grass and fell over backwards. He's now completely and totally quadriplegic. His wife and three little children visit him every weekend.

We have our own Hells Angel. He's probably in his early thirties and has more tattoos on him than I have epidermal cells. Kyle doesn't talk a lot but his girlfriend does. She's a study in black leather. She wears calf-length black boots and skin-tight black leather pants. Her black leather jacket is lib-

erally studded with brass spikes. She looks more intimidating than Kyle and probably answers to the name Big
Momma. I saw her and Marion today on the bench outside
having an animated conversation. Sure would like to know
what they have in common.

Kyle was motoring along on his Harley minding his own
business, like you would, when a car knocked him thirty feet
from where it first hit him. Then the car sped away without
stopping. He, too, is paralyzed from the neck down. I ask
him if the driver was ever found.

"Not yet," he says, almost thoughtfully. "But it makes
no difference. My buddies will find him sooner or later.
Then he'll pay."

The way he says it sends a chill up my spine. So my
spine is paralyzed. I know the chill went up it just the same.

Today a new patient joins us in the dining room. Being
my friendly self I go over and sit at his table while Marion
gets our dinners from the cafeteria.

"Hello," I say. "My name is Ed. Been here long?"

"Today."

"Welcome to the hotel." The standard greeting to new
arrivals. "How'd you get your injury?"

"Shot."

"Oh?" I'm too stun to be daunted. "Accidentally, of course."

"No."

At this point, an effervescent Marion joins us with
the dinners.

"Hi," she says, "my name is Marion. What happened
to you?"

"Shot."

There's no way I can warn her against what I know
she's going to say next.

"Accidentally, I suppose." She says it confidently.

"No."

Marion looks at me, reads my face and lapses into
silence. We never see our new friend again. Must have been
a day patient.

He is the exception. Most patients are only too happy to
explain what happened to them and ask the same question
of you. We like to compare notes.

One would think that Scarbrae is a depressing place. The list of tragic accidents and spinal cord diseases is repeated over and over. Boys of fourteen, girls of eighteen, young women in the prime of life, men of seventy—all paralyzed for the rest of their lives unless science pulls off a miracle. But most aren't putting their lives on hold waiting for that big event. They have no time for that attitude.

"If the cure comes, it comes," they say, "but I'm not sitting around waiting for it."

Scarbrae is actually almost a joyful place. Patients inspire each other with their own little acts of daily courage. Relatives, too, talk with each other and share their frustrations and fears.

People in wheelchairs from outside Scarbrae sometimes play basketball and rugby in the gym at night. Most of us have seen wheelchair basketball either live or on TV. But I couldn't wait to see wheelchair rugby. I think Australian-rules rugby is rough until I see this. The boys line each other up from ten or fifteen feet away and go crashing into the chairs of the opposition. Occasionally a chair and its occupant get smashed to the floor, but the player hauls himself back in his chair and carries on.

It's fascinating, and I get so carried away by the action that I lose what little sense I have.

"How come you fellows don't wear shin pads?" I ask one of the players when the game is over. He looks at me for a long moment.

"Pain in the lower extremities is rare among us," he says with a grin. "I wouldn't be that brave if I could feel anything."

Way to go, Smith.

I admire most the sip-and-puffers. These are people so severely injured that they have no neck movement. They operate their wheelchairs by puffing and sipping into a small tube. Puff and the chair moves forward. Sip and the chair moves back. Puffing and sipping in different combinations makes the chair move left and right. Simply amazing.

This evening out of curiosity we are attending a seminar given by people who race sailboats. Until you see it you can't believe it. But there they are, sip-and-puffers sailing one-person sailboats competitively, and handling the sheets, the boom and the rudder by the same method they operate their chairs. The only concession made to their disability is that the keel is specially designed to keep the boat from over-turning.

We get to know a sip-and-puffer named Stockwell. He breezes into my room one evening and introduces himself. A blanket covers him from chin to toe against the cool autumn evening. On his lap is a briefcase. Stockwell explains that he's on his way to a job interview. He's already got a job, but it's become rather boring and he's looking for something new.

He likes to talk about his sexual experiences. We discover the following segment on one of the numerous self-help videotapes produced by Scarbrae and available to all the patients. This video features Stockwell:

"I wanted very much to try making love, but where could I find a woman with enough courage and pizzazz to go to bed with me? And then one day Jane appeared. She was pretty and young and we were obviously attracted to each other. When I finally got up the courage to ask her about sex, she readily agreed. In the bedroom, she helped me undress and get into bed. She took off her clothes and got into bed with me. Then I got so excited I shit myself. Both of us knew there was nothing I could do about that, but it kind of put a damper on the romantic mood."

Ken is paraplegic and very athletic. He loves wheel-chair basketball and rugby and plays both with great intensity. We've heard that he can change the wheels on his chair without getting out of it. I'm just a bit skeptical about that, but one night in my room Ken gives us a demonstration. Balancing himself on the one wheel, he takes off the other, waves it around for effect and then puts it back on. If we hadn't seen it we wouldn't have believed it. We're also told Ken can take his chair up esca-lators. After the wheel-balancing trick, we can believe anything.

Erika and a friend were riding in a horse-drawn buggy on her farm in northern Ontario. Suddenly something frightened the horse and it bolted. The two women were thrown out of the buggy and landed in ditches, one on either side of the road. The friend got to her feet and dusted herself off. Erika lay in the other ditch with a broken neck. Now she's paralyzed with only limited movement in her hands and arms, and at the moment can do little for herself.

Erika and Robert, a professional photographer, have been a couple for some years. He doesn't miss a weekend coming to see her and shortly after the accident he asks her to marry him.

"I've asked her a dozen times," he confides to Marion, "and she still hasn't said yes. But I'll be there for her, married or not, for as long as she'll have me."

I think of the woman whose husband left her and her two little girls shortly after the accident that left her quadriplegic, and I compare him to Robert. But there is no comparison.

It's Erika and I who begin the NGA thing. It grew out of some conversation abut what is hopefully our temporarily enforced celibacy. Anyway, we take to greeting each other in the corridors with "NGA."

Naturally other patients become curious and ask about it. So we explain it to them. Before long other people are using the same greeting.

"NGA, Bill."

Next thing we know, a small but enthusiastic club is forming and the greeting sometimes gets expanded.

"NGA, rah rah rah!"

I don't know if the movement continues after the two charter members depart the scene but it's fun while it lasts. NGA?

Not Getting Any

Unfortunately, quadriplegia claims its share of failures as well as triumphs. Not far from here is an overpass where, I'm told, more than one patient from Scarbrae has put a sudden end to their torment. Living in the city is a former world-class athlete who was struck down by a motor vehicle and became quadriplegic. People who know him say he's a bitter and broken man who has no joy in his life and no hope for his future.

Not everyone has the strength of will and the spirit to overcome the challenges of paralysis. And no one of us does it completely, or all the time.

Barbara Turnbull drops by this evening.

Eighteen-year-old Barbara was working in a convenience store when two men held it up late one night in September of 1983. As they entered the store, one of them in a senseless act of violence fired at the young woman behind the counter. She recalls lying on the floor in a pool of blood and wondering what had happened.

All of Canada watched and waited as Barbara fought for her life, and later learned to live with being paralyzed from the neck down. With the kind of courage and determination most of us can only marvel at, she earned a degree in journalism and was valedictorian of her graduating class at the Arizona State University. Today she's a reporter with the *Toronto Star* and devotes much of her time to supporting various charities and organizations involved in spinal cord research. Her book, *Looking in the Mirror*, which I read while still in the Hewitt Centre, is an account of her struggle to come to terms with the new realities in her life.

"I will never accept my quadriplegia," she tells us. "When I first came to Scarbrae they showed us a film in which we were advised to accept our injuries and try to make the best of our lives as they were. I was so upset! The day I accept being paralyzed is the day I stop fighting it. And I have to fight it every day to overcome it."

I am so encouraged by her grit and no-nonsense attitude, and more than a little impressed that she took time to come and visit me.

Jennifer arrived today on one of her many jaunts up from Boston. In the eleven months since the accident she hasn't missed any opportunity to come see us, even if it's only for the weekend. I tell her she's a glutton for punishment, but we're always delighted to see her. In fact we've come to depend a great deal on her visits for the morale boosting we often so desperately need.

Late in the afternoon she says she has to run downtown to get something for somebody, but she doesn't intend to be long.

"I'll be back right after supper." Who am I to protest? She might be getting something for me.

After the meal, Karen and Ivan drop by on one of their twice-weekly visits, and we decide to go out to the dining room for a coffee and a chat. Nearby, four older men are enjoying a game of cards. In another corner of the room a patient is having a visit from friends. We've just recently discovered that the dining room is as good a place as any to entertain friends and family. Empty tables and chairs are always available, and the coffee machine and soft drink dispensers are close by. For patients on the wards, the dining room is one of the few places they can have relative privacy, although it isn't quite up to scratch for conjugal visits.

As the evening wears on, we are keenly aware that Jennifer hasn't yet returned from downtown. But talking with Karen and Ivan is helping keep our minds occupied for the moment.

Suddenly, the lights go out. The room is left in semi-darkness with the only light coming from the lobby. There is muttering from the card game, but the players pick up their cards and wander out.

"Must be later than we thought," Ivan says, as he and Karen prepare to leave.

"Can't be that late," I reply. "Let me go check it out."

I wheel out to the reception desk.

"What happened to the lights?"

"Security just turned them off."

"Why in the world would they do that? There were several people in there."

"I know," the receptionist answers, "but they turn them off every night at nine. That's the policy."

They do? It is? At nine o'clock? I can't believe it!

No one came in to say, "Sorry, folks, but we have to turn the lights off now." Or, "Sorry, people, but you have only ten minutes before we have to turn out the lights." Nothing! Just sudden darkness.

I guess being in a private room has isolated me from the rules and regulations that govern everyone on the wards. The staff has allowed Marion and others to come and go in my room as they please, and since the coming and going is often after visiting hours, I've appreciated that consideration. But this is too much.

Marion takes advantage of a ride to her motel with Karen and Ivan in case Jennifer goes directly there. After saying good night, I wheel out the corridor towards my room and almost collide with the night supervisor. She's a large and pleasant-faced young woman named Tricia Seaboard with whom I've gotten along well. But now I'm just a little bit steamed. The fact that I'm worried sick about Jennifer doesn't help my attitude at all.

"Is this a home for wayward teenagers or what?" I demand of Tricia. I don't wait for an answer.

"The patients in this place are adult human beings who have no problem with their mental faculties and who do not deserve to be treated as children. In fact, most teenagers have a much later curfew than nine o'clock. I know this isn't your doing, but someone has to be told that this is ridiculous. Apart from that, the utter disdain shown for everyone concerned by the security people is beyond belief."

I don't know if I've caught her at a bad time or not, but her fair skin reddens in anger.

"When Christmastime comes, it'll get worse than this. We'll have fewer staff and all patients will be individually scheduled for being put to bed. That will be very early for some." Her look says I can look forward to being included among the "some."

"Actually," I reply, "I can understand that problem when you have only a few staff," and wheel on into my room.

Jennifer still hasn't arrived. Now I'm getting very worried and wondering what to do.

Shortly after the ten o'clock deadline for visitors, when I'm about to go look for her myself, I hear something rattle against the window. I peer out through and see Jennifer as close as she can get to the building trying to get my attention. When she sees me, she gives a thumbs-up and waves good night before heading over to the motel and her mother's room. I'm almost giddy with relief. I get almost giddy with anger when she phones a short time later and tells me what's happened.

The time passed downtown much more quickly than Jennifer was noticing, and this coupled with taking the wrong bus a couple of times made her later than she intended. She decided to stop off at Scarbrae to say good night and, knowing my tendency to worry, let me know she was okay. A few minutes after ten she approached the security person in the lobby, told her who she was, explained the problem and asked if she could run into my room for just a moment.

The security woman said that since it was just past visiting hours, she'd have to check with the night supervisor for my floor. Fair enough, and the pleasant way she said it suggested there would be no problem. But when she made the call to the supervisor, or whoever, Jennifer heard a very loud "No, no, no, no!" And then, "Under no circumstances is she to be allowed in here!"

Jennifer appealed briefly and then went out and found my window.

Next night, Marion seeks out Tricia and has a talk with her about the incident. Tricia is all sweetness and light and denies the whole thing. But there is no denying what Jennifer heard over the phone, and no denying she wasn't allowed in on someone's authority, with that authority being very upset at the time. In our minds, there is some suspicion that Tricia was still angry with me and treated my daughter accordingly. There is no doubt in my mind, either, that this would never have happened at the Hewitt.

Behaviour of this sort is inexcusable, whether it's from the security people, the supervisors or anyone else. It shows a callous disregard for the welfare of both the patients and their families. Granted there have to be rules, but blind obedience to rules is as bad or worse than having no rules at all. And when emotion overrides professionalism, the results can be nasty indeed.

Marion spoke with Tricia. I plan to protest to a higher authority.

33

In Ontario, or at least this part of it, they tend to refer to the noon meal as lunch and the supper meal as dinner. I have some problem adapting to this terminology. Marion absolutely insists on the noon meal being dinner and the later meal supper, just as it is back home. Probably one of her means of clinging, however precariously, to The Rock. Part of my own confusion, therefore, arises from having to continually cope with two different sets of meal vocabulary. Part may be due to innate stupidity.

Whatever they're called, the two meals in question are the gastronomic and social highlights of the day. Everyone crowds into the cafeteria and you find yourself with different dining companions almost every meal. This is sometimes nice and sometimes not so nice.

An interesting dynamic is that there are some people who are never to be found sitting with certain other people. I don't know why. Perhaps because they have nothing in common and they're uncomfortable in each other's presence. Our Hells Angel friend is almost always alone, except for his studded-leather girlfriend. If you're inclined to think this is an unfriendly, unchristian and ungodly attitude from the rest of us, perhaps you should try sharing a cafeteria table with a Hells Angel sometime. Those boys are downright scary, even when they're totally paralyzed. It is interesting, though, that none of his biker buddies ever come to visit. I say that in the spirit of humble gratitude, and I know I speak for everyone else here, too.

Most of the rest of us intermingle and get to know each other fairly well. That way we learn whom to avoid in the future: the messy eaters, the garrulous, the unfriendly.

Some patients can feed themselves. Many others, like me at the beginning, cannot and have to be fed. Happily for me, Marion is there at almost every meal and sees that I get sustenance. She also helps other diners by bringing their meals from the servery (yet another unfamiliar meal term) and helping them eat—after I get mine.

The staff depends on volunteers to help with those who can't help themselves. Almost every meal there are two or three such helpers, and some are regulars who keep coming back. Volunteers don't have to pay for their meals, which seems fair enough. Sometimes we see a volunteer only once, and never again. Obviously something scares them off. Might be our Hells Angel. Pretty he is not. Might be me. I'm not that pretty, either.

There are two or three waitresses who get meals from the servery and help people get fed. And there are two or three working inside whom we rarely see.

At first, Marion used to buy her meals from the cafeteria but the staff told her she shouldn't be paying because she takes care of me and helps with other patients as well. If you weren't doing it, they tell her, one of us would have to. No argument on that one from us.

Today, Marion gets me seated at a table and goes to get our dinners from the inside servery. She has selected our food and is almost ready to leave when one of the servery women, a long, skinny supervisor named Hilda, calls loudly from the other end of the line.

"You can have that meal today, but from now on you have to pay for your food like everyone else."

Marion's immediate reaction is one of acute embarrassment and humiliation. Everyone else is silent. Why the change of heart from the staff?

"I don't mind paying for my food," she manages to say, "but it was your staff who told me not to."

She comes back to the table mortified.

Shortly after, a notice appears on the cafeteria doors. In essence it says that only patients are permitted to eat lunch in the cafeteria. Visitors and family must go downstairs to the staff dining room.

My problem, or rather Marion's problem, is that occupational therapy ends at noon at which time the staff dining room opens. Physiotherapy begins at one when the staff dining room closes. If she is to take care of me, therefore, not being allowed to eat in the cafeteria means Marion has to miss lunch.

Certainly none of the cafeteria supervisors lose much sleep over that, but one of the waitresses, a lovely woman named Felicia, sees what's happening. Almost every lunch period after that she comes to my table and places food in front of Marion.

"Now," she says, like a mother telling her reluctant child to eat his dinner, "you eat that and I don't want to hear anything else about it."

One Felicia can make up for a great many Hildas.

Then Marion remembers a discussion she had with one of my nurses a few days before that. Somehow in the conversation Marion mentioned that she was getting her meals free of cost. Gloria reacted strongly.

"Why should you be getting free meals?"

"I guess because I take care of Ed and help with other patients."

"You're not a volunteer," Gloria says flatly. "You're a wife and there's no reason you should be getting anything free."

Marion had nothing to say to that, and the incident went out of her mind. There's no proof that Gloria had anything to do with this, but the coincidence is remarkable.

One Felicia can make up for many nasty nurses, too.

Marion

It was just as well Ed didn't know how I got home every night.

I told him all I had to do was walk across the Scarbrae parking lot, go through a fence, cross another small parking lot and I'm there. That was true as far as it went, but the whole truth went a great deal further.

Ed always insisted I leave his room before dark or get a taxi. As soon as the light began to fade he'd be on my case.

"It's time to leave if you're not getting a taxi. It's getting dark outside."

"It only looks dark because the lights are on in here."

"It *is* getting dark," he'd insist, until finally I'd throw in the towel and agree to get underway. Sometimes I'd wait too long and Ed would demand I call a taxi.

"This is one of the largest cities in North America," he'd say time after time. "No one should be walking the streets alone after dark."

Like I didn't know. I wasn't exactly happy walking the streets anytime after the sun went down.

Home for me for eight months was a room in a tiny motel perched like an afterthought in one corner of a large parking lot. The room had two single beds, two or three pieces of basic furniture and a print of birch trees in autumn dress. It wasn't five-star but it became a home to me for I had no other. If it wasn't my strength, it was certainly my refuge.

I was sound asleep in my bed one night when suddenly I came wide awake. Perhaps another smaller sound had already partially awakened me because I knew immediately what was happening. The door was being opened and had brought up on the privacy chain. Someone was trying to get into the room.

For a few moments I was absolutely paralyzed. I noticed the time on the clock-radio—4:00 A.M. I realized with a chill that went right through me that if someone really wanted to get in that little chain wouldn't be much of an impediment. Then, unbelievably, the door began to inch shut until I heard the latch click and knew that it was really closed. Somehow I managed to call security and tell them what had happened. Not to worry, they said, that was probably the night watchman making his rounds. Okay, I felt a lot better, but then I got to wondering why the watchman would be opening my door when he knew that I was in there every night. It never happened again, but it was a long time before I could once more easily go to sleep in that little motel.

Our greatest support all through the months we were at Scarbrae was the number of people who took time out to visit us. Many were relatives, some were expatriate

Newfoundlanders whom we hadn't seen in a long time, and others were friends of friends or had just heard that Ed had been transferred to Toronto and came to visit. Three men from Springdale came in one night with a great platter of Newfoundland seafood. Ed couldn't get over it. If friends were visiting Toronto from Newfoundland they usually made sure we were on their list of places to go.

The people who had a special place in our hearts were those who came frequently and regularly, including some retired clergymen who were originally from Newfoundland. One Sunday afternoon, Ed's room seemed a little more crowded than usual and I looked around to see who was there. I couldn't believe it when I counted no fewer than five retired United Church clergymen, including Ed's father. In addition to his mother, three of the others had their wives with them.

Ed later said that he probably should have chosen that time to drop dead because if five clergymen couldn't propel you into heaven, even if they were retired, nothing could. He thought that was funny, but I wasn't amused. Anyway, added to the clergy were the Gills, Ed's sister, Pat, and another friend. There was also an older man nobody seemed to know, but that was all right. In fact, it happened more than once that people appeared and disappeared without ever telling us who they were.

We got to be good friends with the Freedmans. Glenda's car had also gone off the road because of black ice within a couple of weeks of our accident, and she had suffered similar injuries to Ed's. She had a dazzling smile and both she and Norm were great personalities.

Meeting Glenda and Norm led to one of the great coincidences of my life.

Two of our closest friends at University in the early '60s had been Vi and Al MacGregor. After college we sort of drifted apart as people tend to do. For some reason, they decided to send us a Christmas card this year, and Kathy, who was looking after our mail at home, recognized the name and gave them a call. Vi immediately called Scarbrae and Ed answered the phone.

"What in the world are you doing there?" she cried.

Ed rarely gives a straight answer where a twisted one will do.

"Oh," he said blandly, "I'm doing some research on the health care system in Ontario from an inside perspective."

I don't remember what she said in response to that, but little did I know she took Ed quite seriously. I thought Kathy would have told her what had happened. Anyway, in just a few hours Vi and Al were in our room and got the fright of their lives when they discovered the real reason we were there. When we all settled down, it was as though the intervening thirty-one years had melted away. We talked and talked as we did when we were two young couples just married and without a care in the world.

Sometime in that conversation, we mentioned our new friends, Norm and Glenda Freedman, and got an immediate reaction.

"Norm is my dentist!" Al exclaimed.

"And," added Vi, "he was mine until I went to work with another dentist."

In a city as large as Toronto that was something of a coincidence and we marvelled at it as people do with such things.

Two days later my brother, Fred, and I were shopping in a downtown mall when Fred stopped dead in his tracks.

"My God, Marion, look who's coming there!"

I recognized him immediately. Ray Homer had been in my brother's class since kindergarten and I had known him almost as long. He had been a student at Mount Allison when we were there, but we hadn't seen him since. The coincidence of meeting the MacGregors and Ray after thirty-one years within three days of each other in a city of four million people was almost too much to be believed, but there it was.

We chatted for a few minutes and Ray mentioned that he lived in a certain area of the city. A large bell started clanging in the back of my head although the odds against what I was thinking were too great to even contemplate.

"You don't by any chance know a Doctor Freedman?"

Even as I asked, I was remembering the fellow at Scarbrae who, on learning Ed was from Newfoundland, had a similar question.

"You're from Down East, eh? You don't happen to know Peter Leblanc in Moncton, do you?"

My question to Ray was about as stupid, but he answered without the slightest hesitation.

"Lord, yes, he's my dentist."

I don't know what the odds are of meeting three people within three days in a very large city whom we knew in university a lifetime ago, and all of whom had the same dentist who just happened to be a new friend of ours. Ed said it was the same as being hit on the head in Toronto by an apple thrown by your brother-in-law in the Annapolis Valley who was aiming for Manitoba.

The Gills, Ivan and Karen, who had visited us at the Hewitt Centre last summer, were in a category all by themselves. Ivan, too, had struck black ice five years before on his way to work in Oshawa and like Ed was quadriplegic.

Their devotion to us knew no bounds.

They visited us at least once a week, usually twice a week and if we were really lucky they turned up three times a week. Karen almost always brought delicious food that would tickle the palate of any Newfoundlander. Often it was fish, fat and teddies, as Ivan called it, one of Ed's favourite dishes. On Ed's birthday they arrived with a large barbecued salmon which we ate out in the cafeteria to the obvious envy of everyone else. The smell of freshly cooked salmon must have driven them crazy.

We spent many pleasant hours together talking about our respective situations and how we were coping. Having walked some distance down the road we were just beginning to travel, their experience and advice was invaluable. Apart from that, whenever we needed something or had to go somewhere, they were there. Nothing seemed too much trouble. In so many ways, they were an absolute godsend to us and our debt to them is enormous.

Karen is nothing short of amazing. Her dedication to Ivan is complete and unending. She looks after him herself twenty-four hours a day and often has a crowd at her house to feed besides. Many of the more than twenty siblings which she and Ivan share between them live in the same area and are frequent visitors. She never seems to get tired or let anything get her down, although I know she must feel both tired and down at times. But as a human dynamo, very few are her equal.

We were able to hold onto our sanity in no small part because of friends old and new, and also because we knew that sometime we'd be heading home to Newfoundland, or at least I thought we would. Ed's doctors were already making noises to the effect that we should move to a larger centre when he's discharged where his unique health problems might be better understood. I could see the sense in that, although I wanted to go home to Springdale, too. But he was having none of it.

"There's such a thing as length of life," he said to me one day when I ventured to bring up the topic, "but much more important than that is quality of life. I want to go home where our family and friends are."

And he never once swerved from that determination.

———————

Marion has been suggesting for some time that I come over to the motel and see where she spends her nights. Today I decide to go.

The afternoon is warm and sunny so I wheel over. Later tonight when it gets colder I'll get a WheelTrans bus back. In the meantime, the trip to the motel is a most enlightening experience. I ask Marion to show me the route she takes when she walks.

The first stage is across Scarbrae parking lot. That's not so bad because it's well lit and there are always lots of people around. That parking lot is separated from the Heart Rehabilitation lot by a fence which runs perpendicular into the backyard fences of the people on the next street. Between the two fences there's a small gap which Marion found she could squeeze through and thus not have to take the long way around via the street.

For some reason someone is trying to keep her from using that little opening between the two parking lots. Sometimes a tree branch or something is placed across it which Marion promptly removes. One night while her brother, Fred, was visiting in my room, she casually mentioned that her passageway had been wired shut. Fred said, as she knew he would, that he happened to have wirecutters in his car.

"I would never ask you to do anything you shouldn't," Marion said innocently, knowing full well that she didn't have to. But the next time she took her normal route the wires were all neatly cut and she could pass through without difficulty. At that point, whoever was trying to close the opening gave up.

From the Heart Rehab lot, which is very much like the Scarbrae parking lot, she takes a sidewalk up to the street where the motel is situated. The first thing I notice is that the sidewalk is fringed with thick, high hedges, the perfect hiding place for someone with evil intent toward a woman walking alone in the dusk. Marion seems unperturbed.

From there, she has to cross an almost deserted street to get to the parking lot of the Children's Rehabilitation Centre and the motel. This parking lot is almost totally empty by the time Marion gets there at night. The small, one-storey motel is at the far corner of that lot with nothing else near it. That doesn't bother me too much until I discover that vehicles can't get into that parking lot after business hours and many who take Marion home, friend or taxi, have to let her out on the sidewalk. Then she has to cross that great empty space to get to the motel. Behind the far end of the building is a wooded ravine which is totally unlit. The ravine runs behind the parking lots and the buildings and eventually is intersected by one of the Scarbrae walking paths.

Lovely. So far I've counted several hundred places where a woman alone should not be walking when it's almost dark, including the motel. Marion admits that getting across the parking lot and to her room on the far end of the motel is the scariest part.

But then she admits something even scarier. She's discovered that there's a lovely little path through the woods which skirts the edge of the ravine and takes her right to Scarbrae. Some mornings, she tells me, she takes that path because it's shorter and such a nice walk.

Nice walk! The whole population of Kingston Penitentiary could hide in that ravine and kidnap half of Toronto without ever being seen. I can't believe she's actually taken that route, but she's not doing it anymore, she says, because it's occurred to her as well that walking that path alone might not be totally safe, even in daylight.

On a five-star rating basis, the motel itself might merit a half star. One woman who was offered a room there refused because she said there were ants in the rooms. Marion says that this was true, but her response was to buy a can of Raid and declare war. The room is a little sparse but Marion says she doesn't mind that at all. After a few months it's become her home because that's the only place she has for herself.

I understand what she means, but I also understand that being in the middle of one of the largest cities in North America, she puts herself at risk every time she walks to that motel, especially when it's late in the day. Marion minimizes the danger when we talk about it, but I'm sure she knows as well as I that the danger is there. I know, too, that she does it because she feels she has no choice.

Neither one of us has any choice.

34

I promised myself when rehabilitation began last February that I'd be home for Christmas. You'd think I could keep a promise to myself if no one else, but finally I know that's not going to happen. This road I travel has already been much longer than I ever thought, and seems to stretch on beyond where I can see its ending.

I have as much chance of being home for Christmas this year as I have of being salesman of the year for Adidas running shoes.

Toronto is lit up for the holidays like a giant Christmas tree. We've been downtown a couple of times and the difference between it and downtown Springdale is quite noticeable. More businesses, for example, taller buildings and probably more traffic. The whole area seems more crowded, perhaps because although Springdale is large enough to have a Santa Claus parade, it isn't large enough to have a traffic light.

The residential areas are strangely inconsistent. On some streets, almost every house has a Santa Claus on the lawn or a Christmas tree on the porch. On others, hardly a house seems to have been touched by the Christmas spirit. Still other streets have a mixture of houses with nothing and others with everything. The same is true for downtown. Some stores are lit up like Roman candles and others are as plain as they are in June.

A friend explains it to us by suggesting that Hindus and Muslims and Jews, among others, don't seem to have the same interest as Christians in dressing their places up for Christmas. Possibly, but you don't have to be Christian to believe in Santa Claus and eight tiny reindeer. In fact, when you get right down to it, Santa and all his retinue have about as much to do with the birth of Christ as they do with the birth of Mohammed or Moses. I suppose that in the popular culture of the day, Christ and Santa Claus are seen as two brothers in the same family.

In October, we saw everyone—Christian, Muslim, Hindu and Jew—coming together in the decorating bit. Every culture, every faith and every persuasion believes in the Great Pumpkin. Households are festooned with ghoulish depictions of executions and gory murders. Bloody skulls have hatchets buried deep between staring eyes. Gaunt bodies with protruding eyeballs and lolling tongues hang by the neck from skeletal tree branches. Witchcraft as the dominant religion is practiced universally. Perhaps the lesson here is that while few of us can agree on the ultimate nature of God, everyone sees the devil from the same perspective. Whatever, it's good, clean fun for the children, eh?

The multicultural and multi-religious groups that make up the Greater Toronto Area seem to have found a way to live together in peace. More power to them. I'm all for peace. Like all peace, this one seems to have come at a price, that price being that all faiths and cultures are in danger of being reduced to the lowest common denominator.

I give you a case in point from a Christian perspective. Scarbrae, which is a cultural microcosm of the GMTA macrocosm, has a lovely Nativity scene in the lobby. Christians here are probably outnumbered three to one, but nevertheless, there it sits with the standard complement of shepherds, angels and wise men proclaiming peace on earth, goodwill toward men. For some time that display bothered us, but we just couldn't figure out what was wrong. We looked at it and talked about it, but something was missing. And then one day Marion sees it: the manger is empty. There is no baby Jesus.

When we ask about it, we are told that the Centre doesn't want to offend other patients who are non-Christian. That's fine as far as it goes. But it's no small irony that in order to achieve peace on earth and goodwill in Toronto, the Prince of Peace has to be taken out of the picture.

Marion decides that our room (she spends almost as much time here as I) must be decorated for Christmas. She doesn't let a little thing like not being in our own home slow her down much. Christmas cards are stuck to the cement block walls as they come in, and they are really coming in. Before long, one twenty-foot section is completely covered. Special decorations in the form of a paper chain made for us by our two granddaughters, Samantha and Robyn, are strung from the four corners of the ceiling to meet in the middle.

Finding a tree is a bit of a challenge for Marion, especially since the powers that be have decreed that no trees of any kind will be allowed in the rooms. These include artificial trees of all types and sizes, even those made from fire-retardant materials. This sort of negates the fire hazard concern, but the powers that be, like powers that be everywhere, see no reason to bow under the weight of common sense and are adamant. No trees of any kind will be allowed in patients' rooms or on the wards.

Marion isn't prepared to take this sitting down or lying down or in any other body posture that might indicate retreat. We've always had a Christmas tree, she says, and by damn we'll have a Christmas tree this year, too.

The creative Marion goes into action. Downtown she finds some beautiful green Christmas garland which, she is assured, is made from fire-retardant materials. She brings back a pile of it and seeks out one of the powers that be.

The nursing supervisor tells her that while Christmas trees are not allowed, Christmas garland, especially the fire-retardant kind, is perfectly okay. It's all Marion needs to go to work.

In the corner opposite my bed, a magical Christmas tree begins to grow before my very eyes. Using green Christmas "rope" and working from the top down, she tapes first short and then progressively longer lengths of rope across the corner until the longest piece on the bottom forms the base of the tree. Since Christmas lights are also prohibited (and this does make sense because of overloaded circuits), one of the more empathetic staff, who shall remain nameless for his own protection, presents us with several strings of battery-operated lights. Now, not only does Marion have a Christmas tree, she has a Christmas tree sparkling with beautiful Christmas tree lights.

Everyone—staff, patients, visitors and stray dogs—is invited into our room to see the Newfoundland Christmas tree, as it gets to be known. When people ask Marion why she put so much effort into making the tree, her reply is immediate and honest.

"It's a matter of culture," she says, with a fine sense of irony. "Surely Torontonians can understand that."

One of the women working in the administration office is so delighted that she wants a share in the ownership of the project.

"You're from Newfoundland and I'm originally from Newfoundland," she tells Marion, "and as far as I'm concerned that makes us family."

That's a sentiment perhaps only a Cape Bretoner would understand.

Today, a large, thin, cardboard package arrives. It's obviously from Springdale and we open it eagerly. Inside is one of the most wonderful Christmas cards we will ever receive. Two pieces of cardboard, about twenty inches by fourteen, are taped together to open like an ordinary card. The outside cover has a watercolour painting of the scene one sees through our dining room window. Painted by local artist, Doug Downey, it's bright and cheery and makes us homesick. But there's another surprise inside. Almost everyone in our church, Grace United, has signed their names to a Christmas card from the congregation. It's impossible to say how much that card means to us. It lets us know again, as if we could ever forget, that our friends and our church family still remember us and are wishing us home.

Tonight, a truly wonderful surprise. We hear footsteps in the corridor outside and look up to see Arthur Fielding and a tall, dark-haired woman entering the room. It's the first time we've seen Arthur since his memorable visit last summer at the Hewitt, and we're more than pleased to see him. He introduces the woman as Val and as the evening progresses it becomes obvious that they are very much a couple.

Arthur is such a mysterious person that we try hard to find out more about him.

"Where do you live?"

He names some island just off Vancouver Island and says that's where he and Val spend most of their time, except when they have to fly to Montreal or Toronto on business.

"What is it you do, Arthur?"

"As little as possible."

"But what do you do for a living?"

"A little of this, a little of that."

Try as we might Arthur will say nothing else. He doesn't seem irritated by the questioning, but he does seem determined not to tell us any more.

"I've got something for you," Arthur says to Marion. I've been looking at the cardboard carton he brought into the room with him, but Val produces a different kind of package and gives it to Marion. It turns out to be a beautiful miniature Santa Claus about two feet high. Marion is delighted.

"And I have something for you," Arthur says to me. He goes on to explain that he's become quite interested in a book entitled *Conversations with God.*

"It's a whole new approach to our relationship with God," he says, "and it's changed my life. I'd like you to read it. In fact," he goes on with some enthusiasm, "I brought along the cassette tapes that go with the book."

"I'll look forward to reading and listening," I say.

"And," his face is lit up like a boy's, "I've also brought along a videotape of some of this man's lectures. I think you'll find them fascinating."

"I'm sure I will. Thanks for bringing all this. I'll get a VCR and monitor from the library tomorrow and watch it."

"No need," he grins, "I brought both with me."

So that's what's in the cardboard box. I watch as Arthur opens the carton and hauls out a combination 13-inch television and VCR. He plugs it in and inserts the videotape.

It is interesting, and I do resolve to read the books and listen to the tapes.

After the videotape is finished and we've discussed at some length the author's viewpoints on God and humankind's relationship with the Creator, Arthur and Val prepare to leave.

"What do you want me to do with the television-VCR when I'm finished with it?" I ask.

"Do what you want with them," he smiles. "They're yours."

And then they are gone.

Tonight there's a carol-sing in the gymnasium. We're really looking forward to it because that's the only activity Scarbrae has planned for Christmas. A girl's choir from one of the local high schools will be performing and leading the singing.

Strange the things that bond people to each other. Tonight it's the music and the singing. We see each other as having common interests and traditions that we can share, and people who were just acquaintances suddenly become friends.

About halfway through, a new patient is wheeled in on her bed. After a few minutes, I go over to say hello and welcome her. Erika has a high cervical break and arm and hand movements are minimal, but she can still smile. She lives in Northern Ontario, but her mother was from PEI. That gives us an Eastern connection.

After the carolling we chat awhile among ourselves and with the students, and then feeling full of the Christmas spirit head back to our rooms. Ours holds a most unpleasant surprise. The ceiling decorations which our grandchildren had made for us are stripped from the ceiling and dumped in a corner. They are so crumpled as to be useless from then on. We know what's happened. Someone has taken them down because they're paper and deemed to be a fire hazard.

Interestingly, the dozens of paper cards on the walls are left untouched.

Marion is upset and sets out to find who's responsible. It isn't that we don't understand the need for fire safety. But they could have approached us about it and we would certainly have understood if they had a problem. Now it looks as though they waited until we were out of the room to do the deed. The staff tells us that someone from Occupational Health and Safety was doing a regular safety check of the rooms and ordered the decorations removed. Okay, but they could have been more careful with the paper chains. Or let us take them down ourselves.

Kathy

I'm not sure exactly when I decided we should go to Toronto for Christmas, but when I mentioned it to Rod early in December his response was immediate.

"If that's what you want, that's what we'll do."

We had some difficulty getting seat sale airline reservations that late, but with Robbie's help we found a travel agency that could do it. I wanted this to be a surprise for Mom and Dad so we told practically no one else. The plan was to fly out of St. John's on the twenty-third and be in Toronto that night. That meant catching the earliest car ferry from Fogo Island to Farewell and then driving for five hours to St. John's that same day. It would be a long day but absolutely worth it.

The closer the time came, the more excited we got. Samantha was old enough to understand and was thrilled. Robyn was still only a toddler, and Nicholas had more than a month left to be born. What a Christmas this promised to be!

And then disaster struck.

The fickle Newfoundland weather turned sour. Two days before we were scheduled to leave, the forecast gave for high winds on the twenty-third.

"We can't take a chance on the wind being too strong for the ferry," I said to Rod. "We'll just have to leave on the twenty-second."

The day before, we loaded everything into the car, including the Christmas presents that Mom had already sent, and prepared to leave before dawn the next morning.

We awoke to the sound of the wind whistling around and in under the eaves of the house, and my heart sank. The storm had come early. We got the kids out of bed, crammed the last things aboard the car and at 5:00 A.M. we were sitting in the lineup of cars waiting to board.

Then came the crushing blow. The PA system at the terminal announced the ferry could not leave because of the high winds. The disappointment was overwhelming.

I told myself that if the storm had come a day early, perhaps it would also be over a day early and we could leave on the twenty-third as we had originally planned. All that day I kept watching the harbour through the window for some sign of the winds slackening. But the white foam blowing off the tops of the waves showed no sign of abating by the time it was dark and I could see no longer.

Although the wind shrieked all night, we were again in the lineup for the ferry before daylight, and once again were sent home because the seas were too high for the ship to leave the terminal.

But I wasn't ready to give up. We phoned the owner of a fishing boat to see if he would take us across to Farewell.

"I'd like to help you out," he said with genuine regret, "but the seas are just too high to risk it. If the winds die down before evening I'll take you over."

Then I remembered that a friend of Dad's in Springdale owned a couple of small planes. Perhaps he could help. But his answer was the same. The winds were just too high for safety, but if they dropped at all he'd chance it. It was a measure of our desperation that we were willing to try anything.

By dark the winds were still howling out of the northeast. Our one last hope was that the ferry could get across the bay in the morning, Christmas Eve, and we'd make it to St. John's in time to catch the direct flight to Toronto that evening.

Once again our hopes were crushed. When I called Air Canada to change the reservations I was told that we could not transfer our tickets from the twenty-third to the twenty-fourth. I explained our situation and why my parents were in Toronto, and how important it was that we get to Toronto to be with them. I pleaded that this was our last chance and to please make an exception for us. But all in vain. There were no exceptions, said Air Canada. It was policy. Since the plane was only half full, we could have the seats if we were willing to pay full price. That would amount to over $8000 and was so far out of reach we couldn't even consider it.

Then I did give up. There was just no way we could be in Toronto for Christmas. Sobbing, I telephoned Mom and told her all that had happened. I wasn't ready for her reaction, although knowing Mom I should have expected anything.

"Give me ten minutes, Kathy," she said and was gone.

But not even Mom could work miracles in ten minutes.

Marion

When I hung up from talking to Kathy I was even more upset than she was. I could see them in that little house on Fogo Island, whipped by the winds off the North Atlantic and drained by bitter disappointment, their own Christmas in ruins. Kathy had done everything she could and both her family and we deserved better. Then I got mad. That damned Air Canada again!

Suddenly I remembered our own guardian angel, Arthur Fielding. We had been telling him about our troubles with Air Canada when he had visited a few nights ago, and how we hadn't heard from them since writing their CEO more than a month before.

"I just happen to have the phone number of Air Canada's CEO," said Arthur. "If you don't hear from them soon, use it."

I wasn't even surprised. Arthur seemed to have connections everywhere.

I didn't tell Ed anything. If I could pull this off, the surprise would still be good for him. I found another phone and dialed the CEO's number. The person who answered was an executive assistant, he said, and what could he do for me?

I told him. In good plain English, I told him. He heard me out in silence.

"There isn't much I can do," he said politely. "That's our policy."

"Perhaps you should speak to your boss," I said, as riled as I've ever been, "and remind him that we haven't had a reply to our letter yet."

"Letter? There's a letter? What's it about?"

"A lawsuit," I said shortly. "Look it up."

He asked me to hold, and was gone perhaps five minutes. It was the same person who returned, but the voice and the attitude had undergone drastic change.

"We don't usually do this, Mrs. Smith," he said, "but under the circumstances we will make an exception. Tell your daughter if she can get to St. John's tomorrow she can have the seats using her original tickets."

I thanked him and called Kathy down on Fogo Island, now separated from us by less than an hour of windswept water.

It is Christmas Eve. Robbie is here and Jennifer with her friend, Ian. We are out in the cafeteria sitting around a table and planning tomorrow's Christmas dinner. The turkey is ready, and Marion will put it into the oven at the motel first thing in the morning. Gifts have been wrapped and labelled and delivered to Marion's room. Everything seems to be well in order, and then I notice that Marion is missing from the table. Jennifer has seen her leave and goes after her. Rob and Ian get up and go out as well.

I am left all alone at the table on Christmas Eve. What in the world is going on here?

And then I hear it.

To you and all your family,
Your neighbours and your kin,
May all your days be happy
With a joy that never ends...

It's a verse from an old Partridge Family Christmas album that our family has played every Christmas since the children were tiny tots. Someone's singing it, and then I recognize children's voices. Before my mind has time to take that in, I see them. Kathy, with little Robyn in her arms, and close behind Samantha Rae and her father, Rod. Bringing up the rear at a discreet distance are Marion, Jennifer and Robbie. Their wide smiles say it all. They've known about this all along and been saving it as a surprise for me.

I cannot believe it! Kathy and Rod and the children are here for Christmas! From a tiny rock out in the North Atlantic Ocean called Fogo Island, off the northeast coast of Newfoundland, they have somehow materialized here in Scarbrae in Toronto. As Sam and Robyn climb up on my knee for hugs and kisses, I try to embrace them with my arms, but have to be content with taking them into my heart where they already are. Two of our three grandchildren, three of our four children are with us on this blessed Christmas Eve. It is more than I thought, more than I dreamed.

I realize now that Marion had gone out to the lobby earlier to wait for them, and when they arrived, Rob and Jennifer left so that I might be alone when Kathy and her family made their entrance.

That night after everyone has calmed down and we're more or less settled, the children climb up on my bed for the traditional reading of *The Night Before Christmas*. I've been reading that beautiful old poem since our kids were old enough to understand, and even before that.

I am grateful to an unseen God that I am still around to do it.

On Christmas Day, the WheelTrans bus picks me up early for the short trip to Marion's motel. The motel kitchen is almost like any other kitchen on this day, except smaller and a bit more crowded. The original five of us have jumped in number to nine. But that's not all. Marion has discovered two parents whose son was in a snowmobile accident yesterday north of Toronto, and last night was transferred to Sunnybrook Hospital, just behind Scarbrae. He'll survive, they say, but they still don't know the full extent of his injuries.

Marion has invited them to have Christmas dinner with us. She doesn't bother to consult with me first because she knows what I'll say, even when the parents turn out to have two older children with them. Now we are thirteen, but that bothers no one and Marion least of all.

The dinner is excellent. Somehow everyone finds a place around that tiny table in the tiny dining area of that tiny kitchen. We would have been crowded with five, and I reflect that the miracle of feeding the five thousand with a few fish and some bread was perhaps a miracle of generosity and sharing. Our new friends leave immediately after dinner to go see their son at the hospital.

The format for the rest of the day is dictated by family tradition. The stockings are opened in the morning before breakfast. The handing-out of presents takes all afternoon because we have to "ooh" and "ahh" over every single one. Then we spend the evening hours playing games and generally relaxing.

By the time I leave to go back to Scarbrae later that night, everyone's tired but in full agreement. This has been one of our best Christmases ever.

"You need a haircut badly," Marion says one day shortly after Christmas and before Kathy and her family leave for home.

"Yes, Dad," adds Kathy, "your bed-head is by far the worst in Scarbrae."

I recognize the hyperbole, but the other term is not familiar to me.

"What's a bed-head?"

"A bed-head," chimes in a nurse, "is when the hair on the back of your head gets all scrunched up from lying on it overnight. You've got one of the worst cases I've ever seen."

I'm trying to think of a comeback to this when one of the orderlies comes in.

"You need a haircut Meester Smith," he says. "You have a very bad..."

"I know, I know," I say impatiently. "I have a bed-head."

"You have a very bad bed-head," he corrects, and moves quickly out of the room.

This is obviously a conspiracy engineered by my wife and daughter. I'm reasonably sure that had Toronto Mayor Mel walked in at that point, he would have made some reference to my needing a haircut because I have a bad bed-head.

I'm beginning to get the point, although I don't need much prodding. When you can't see anything near or far without giving your head a vicious toss to get the hair up out of your eyes, chances are you need a haircut.

"So where's the nearest barber and is he accessible?"

I watch daughter, wife and nurse exchange satisfied glances.

"Actually," says the nurse as though it were right off the top of her head, "there's a barbershop down in the basement. Once a week students from the hairdressing course at a local college come in and cut the patients' hair."

"Are they any good?" asks Marion.

"I've never heard any complaints," says nurse.

"Okay, I'm ready. You've all convinced me. I need a haircut. When are these people due to come in again?"

"They're down there now according to the notice board." Kathy slips on her shoes. "I'll go down with you."

Isn't that a sweet little coincidence!

Don't tell me humans don't have a sixth sense. I smell trouble the moment we get off the elevator. There are two young female barbers in the salon. One is working on the hair of a woman patient I know, and the other is standing by an empty chair with a towel on her arm and anticipation on her face.

"I brought my own chair," I say lightly, but get no response. No sense of humour again.

"Hello," says my hairdresser, and I understand why she didn't respond to my little witticism. Her speech is so heavily accented that she obviously knows little English.

"Hello. Don't cut it too short. Just make sure all the long parts are shortened."

I don't know what I'm thinking, or why I don't realize that with her limited understanding of the language she mightn't know what I'm saying.

"Okay." Again so heavily accented that the one word is almost hidden.

She fixes the cover sheet around my neck, picks up the clippers and goes to work. I relax, which is my third mistake within the last half-hour. The first was coming in here, and the second was staying.

I look in the mirror and see Kathy sitting behind me reading a magazine. I hear the hum of the clippers. I see her glance up. Her eyes open wide, then one hand flies to her mouth and her shoulders start to shake. The magazine jerks up to cover all her face except her eyes which are fastened on the back of my head.

Something is definitely wrong.

The barber, however, seems to know nothing about it. She's working merrily away and humming happily to herself as though she were cutting Bill Gates's hair and expecting a healthy tip. The magazine remains firmly in front of Kathy's face, although from time to time I see her eyes peering briefly over the top. I can see nothing in the mirror of what's happening to me.

Finally she's finished. She whips the cloth off me with a flourish, turns the chair around sideways so that I can see the effect for myself and stands back as if inviting the whole world to see the excellence of her handiwork.

The first thing I think to do is rescind the invitation. The second is to wonder if killing a barber is justifiable homicide. The third is to find a place to hide.

The woman has scalped me. It wouldn't be quite so bad if she had scalped me consistently. But she hasn't. Some parts of my head are shaved close to the bone. In other places there's enough hair to hide a small bird. I am an apparition.

There is no point in complaining; she wouldn't understand. I give her fifteen dollars and she flashes this brilliant smile and speaks the only other two words of English she knows.

"You happy?"

Happy? Me happy? Of course I'm happy! I'm happier than a pig in doo-doo. I'm so happy I could dance a little jig. Why, if I were any happier...

"Yes, my dear, I'm happy." The words just about choke me.

Kathy looks as though something's choking her. It's not until we get out into the hallway that I realize she's laughing. Laughter comes bubbling out of her like water through a broken water main. She's in absolute hysterics.

I don't need to ask why.

The woman who was having her hair cut catches up with us. Her daughter is pushing her, or pushing as much as one can when one is doubled over in laughter. I look at her mother's head. Were it not for the fact that I have suffered a similar fate, I'd be letting off a few guffaws myself. She and I look at each other in perfect empathy, then she goes her way and I go mine in silence and in misery.

Norm and Glenda are in my room with Marion when I return. There is a long, awkward moment. Marion is in shock. Glenda obviously doesn't trust herself to speak. It is Norm who comes to the rescue. He's about to put it all in perspective.

"Do you know the difference between a bad haircut and a good haircut?" he asks with a grin.

I shake my head.

"About two weeks, normally. In this case..."

Norman, you are a pain in the butt.

35

I've been a fan of the Toronto Maple Leafs since I was six years old. I had no idea at the time who or what the Toronto Maple Leafs were, which is much the way I feel now except for different reasons.

On Saturday nights I was usually allowed to stay up until the news was over and Father himself went to bed. Sometimes he was a bit slow in turning off the old Zenith battery radio and I'd catch an excited voice.

"Hello Canada and hockey fans in the United States. This is Foster Hewitt in the gondola at Maple Leaf Gardens where the Toronto Maple Leafs are leading the Montreal Canadiens by a score of three to nothing. There are two minutes and thirty-nine seconds left in the first period and the Leafs are on a power play... Here's Kennedy leading a rush out of his own end... he passes to Sid Smith... Armstrong is in all alone... He shoots..."

And that's as far as Foster Hewitt ever got before Father turned him off. Not much you can learn about hockey that way, but it sure sounded exciting.

Truth is, I didn't know much about the United States, either. I had a vague idea about Canada, enough to know we weren't part of it, and I used to wonder why Foster Hewitt never said "hello" to hockey fans in Newfoundland.

Then one day when I was nine years old my father told us excitedly that we had joined Confederation and were now a part of Canada. That was great news! When Foster Hewitt said hello to Canada and hockey fans in the United States, I knew he was talking directly to me.

When we moved into a house with electricity and didn't have to conserve battery power I learned what hockey was all about. From then on, I spent every spare moment on the small frozen pond behind Ray's house chasing a wooden puck with the other boys. That's when I became a rabid Maple Leaf hockey fan.

On Saturday nights I'd go to bed a couple of hours early and lie there listening to "Trans-Canada Hit Parade." On my wall was a picture of actress Piper Laurie, my current romantic fantasy. But nothing compared with the glorious anticipation of the moment when Foster Hewitt said hello to me and hockey fans in the United States.

When free agency and rapid expansion tore the heart out of the game for me, I lost interest in the Leafs and hockey in general. But enough of the childhood magic remained that when Rob came to spend Christmas with us in Toronto, we got tickets for a game in the new Air Canada Centre.

So here we are, on a bitterly cold and windy night making our way across the parking lot, past the squatting homeless with their heart-wrenching little cardboard signs, past the weird, rusty-looking structure in front of the Centre and in through the gates. I forget all about my cynicism regarding modern sport, hockey included, and am as excited as a boy. Somewhere in this very building the fabled Maple Leafs are getting ready for the game. Okay, so I can't call more than two of them by name and they probably don't even know I'm here, but that's all right. I know we're all under the same roof and boyoboyoboy it's better than lying in bed on a Saturday night when I was eleven years old and looking at Piper Laurie and waiting for Foster Hewitt to say, "Hello Canada and hockey fans in the United States..."

Foster isn't here, I know. His ghost is sitting in the gondola in the old Maple Leaf Gardens calling a game in which Johnny Bower is unbeatable and Tim Horton is stopping the opposition cold at the blue line and The Big M is eating up the ice with those great strides.

The Centre is an exciting place, with all the vendors and the great crowds and the noise. We board the elevator for the third level and I feel Rob's big hand on my shoulder. He knows I'm still iffy about elevators. I remember carrying him across brooks when he was a small boy and we were on our way to our favourite fishing hole. Now Rob is helping me to cross my river and I'm as secure with him as he was with me.

We find our way to one of the wheelchair-accessible seating areas. To my surprise and joy we have a great view of the ice surface. The lighting is a little dimmer than I expected, but the blue lines and centre ice line are clear, as are the advertisements along the boards.

Suddenly a dazzling, white light illuminates the ice a hundred times brighter than before, and almost immediately the Leafs come pouring onto the ice, caught sharply in the brilliant glare. I just wish I knew who they are, but the helmets hide their faces and I don't know their numbers. In the old days, I knew Tim Horton was number 7, Gordie Howe number 9 and Bobby Orr number 4. And because they didn't wear helmets, I knew their faces as well as I knew my own. These players are strangely anonymous.

Rob goes off and gets us a beer each and we settle back to enjoy the game. After the novelty of being where I am wears off a little, I begin to realize something's missing out on the ice. Rob explains it for me in his own inimitable way.

"The players on both teams each have a dozen eggs sewn inside their jerseys. The one who has the fewest broken at the end of the game gets a week off."

The Leafs take an early 4-0 lead, and the rest of the game has less action than the world figure skating championships. Rob and I are disgusted, as are most of the fans in the Centre. Nevertheless, attending my first NHL game with Rob is still a great thrill and I wouldn't have missed it for the world. Next morning Leaf coach Pat Quinn describes the game as pitiful. I gain a measure of respect for at least him.

The leap from hockey to live theatre in two nights isn't a big one. The acting in the Leaf game was as serious, if not as effective, as in *Les Miserables. Les Miz,* as it's known for those who can't pronounce "miserables," is one of the most popular musicals ever to hit the stage.

The Princess of Wales Theatre is richly appointed for someone impressed with the Air Canada Centre. Again, I have this wonderful sense of anticipation. I've always wanted to see a musical onstage rather than on film, where they have about the same status as a Roy Rogers western, and now it's about to happen. Marion and I have excellent seats in a row from which a couple of end seats have been removed for wheelchairs. Jennifer and Ian, Rob and Kathy are seated some rows behind us. Rod is back at the motel babysitting the children.

An usher touches me on the shoulder.

"I'm sorry," she says, "but I must ask you to move. Some people behind you can't see the stage."

"Isn't this the place for wheelchairs?"

"Yes, but you're higher than normal and they can't see over you."

Marion isn't happy.

"Don't let them move you around just because you're the one in a wheelchair," she whispers.

Still, it seems unfair to block the view of other patrons when perhaps a slight adjustment in seating arrangements can resolve the problem. I ask where they want me to go, and the usher directs me to a place farther back in the theatre and at the very end of a long row. When I look up, I find a post between me and the stage. I realize, too, that Marion won't be sitting by me. Something wrong with this picture.

From the corner of my eye I see Jennifer approach the same usher and point to me. I know she's objecting to my being moved, but the usher is shaking her head. With Jennifer around I'm never alone or helpless, but I have to begin standing up for myself in situations like this. I catch the usher's eye and beckon her over.

"I can't see half the stage from here," I tell her.

"Well, sir," she says, vaguely looking around, "I'm not sure what we can do about that."

That really ticks me off. The guy in the wheelchair has to be separated from his wife and put behind a post so that other people can see clearly?

"I know what to do about it."

I don't get upset very easily, but now I feel the anger rising in my throat like bile.

"I'm going back to sit by my wife and I'm not moving again."

"But sir, the people behind you can't see."

"Then move them."

Marion is delighted, and as I move my chair in next to hers, she turns in her seat to look up at me and says fervently and quite unexpectedly, "I love you!"

She says it the way she used to when we were college students standing on the stairwell of Palmer Hall, the women's residence. We'd be trying to grab a few more moments of holding onto each other before I was told by the house mother (who wore sensible shoes) to vacate the premises.

"I love you!"

That in itself is worth the trouble.

I haven't read all of Victor Hugo's great story of suffering and revolution, but the main character's name, Jean Valjean, is setting off memory vibes. Where have I heard it before? And then it hits me. Jean Valjean and the Bishop! Of course. In one of my old school textbooks a hundred years ago there was a short excerpt from Hugo's novel. The escaped convict, Valjean, seeks shelter in the Bishop's house. The Bishop, not knowing who he is, takes him in for the night. Valjean gets up early and takes all the rich silverware he can find before leaving. But he doesn't get far. He's arrested and tells the police the Bishop had given him all the gold and silver utensils. The police take him back to the Bishop and ask if Valjean's story is true. Without a moment's hesitation, the Bishop replies that it is true, and he takes a silver chalice and gives it to Valjean saying, "You forgot this, my friend."

I have never forgotten that little scene, and as the complete story unfolds before us onstage I am totally captivated by the drama itself, and Colm Wilkinson's magnificent voice.

Later that same week, we take in *Phantom of the Opera* and are treated to Webber's wonderful music and the production's breathtaking special effects.

I'd never willingly choose big-city living over small-town Springdale, but this past week has shown me that the city has its advantages, and they are not to be lightly dismissed.

36

It's decision-time for ordering my wheelchair and van. Big deal? Let's put it this way: together they will eventually cost us in excess of one hundred thousand dollars. Thinking about that too much causes me to break out in a cold sweat and begin trembling all over. Then the nurses tend to get excited and start taking my blood pressure and temperature and sugar level and inevitably order me back to bed. They don't seem to believe me when I tell them my condition is caused entirely by being financially challenged.

We're looking first of all for a chair that will raise me to a standing position. Recent research shows that standing is important from several perspectives. It puts you at eye level with everyone else at a cocktail party. It makes you feel less conspicuous in church when everyone's on their feet and singing "Stand up, stand up for Jesus." Chiefly, however, it redistributes the body weight from the back and bottom to the feet, thus reducing if not eliminating the possibility of pressure sores.

Pressure sores or ulcers are the chief enemy of the wheelchair-bound person. If not caught immediately, they can eat through the flesh to the bone, often requiring plastic surgery in places where you'd rather not have an itch, much less surgery. The condition can take months to correct and more months in bed to recuperate. Pressure sores are to be avoided like the plague. Pressure sores *are* the plague.

The standing position also regroups the organs of the body as they would normally be relative to each other. This achieves other desirable results, among them a reduced tendency to osteoporosis. I have yet to see the connection between the two, but hell, who am I? We are told by people who have lived overseas that most clinics in Europe and Scandinavia will not discharge patients until they've purchased a chair with standing capability. Given the cost of some of the chairs we've seen, clinics in Europe must have some very long-term patients.

Not only is the standing feature important from a health perspective, but also it should be useful to me in public and after-dinner speaking which I hope to be doing as much of as before. I may even up my fees. The more expensive you are, the more people want you.

The chair should also tilt and recline so that the pressure on my skin gets distributed as evenly as possible while I'm sitting up which, let's face it, is anytime I'm not in bed. The cushions on which I sit will be customized to my body contours by computer to identify higher stress areas and again reduce the possibility of pressure ulcers. Does this mean I get to sit on a copier and have an 8x10 glossy made of my bottom? That's not a bad idea for a Christmas gift. I know one or two people who might appreciate it, especially with a little note attached inviting them to "kiss this."

We look at several chair models before deciding on one. The only prohibitive factor is the cost, thirty-seven thousand dollars. I think it's prohibitive, especially given the fact that as yet we have no settlement with the insurance company. But Marion insists that if I have to spend the rest of my life sitting in a wheelchair, we have to get the best that's available in terms of health, comfort and practicality. She does make sense.

The chair we're looking at is built in Sweden, brought over to the United States for further work and then delivered to Toronto for the final touches and the accommodating to my specific physical needs. The process will take many weeks, which is an indication of the state of my physical needs. Since my tenure here is now resting solely on getting me fitted into a chair, it's important that we order it as soon as possible. I don't want to be here next Christmas.

About this time we run into a problem. Everyone in Scarbrae wants to know exactly how we intend to pay for the chair, and takes an active interest in finding out. Our feeling is that, as the song goes, it's nobody's business but our own. The company from whom we're buying it might have a legitimate interest, especially given the cost of the thing, but that's about it.

We're told the physiotherapist needs to know. Why on earth would that be? The social worker is adamant that we should go through her department to set up the sale. The doctor wants to know. The whole damn team wants to know. Not their concern. We resist any and all attempts from people other than the company to look into our financial situation, and that causes a major flap. What have we got to hide? Why do we not trust anyone? Our response is, what business is it of yours? The harder they press, the more stubborn we get. That's probably another Newfoundland peculiarity.

We might be more inclined to answer their questions if we ourselves had a clue about where the money's coming from.

We know that this is causing major upset, but we have no idea why or how much. Our friends in the psychology department tell us that it's all a matter of control. The institution is used to having a major influence in all aspects of their patients' lives, and can't understand why we resist it. Consequently they're trying to find out why it is that we're being, in their view, so secretive.

Then one day a worker in the office draws Marion aside.

"I can't be a part of what they're doing to you," she says.

"What do you mean? Who're 'they' and what are they doing to us?"

"All I can tell you is that any faxes that come in for you must be given to them before they're delivered to you. They say they have to find out what's going on."

Marion can't believe what she's hearing. They would actually intercept faxes intended for us? Isn't that illegal? Isn't that the same as tampering with the mail? It is certainly highly unethical. And what do "they" think we're up to? Don't they understand the principle of privacy? Don't they know we simply want to manage our own affairs, as we've always done? We're not "up to" anything.

We discuss what we should do about this, and come to the conclusion that we will bide our time, as my grandmother used to say. In the meantime, our friend in the office will put a mark on any fax that she has to hand over to them so that we'll know which ones they've seen. We still don't know who 'they' are specifically, but we have a pretty good idea. Later, this person who's befriended us will confirm our suspicions.

The physiotherapist must sign the prescription for any equipment before it's forwarded to Blue Cross, which is fine. That's her job. But the prescription is delayed because they're all in a blue funk about what we're up to.

Our family meetings have become rather cool. Again, if this is a team, we are decidedly the football. The powers that be want us out of here yesterday, although not as much as we want to be gone, but Doctor Lingworst has promised we won't be discharged until the chair is here and fitted properly for me. Despite our problems, I believe him to be a man of his word.

We are told by senior people in one of the departments that policy regarding length of stay in Scarbrae is being changed drastically. From now on, patients will not be permitted to stay more than two months. No wonder they're getting impatient with me. Needless to say, this policy change is causing some upset among front line staff who believe it not to be in the best interest of most patients.

Today a representative of the U.S. company through which the chair is ordered is meeting with us to show some units that are similar to the one we want. Since these chairs are relatively unknown, there is a crowd of onlookers. Some of the OT people, salespeople from the company here in Toronto, several patients and others whom I don't know have collected to watch the show.

We look at a model which not only stands me up but also can be driven in that position. However, I'm not fussy about moving around like that, and besides it does little else. I need one which will at least tilt me back from a sitting position as well as stand me up. So they sit me in another chair which does tilt, but the American chap has a problem.

"I can't tilt you in this," he says, "because I forgot to bring the headrest for it."

I'm buying a thirty-seven-thousand-dollar chair, and I can't try it out because the salesperson forgot to bring the headrest? I'm not impressed, but if it's at the company's Toronto offices, perhaps we could send someone for it.

"Where is the headrest?" I ask.

"In the trunk of my car."

I still don't twig to this. He probably left his car at the company's office across town and we might be able to get it later today.

"And where's your car?"

"Out in the parking lot."

I'm not sure I'm hearing him correctly. Did he say "out in the parking lot"? He's not willing to go out to the parking lot to get a piece of equipment for a thirty-seven-thousand-dollar chair? I don't believe it. I simply don't believe it. In the meantime, he's showing some irritation at this line of questioning.

"In the parking lot here at Scarbrae?"

He stares at me directly. It's a "you want to make something out of it?" stare.

"Yes."

"Then why don't you run out and get it?"

His answer is as immediate as it is nasty.

"Why don't *you* run out and get it?"

Perhaps it's frustration. Perhaps it's the classic case of the big guy beating up on the little guy (little guy in wheelchair, big guy towering over him). Perhaps I'm just tired. I only know I've had enough of this man. He has only to see my face to know he's gone too far.

"Just kidding," he says hastily, "just kidding."

I return his stare with a glare of my own.

"You're not funny." My voice is as cold as I can make it. "You're just not funny."

Now he turns belligerent. His eyes bore a challenge into mine. I'm aware that all conversation has stopped. Everyone is watching to see what happens here. The tension in the room is palpable.

"Can't you take a joke?"

I know as well as he that his words were totally without humour.

"You're not funny," I repeat. "To someone who has no legs and no feet you are not funny at all."

I guess he feels he has to save face in front of his audience. He turns to face me front on, and proceeds to try and stare me down.

My God! We used to play this game as children. I can't believe we're into this childishness. But it's his choice of weapons and I have no intention of backing down. More than thirty years as parent and teacher have prepared me well for duels of this kind. Besides, and this is getting to be more and more important to me, when I'm put down, others who live with disabilities are put down, too. We all have to advocate for each other where we can, and this seems to be my turn. The patients in chairs in this little group are watching. If I lose, they lose.

I don't know how long our eyes are locked. Marion says it's no more than a minute or so. But a minute is a long time when you're waiting for it to pass, and I'm beginning to wonder if I've taken on someone who's stronger than I. Then I remember this was his idea and that's a whole lot different. No way is this man putting us down.

Without so much as a flicker of warning his eyes suddenly drop and he turns away. The tension goes out of the room like the air out of a balloon. Talk begins again in bits and pieces. Marion is smiling broadly. That means I didn't make a total fool of myself.

This man and I exchange no further words, and when he leaves I know I won't see him again. I can live with that. Bad enough I have to buy a chair from his company.

Our final choice is a chair that will stand me up, lift the chair vertically while still in a sitting position and tilt me back. The cost of the chair rises with each option until it reaches forty-six thousand dollars. Now it's worth much more than an Explorer and it's not even four-wheel drive. I think this is exorbitant, but we seem to have little choice.

For the past several weeks the Blue Cross people have been assuring us that they have no problem paying for a chair of this kind. I'm surprised, but they assure us that they've ordered thirty-thousand-dollar chairs in the past and expect to pay more for them now. What they need is a prescription from Scarbrae stating that this equipment with its options is necessary to my good health and overall well-being.

In Newfoundland, such prescriptions are categorized as recommended or not recommended. In Ontario, they're listed as essential or recommended. Essential indicates that I blessed well must have this to survive, and recommended states that, while it is recommended for my health and well-being, I could probably survive without it, for a while anyway.

We explain the situation to our doctor and ask him to just list all equipment as recommended. We are not asking him to do anything illegal or even misleading. Even if he explained the Ontario system relative to the Newfoundland system and how the different categories relate to my situation, it would help considerably. If he does that, we are told that Blue Cross will have no problem paying for the chair. If, however, he sticks with the essential and recommended categories, recommended will be read as not necessary. But the doctor says he can do none of that and sends the prescription with the Ontario categorization. The result is that Blue Cross will pay only fifteen thousand dollars out of the total forty-six thousand. The rest comes from our pocket. Are we grateful to our doctor? Are we grateful for root canals?

Selecting a van is an even more complicated process. Several factors narrow down our options. First, the wheelchair weighs three hundred and seventy-five pounds. With me in it, the total weight approaches six hundred pounds. That's a heavy weight for a van to carry on one side. It's an even heavier weight for a wheelchair lift to handle. I insist on wanting to ride in the front passenger position. One of those days I want to drive it, but for now I'm content to be a passenger, a passenger in the front seat.

Another factor is my height when I'm sitting in the chair. Most people in wheelchairs have their vans lowered four to six inches and the roof raised another few inches to give passengers lots of headroom and a proper view out the windows. This poses little or no problem for the average wheelchair traveller. But in an ordinary full-size van modified that way, my height is such that my line of sight is above the windows. I learned all about that, you'll remember, from Air Canada last summer. I'm one of those people who always have to see where they're going, which might also be an asset when I get to drive. For me to see out the windows, I must be lowered some ten inches, which means the floor of the vehicle must be lowered ten inches.

After diligent researching, and the help of some friends, we discover that only one company in the world will modify a vehicle to that extent, and get me into the front passenger side at the same time. That company is in Indiana. More research reveals that the Canadian Transportation Agency hasn't approved these modifications because the necessary crash testing hasn't yet been carried out in Canada. This means it would be illegal to bring a vehicle so modified into Canada from the United States. I suggest that we could offer to do the crash testing ourselves, but this goes over like expelled intestinal gas in church. We could always take a chance that our vehicle wouldn't be checked at the border, but since the going price for a full-size van so modified is roughly seventy-five thousand dollars, the possibility of having it confiscated is just too great. It isn't likely Blue Cross would reimburse us for that.

We are becoming increasingly frustrated. We must have a van, and it must be capable of seating me in the front, and allowing me to see out the windows. That's bottom line. What to do, what to do.

And then this friend steps in.

Delano dropped by for a visit shortly after we arrived at Scarbrae. An accident fifteen years ago left him quadriplegic with paralysis similar to mine. Five years after his accident he married, and is now a successful businessman. His latest business venture is as a partner in a company which makes wheelchair lifts for vans. I envy his energy and charm, and hope I can become as strong.

Delano belongs to a popular fundamentalist church here in Toronto. Since I'm about as far from being a fundamentalist as I am from being a marathon runner, we have some interesting talks. He begins dropping in every Sunday and stays two and three hours while we discuss our different perspectives on homosexuality, belief in a literal interpretation of the Scriptures, abortion and the like. While we argue and debate strenuously, we never become angry or upset, and I think each of us looks forward to our conversations.

Delano maintains that after his accident his life changed completely. He states unequivocally that he's a better person today than he would have been, because as a young man he was completely self-centred and cared only for himself. Now, he says, the focus of his life is others.

"Good for you," Marion says, "but Ed was never selfish. He's always been a good person who tried to help others as much as he could. How do you see God's plan fitting his life?"

Interesting. Never knew she felt that way. Never knew I'd given her reason to.

Delano doesn't have an answer for that at the moment. As with all other issues on which we differ and usually reach an impasse, he says he's struggling with that.

As we again research the van issue, Delano is more than helpful. With our frustration increasing each passing day, and our problem seeming no closer to being resolved, we count on him for advice and direction.

But finally we reach a dead end. There seems to be no way we can have a van with the modifications we want. Not only will I not get into the front passenger position, but also it seems I won't even be able to see out the windows. It's a low point for us both.

It's Delano who comes to the rescue.

"I've been talking to the people over at our place," he says one day out of the blue, "and while they've never done it before, they say that if they can't lower the floor of a van nine or ten inches, they shouldn't be working for me at all."

This is fantastic news. Delano is certain they can make the necessary modifications that will allow me to see out the windows and also get me into the front passenger position. We are absolutely delighted.

There's only one possible hitch. The Canadian Transportation Agency must first agree to the conversion. Delano says he will approach them with the proposal, and explain my particular circumstance. Within a few days he tells us that the conversion process has been approved on a one-time basis only.

The next step is finding a van. Our friends, the Gills, tell us we should have a three-quarter-ton vehicle because the half-ton suspension won't be heavy enough to carry the combined weight of lift, chair, me, driver and any other passengers. Apart from that, it must be capable of having the floor lowered ten inches. Arthur Fielding's associate contacts us again to say that Arthur wants him to assist us in finding the right van. He and Delano reach the same conclusion: the only vehicle that will accommodate my chair, sit me in front and allow me a clear view through the windows is the GMC Savana.

Savanas are scarcer than federal PCs. It takes almost a month to come up with a van fitting the requirements. Although we haven't seen this vehicle for ourselves, we authorize Delano to purchase it from the dealer and begin work on the modifications. There doesn't seem to be much point haggling over colour schemes and the like, and Delano assures us that we've gotten the best possible deal from the GMC dealer in question. He promises that we'll have the finished product no later than the first week in July. I tell Marion we'll be lucky to get it this summer. I've been on the receiving end of such promises before, and while they're made with the best of intentions, they rarely come through at the desired time.

We relax. The chair is due any day and the van is under construction. All we have to do is find some money to pay for it all.

37

Dr. Lingworst is standing by my bed, hands shoved into the pockets of his white lab coat. Several pencils and pens are sticking out of the breast pocket together with an empty eyeglass case. The glasses are perched on his nose. The only thing missing from the classic doctor image is the stethoscope. Without preamble he speaks.

"You have a life expectancy of fifteen years."

Excuse me? I have what? A life expectancy of fifteen years? What's this all about? Is he giving me a reprieve or pronouncing sentence? While I'm momentarily pondering this, he enlarges slightly on his previous statement.

"A man of your age and with your level of injury has a life expectancy of fifteen years."

I know some kind of verbal response is expected here so I think carefully before I speak. Fifteen years from now will make me seventy-three. That's three years better than the Bible offers at three score and ten. Could be worse.

"That's good," I say soberly. "I'll take it."

The doctor is not amused.

"This is very serious, Mr. Smith. The insurance company wants to know your life expectancy so they can better estimate how much it will cost to maintain and support you for the rest of your life."

A hell of a lot more than they're going to admit, I think to myself.

"I see," I say aloud. "On what do you base this fifteen-year thing?" And why, I think to myself, should I care?

"There are many factors involved in arriving at this projection. For example, smoking."

"I don't smoke." I think this might be important in my own individual case.

"Alcohol abuse."

"You probably drink more than I do."

"Drug abuse."

"I don't abuse drugs, drugs abuse me." He doesn't so much as smile.

"Another factor is suicide."

"We don't do suicide," Marion interjects, "although it's a thought. Perhaps we should skip all other factors and go directly to suicide. Do not pass GO, do not collect $200."

He still wasn't smiling. Probably not a fan of black humour. Might never have played Monopoly. I try to explain my position a little more clearly.

"Look, I'm having trouble taking this seriously. Perhaps in fourteen years I'll be more concerned about it. In the meantime, most of the factors you mention don't apply to me. How does it look for me specifically?"

"I don't know," he says. "These criteria were developed by Dr. Oldthing when he was doing research here back in the '50s."

"The '50s? Your prognosis of my future is based on statistics gathered almost fifty years ago? What application would they have now?"

"We believe these figures are still reliable," he replies rather stiffly, "but I will look at them again."

Marion and I share a laugh about the whole thing and promptly forget it.

Next morning he appears again.

"I have studied the factors having to do with life expectancy from your individual perspective," he announces, "and am prepared to revise my conclusions."

"And...?"

"I now believe your life expectancy to be nine years."

Nine years? I've lost six years overnight?

"Good heavens," I say in mock desperation, "if this keeps up I'll be dead by the weekend."

Dr. Lingworst doesn't smile. Instead he simply turns and leaves the room.

Oh well, easy come, easy go.

But I have a more measured response. Is this man for real? What kind of doctor yanks a patient around like that? If I cared about his prognosis at all, I'd be a basket case by now. One of the reasons I'm not is that Marion has discovered in the library some research that was done in 1985 by respected medical people in this field which states plainly that if a person with quadriplegia is given the proper care and support, life expectancy does not differ significantly from that of the general population. Both the date of this research and its findings are much more attractive to me than the work done by Dr. Oldthing half a century ago.

In the Scarbrae lobby is a large mural entitled *The Early Years* which gives a written and pictorial history of the hospital from when it was founded shortly after the Second World War up to 1975. I read the text carefully and am immediately struck by something. There is no mention of quadriplegia. Surely not everyone who was wounded in war or injured by accident wound up being paraplegic. Paraplegia, being paralyzed from the waist down, is bad enough. The person who has quadriplegia can be so badly paralyzed that he can't even breathe on his own, much less have any use of his arms and hands. So why is quadriplegia not even mentioned?

I was so curious about this apparent omission that I asked one of the Scarbrae staff about it.

"Those who had quadriplegia during that time are not included there," he said, "because before 1975 they did not survive. Exceptions were rare."

That was a sobering thought and made me happy I wasn't born before my time. At the same time, it showed Dr. Oldthing's research from the middle '50s to be somewhat antiquated. When we point this out to Dr. Lingworst, however, he sticks to his muskets and refuses to acknowledge the more modern research. So much for being up-to-date.

38

<u>Marion</u>

When Ed finally agreed to come to Scarbrae last August I was overjoyed. His progress at the Hewitt Centre had slowed to the point where they were about to discharge him. The main problem, of course, was his frozen right shoulder which was preventing his right arm from gaining more range. Quite apart from that, we felt that Ed had not given his therapy a fair chance since much of the time he had been lethargic and non-cooperative. He wasn't to blame because the medication he had been on for so long kept him in that state. When he took himself off that pill he became more alert and concerned, but it was too late. Only a month remained of our stay at the Hewitt.

Scarbrae with its experience and expertise in spinal cord injuries was, I thought, exactly where Ed should be. Surely here he would make the progress in his rehabilitation necessary to prepare him for life with quadriplegia. But we had been here more than five months and from a therapy point of view, he was making no more progress than he had back in Newfoundland. He was certainly benefiting from meeting the other patients day after day and realizing what was possible when one really tried. There's no way to overestimate the importance of that. But physically he had gained very little in strength and flexibility, especially in his frozen right shoulder.

Ed was getting frustrated, too. Since coming to Scarbrae he had really thrown himself into the therapy sessions. When his scheduled sessions were over for the day, he could be found in one of the weight and exercise rooms. No one could say he wasn't giving it the old college try. Still, the range of motion in that right arm was increasing hardly at all, and it was obvious that if we couldn't find some other form of therapy nothing very much would change.

Ed wanted to try different kinds of exercise that might help him overall. Most of these I dug up in books in the library which many of the patients didn't even know existed. I found it quite by accident. Much of what I learned about quadriplegia I found in the books in that little out-of-the-way room. I'd read them carefully and then summarize what I had read for Ed.

Our team wasn't exactly supportive of these efforts. They, it seemed, decided themselves what a patient could and could not do and the patient was supposed to adhere strictly to that regimen. Both of us got quite sick of hearing, "For a man of his age and with his level of injury he can't..." At one point, after hearing this for the nth time, I could contain myself no longer.

"I don't know about Ontario," I said to the team, "but in Newfoundland a man of fifty-eight is still alive."

Ed and I were quite puzzled by that attitude. Our understanding of rehabilitation was that it consisted, at least in part, of trying new things until something was found that worked. Obviously that included a fair amount of failure. But if Ed wanted to do something which they didn't approve, they were totally non-supportive.

Gardening had always been an important part of our lives. We grew many of our own vegetables and enjoyed the work and the harvest. It was natural that Ed would want to try his hand at planting seeds, so we asked the staff person responsible, Robyn, to help us find tools and methods that would help. She became quite enthusiastic and together we planted cucumbers and tomatoes with Ed learning to do much of the work himself. In retrospect, this was one of the most significant activities in Ed's whole rehabilitation because he learned that he could continue with one of his favourite and most rewarding hobbies.

After almost six months, I'm still in a private room. I really don't know why and I haven't asked. My ties to the Health Care Board and the Church Board of Management were severed, at least temporarily, when we left Newfoundland last August so I haven't needed the privacy from those perspectives. And while we have lots of visitors, it's nowhere near the steady stream we had at the Hewitt. The marathon Trivial Pursuit games don't happen up here, and neither do the great singsongs. On the face of it, the need for a private room doesn't exist.

This is not to say I don't enjoy the convenience. Conversations with Marion are private and I can meet the psychologist and other staff whenever I wish. Indeed, we've sometimes made the room available to other patients who want a little private time with spouse or family. I can't say whether or not some of these visits are conjugal. The staff has been flexible for the most part in allowing visitors to remain longer than normal.

But why am I still here? I wouldn't object strenuously to being moved to one of the wards. Not now. Not after being here long enough to make the good doctor at the Hewitt eat his words about not having a private room when I got to Scarbrae. But I wouldn't do that, of course. It wouldn't be nice.

Marion

The support from the team for the gardening project wasn't exactly overwhelming. Why not? Any old guess will do.

The team told Ed that because of his age and the extent of his injuries he would never be able to use a manual chair. But other patients reminded us that wheeling would be Ed's only physical exercise and he should learn to do it.

We got hold of a manual chair and Ed got into it. His first effort at wheeling was exhausting and depressing. He could hardly move the damn thing, which was what happened at the Hewitt Centre. If Ed managed to move the chair a foot back then, the whole floor celebrated. If he made six feet all St. John's celebrated. Finally, he just gave up trying and all celebrations ceased.

But now it was different. Now he felt he had something to prove on behalf of everyone with disabilities, and especially all fifty-eight-year-olds. And also he had the wonderful patients at Scarbrae to encourage and support him.

The first time he worked like a dog and after an hour made it to his room door. His hands were sore, what he could feel of them, and his spirit wounded, or so he said. But the next day with some urging from me he was back at it again. After an hour he was wheeling to the end of the unit, some twenty feet! Other patients gave him tons of verbal support and urged him on.

"You sure are a dog for punishment!" It was said admiringly.

"You're doing great, but I wouldn't take it out on the 401 just yet."

"You'll make it, Smith, but you'd better leave your room by noon if you expect to get to the cafeteria by suppertime."

He was slow, dead slow. But at least he was moving under his own power. And after many many days he made it to the craft shop and back, all of fifty feet in an hour! Not far, but far enough to show him he could go a lot farther with work, and much faster with practice. He discovered the corridor floors weren't exactly flat. There were hills which he could climb only with great difficulty and after repeated attempts. There were valleys and slopes down which he could cruise with satisfying speed. He got to know the location of each little hill and downward slope and learned which route across the floors would give him the least trouble.

Most of all, he watched the other patients. Those with paraplegia and strong hands had no problem at all and the younger among them went racing up and down the corridors like demented fools. Some were almost as slow as Ed. Our friend, Glenda, was also quadriplegic, but she seemed to have a little more movement and strength in her hands than Ed. She was quite an inspiration to us because she wheeled wherever she wanted to go. This usually included passing Ed in the corridor with a wide grin.

Then came the day of days when Ed wheeled his chair all the way from his room out through the unit, down the corridor, across the lobby and into the cafeteria, all under his own steam. We celebrated with a glass of Diet Coke each and one dry biscuit—shared.

By the time the next family meeting came around Ed was pushing himself up and down the corridor in a manual chair. He wasn't real fast but he was doing it. On the day of the meeting Ed wheeled himself into the little boardroom like Rick Hanson wheeling down the 401. Perhaps not *quite* like that, but he was just as proud. To our surprise there was absolutely no reaction. No one said, " Hey, look at you!" or "Good for you, Smith!" or "You sure proved us wrong on that one!" There was absolutely no reaction at all. I couldn't believe it.

In all the things we found exasperating about Scarbrae this was perhaps the most fundamental. Things were fine until you deviated from the path set out for you. Then, even if you had a measure of success, the team refused to acknowledge it or encourage it. It was the last thing we expected at that institution. When we left Scarbrae the doctor wrote in the discharge papers that our expectations weren't always reasonable and consequently we wasted a good deal of their time and ours especially in trying to garden. Our attitude was that, as the poet said, " A man's reach should exceed his grasp..."

How else do you get better and achieve more?

One day Ed's physiotherapist told me about a new shoulder splint that was designed to extend the range of motion of an arm and frozen shoulder much beyond where normal therapy could take it. There were just two draw-backs: the splint was extremely expensive and available only in the States.

I went to work on the second problem first. The company that made the Dynasplint also made other splints that were distributed in Canada and so had representatives in

Toronto. I called the local office but could get no satisfaction from them at all. They did give me the number for the company's headquarters in Baltimore and after a few wrong turns I managed to find the right person. When I told her about Ed she agreed almost immediately to send the splint to Scarbrae with a salesperson who knew how it was supposed to work. She also told me the reason the product wasn't in Canada yet was that they simply couldn't keep up with the demand in the States. She couldn't have been more cooperative and I was delighted.

Diane was willing to sign a prescription which meant that our insurance would pay for it. That, too, was great news.

We couldn't wait for the splint to arrive. If the claims that were being made for it were only half true, Ed's right shoulder and arm would have to benefit.

The big day finally came. The company representative, whom we knew only as Gerry, brought it into the gym and assembled it under the watchful eyes of the other patients. It looked exactly like a car shock mounted on a piece of plywood with a steel rod coming out of the top and a leather strap attached to the rod. The idea was that the arm could be strapped to this apparatus and moved up a few degrees at a time depending on the patient's comfort level. Little by little, the range of the arm would be extended so that maximum use could be made of it.

The splint was used on Ed's left arm first because the frozen right shoulder and arm still wouldn't rise to the minimum 90-degree angle for attaching the splint. The physiotherapist supposedly would work on that side with more traditional therapy until the Dynasplint could be applied to it. In the meantime, using it on Ed's left arm wouldn't be a waste of time.

Ed enjoyed playing a little game with both visitors and staff. We'd put the Dynasplint up on the bed so that it could be inspected and then Ed would ask them to estimate how much it cost. The answers from people who were wise in the ways of carpentry and mechanics and the like were always in the same ballpark.

"Okay, let's see here. The piece of plywood is obviously second-rate and costs no more than ten dollars at the outside. I don't know what's inside that shock affair—probably hydraulic fluid of some kind. Can't be worth more than seventy-five dollars at most. That steel rod and hinge and a few stainless steel screws might go another hundred dollars. Certainly two hundred dollars would more than cover the materials. Add to that the labour, the expertise, the time spent in developing, plus a healthy profit, and I wouldn't be surprised if it cost you, oh, somewhere around six or eight hundred dollars."

We'd just smile and say nothing. The response to that was always the same, too.

"Okay, knew I was going a bit high there. Let me revise that to five hundred dollars. That's closer to the actual price, right?"

Wrong. When we'd tell them the Dynasplint cost over eight thousand dollars to buy, many refused to believe it. Actually, we were renting the thing for a couple of months to see if it helped Ed's frozen shoulder before hitting on the insurance company. No reason we shouldn't be as careful of their dollars as we are our own. The monthly rental was eight hundred dollars. This thing just had to work.

Week after week Ed's left arm was strapped to the Dynasplint, which he said was quite painful, and the therapist worked, or so I thought, on his right arm trying to get it perpendicular to his body as he lay on the mat. At night in his room we would hook him up again to get another hour or two on the day. Still Diane reported that while the left arm was indeed being extended farther she could get no more range on the right. The sales rep would come in and adjust the splint and try to move Ed's right arm and shoulder, but without significant progress. Once they even sent their company surgeon up from Baltimore to see what he could do but the results were the same. Whatever the problems with Ed's shoulder, the Dynasplint company certainly couldn't be accused of neglecting us.

Finally, shortly before we left to come home, we reluctantly agreed that the Dynasplint was ineffective in treating Ed and sent it back. We were extremely disappointed because it meant that after more than seven months of therapy at Scarbrae, the range of motion in Ed's arms had not improved significantly. We had tried really hard to make it work so there was nothing else to be done.

Before we left I went out to see Ed's physiotherapist, Diane, and have one last chat with her. Both Ed and I were trying to tie up what we perceived to be loose ends before leaving. Ed had asked for and gotten an interview with the newly appointed CEO and spent an hour giving his overall impressions of Scarbrae from a patient's point of view. Perhaps it was presumptuous of us to be doing this, but given our sixteen months in rehabilitation centres, and Ed's long involvement with several facets of health care, we felt that what we had to say might have some value.

I'm not sure exactly what I said to trigger this final response from Diane but when I heard it I just about fell over. It was something about being disappointed over the lack of progress in Ed's frozen right shoulder.

"His right shoulder?" She looked perplexed. "I didn't know Ed had a frozen right shoulder."

"Diane!" I exclaimed. "That's the major reason we came here! Nothing could be done for his shoulder in Newfoundland so we came to Scarbrae with the hope of getting it fixed."

"Well," she said, "that's the first I've heard of it."

This was unbelievable! Since the shoulder was the major problem, it had to have been mentioned in Ed's discharge notes from the Hewitt. Surely the medical staff would pass this information on to the physiotherapy people. And what did Diane think all that business with the Dynasplint was about?

"I can't believe that!"

Diane shrugged as if to say that was all she could do about it.

We had only a couple of days before we left so there was little hope of searching out the truth at this stage. But this has tormented me ever since. If Diane was telling the truth, Ed had just spent eight months of physiotherapy with a therapist who didn't know what was wrong!

It was overwhelmingly beyond belief.

39

I saw dogs today that I couldn't believe.

I've always loved dogs and had one or two all my life. The last one died about four years ago and we didn't get another. That was the first time in recorded personal history we didn't have a mutt around the house.

My parents tell me that when I was a baby they had a large dog named Terry that I'd play with as if it were a doll. Someone poisoned it and although my father had a strong suspicion who it was he could never prove it, which prevented him from doing real damage to the person in question.

I remember the next dog well. I was six years old. We were visiting my grandmother in Lewisporte for a week or so, and another little boy with whom I'd made friends after a fight or two showed me the family dog's litter of puppies. I fell in love with them, of course, and promptly took one home to my parents and asked if I could keep it. They said no, and to take it back. So I did. The next day I took it home again and got the same answer.

I decided to adopt another strategy and waited until the day we were to take the coastal boat out to Moreton's Harbour where we lived. Just before sailing time I ran and got the puppy, hid it under my coat and told no one about it until we were halfway home. Mom and Dad weren't too happy but they couldn't very well throw the dog over the ship's rail so we were allowed to keep her. That's when I discovered deceit can pay.

We named her Lady and she lived with us for fourteen years before she died in puppybirth. You might say she was active right up to the end. No one mourned her more than my parents.

We were living in Halifax when Lady crossed over into canine paradise, and Dad immediately bought an English sheepdog to fill the vacuum, which he also named Terry. Because we were living in the notorious North End and Dad was afraid of break-ins, especially if he wasn't there, he trained the dog to bark ferociously when anyone came near the door. Unfortunately, the dog barked at everyone coming and going, and because of his size he could be quite intimidating. He wasn't very popular with parishioners.

One night Terry was lying on the carpet in front of me when without warning he leaped off the floor and attacked me in the chair. I was able to hold him off until he calmed down, but I had a few scratches and scrapes from his claws. Dad grabbed his 12-gauge shotgun, threw Terry into the car and headed for the city dump with every intention of blowing the dog's head off.

I knew how much my father loved that dog, and when I started to think rationally I knew it was something he shouldn't do. I raced after him in my own car and when I got to the dump, he was just sitting there unable to do the bloody deed. I talked him out of it because Terry hadn't actually attacked anyone else and I knew that shooting the dog would just about break Dad's heart.

That same year, I had my own heart broken when the girl to whom I'd been engaged for more than two years decided she didn't want to get married and the whole thing was called off. To fill that vacuum, I bought a new car and a dog, a beautiful black cross between a German Shepherd and a Labrador Retriever. A few months later Marion and I made up and got married, and I still had the car and the dog. I thought I came out of it rather well. Queenie grew to a large size, was gentle as a lamb and took care of our children as they came along with great devotion. She lived for fifteen years.

Then came Tiki, a small brown mutt who was arguably the most stupid thing alive I have ever seen, including hens. He was Marion's nemesis from day one and remained so until the last day of his twenty years. Holly, a miniature poodle, was exceptionally intelligent and passed over Jordan at thirteen, a year or so before our accident. She was our last pet.

Today I see my first skill dog. She's a beautiful golden retriever and her behaviour is remarkable. When her owner is wheeling his chair, she puts her nose about twelve inches from the large wheel and there it stays, no matter how fast or how slow they go. When the chair stops, she immediately flops down on her stomach, her nose still within twelve inches of that wheel. I see a man stop to pet her, and her owner politely asks him not to while she's working.

I'm intrigued, and inquire further about such dogs. They're called skill dogs for obvious reasons and their skills are enormous. They're trained to open doors, turn on lights, retrieve bottles or cans from the fridge which they also open, pick up things from the floor, use their weight to assist turning you in bed and many other tasks peculiar to their owners' needs. They are so well trained, they swear, that the pooch will poop only where you tell it, and when you tell it. I find this almost as difficult to believe as the Toronto lawyer, also quadriplegic, who says that his dog, a beautiful standard poodle, can actually pick up a coin off the floor with her teeth. I don't know why we don't ask him to demonstrate, but we don't. The dogs also make great companions, especially for people with disabilities who live alone.

Skill dogs are trained in Oakville, Ontario, by Lions International which gives them free of charge to any person who can demonstrate a need. They breed only poodles, Labs and golden retrievers because of their superior intelligence and personalities. Each dog takes more than a year and about ten thousand dollars to train.

The dogs require strict discipline, especially when at work, and have bright pinnies wrapped around their middles like oversize bandannas. When the pinnies are off, the dogs can relax and play around a little. The trainers warn against the dogs becoming pets and forgetting their main purpose. One chap told us he had been in hospital for a few weeks and left the dog with his parents. By the time he got out, the dog was almost completely ruined as a skill dog, thanks to his parents treating it as a pet. Grandparents do the same thing with grandchildren.

I've heard of other animals with certain skills not offered at the Lions' kennels in Oakville. There was, for example,

Pudgie, the trained cat that belonged to a relative of ours. Pudgie developed diabetes. As with humans, he required several medical interventions. The most challenging of these for his owner was that his urine had to be tested on a weekly basis. No problem. She put a tiny little potty—so help me—in the corner of his litter box and taught him how to use it. Don't ask me how, but the missus had no end of clean feline urine samples from then on. But the best is yet to come.

Pudgie had to have his daily injection of insulin. When the time came, the missus would call out, "Come here, Pudgie, it's time for your needle." The cat would jump up on the table, close his eyes, retract his claws and stick his backside up in the air awaiting the procedure. He'd accept the needle stoically and give his owner a friendly little kiss as if to say "thank you." Then he'd prance off across the floor likely singing the praises of Frederick Banting, the co-discoverer of insulin, who was killed in a plane crash not far from where Pudgie lived.

An aunt of ours had a dog that developed heart problems. I had trouble believing that until our daughter, Michelle, had a dog that required psychological intervention. The conclusion reached by the dog psychologist was that he needed company so Michelle got another dog just like him, so alike that she ended up with two dogs seeing a psychologist. Anyway, the vet put our aunt's dog on digitalis and a strict diet which included for lunch a lettuce and tomato sandwich. The dog loved it. I don't know how long he lived but when he died he wasn't real fat. My guess is that he died of malnutrition and not cardiac arrest.

Another lady of our acquaintance loved birds as much as she loved cats, so she had her cat's teeth removed so it wouldn't eat her little feathered friends. Realizing the cat couldn't eat without any teeth of all, she took it to Germany and had it fitted with false teeth for the princely sum of fifteen hundred dollars. I don't know if the cat kept its teeth in a glass of water overnight or used Polygrip to keep his dentures from falling out when they closed over some hapless little sparrow.

But back to skill dogs. The prospective owner is told to wait about a year at home until he knows more about his special and specific needs before applying for an animal.

I'm definitely interested. Marion is another story. When our last dog went mammaries up, she vowed that nothing that barked, wagged its tail and had four legs would ever cross her doorstep again. She stripped every inch of carpet out of our house and replaced it with unpeed-on and unpooped-on fresh, new stuff. I don't know if she'll ever change her mind. Perhaps if I can keep her hopping to the refrigerator for beer, rolling me over at night, and picking up loose change from the floor with her teeth she'll see the need for a skilled animal.

When I do grab an opportunity to talk about skill dogs to Marion, she raises some practical concerns.

"You have this voice-activated computer," she says, "and it prints exactly what you say, right?" She goes on without waiting for me to affirm or deny. "Let's say you're working at the computer and your faithful canine pal is lying on the floor beside you. Suddenly the computer prints something you didn't say and you, as is your wont, will say, "oh shit!" The computer then runs haywire trying to print the polite term for "oh shit," and the dog, thinking you said *go shit*" will run to the nearest neutral corner and do a job. Your blood pressure will go through the roof because you can't kick the dog out the door since you have no legs, and you can't throw something at the computer since you have no hands. What you do have left in abundance is your tongue and I'll be on the receiving end of that. Then I'll get upset and leave and you'll be really screwed. Is that what you want?"

I assume it's a rhetorical question and say nothing.

Discretion is the better part of valour.

40

"You're grounded! You're grounded!"

The shrill voice of the little five-feet-nothing nurse precedes her through the open door. As usual, she's in a hurry. She was probably born in a hurry. She may even have been conceived in a hurry, like most of the rest of us. I have never seen her walk normally. If the corridors were a dirt road, her little feet would be kicking up dust the way a high-speed racing boat kicks up a rooster tail.

"You're grounded! You're grounded!"

She says it almost joyously as she rushes through the door. There is certainly no hint of regret in her voice as she busies herself with pillows and sheets. She is without doubt the busiest nurse on the floor. She may be the busiest nurse in the hemisphere.

Being grounded means I'm confined to bed until further notice. It means I'm not allowed up for dinner. It means I can't get into the pool, which I know is there because I was allowed in it—once.

The reason I'm placed on the inactive list is a small area on my lower back which has been a problem ever since my days—many eons ago—in the Health Sciences Centre in St. John's. It developed one night when a nurse decided to ignore the doctor's orders that I should be turned from one side to the other every two hours.

"He was sleeping so well," she said next morning to Jennifer, "that I didn't have the heart to disturb him."

Very considerate, and I'm not being sarcastic, except the result of not being turned is this delicate skin area that will probably be with me 'til the end of time, or at least the end of my time. That's a heavy price to pay for a night's sleep.

Anyway, it hasn't broken down to be a full-fledged pressure sore, but it has become what we Newfoundlanders like to call nish. The conventional wisdom here at Scarbrae dictates that the patient, namely me, must remain in bed until the skin has toughened up enough to bear my weight again. That's the conventional wisdom at Scarbrae.

In the Hewitt Centre, they used to stick a dressing called Duoderm over the area and let you go your lintsy. "Go your lintsy" is a term my grandmother used to use to mean "go do what you want." My grandmother was also fond of saying, "bad cess to you." I had no idea what that meant until I heard it in an old Irish ballad where it was used as a curse against the hated English. Lintsy might also be Irish, given my maternal grandfather's Irish roots.

At first I allowed myself to think thoughts that would have me pitched out of Newfoundland on my arse if I gave voice to them. Perhaps the Hewitt nurses aren't as progressive as the Scarbrae nurses, I thought. After all, Scarbrae nurses see more spinal cord injuries in one day than Hewitt nurses see in five years. They should know more about it and the relative complications. Perhaps, I said to myself, if my skin problem had been treated in Newfoundland as it is in Toronto it would have been cured by now. But of the four months I've been here I've been grounded almost two and the nish place on my back hasn't changed one way or the other.

The accepted treatment here for a nish area is to turn you on your side, expose your rear end to the elements, set up a fan about three feet from your posterior and let the breezes blow where the sun don't shine. I've asked if there's any way they can combine a sun lamp with the fan so that at least I'd be getting a suntan in places most other people don't, unless they've been on *Baywatch*. It seems to me that if my bum is to be shown in public, it should look as good as possible. No one seems to take my suggestion seriously.

Marion

Ed finally had several weeks free from pressure areas and the resultant groundings, and was able to concentrate on his therapies. Both of us were feeling better about his rehabilitation than we had in some time.

Ed was trying out a wonderful new device called a Freedom Bed. The Vancouver company that makes the bed had one at the Centre for patients to try out if they wished. The great thing about it is that it's programmable to turn the patient from side to side any number of times. We programmed it to turn him on one side for two hours, on his back for another hour and then the other side for another two. The cycle is repeated for as often as necessary. Without it, nurses or orderlies had to come in every two hours and turn him to prevent bedsores from developing on the pressure areas of his skin. When the bed turned him, it was so gradual and gentle he didn't even awaken.

The bed costs in excess of twenty thousand dollars! That's enough to be prohibitive for many people, and normally would certainly have been so for us. But we worked it out. Ed will need to be turned that often for the rest of his life. My hands have been so weakened by rheumatoid arthritis that I couldn't possibly do it. That means we'd have to pay someone to stay overnight and turn Ed the required number of times. For eight hours each night at the going rate that amounts to approximately seventeen thousand dollars a year. In other words, the bed would pay for itself in less than two years. But that's not the best of it.

It's well-named Freedom Bed. Having someone in our house all night every night and coming into our bedroom every two hours would effectively destroy any privacy and intimacy we might otherwise have. We would certainly not be able to sleep together. The toll on our quality of life would be heavy and possibly even unbearable. The Freedom Bed would allow us our privacy—if it proved consistent and dependable.

We had it for almost two weeks, the length of the trial period, and it performed faultlessly.

Then one morning I arrived in Ed's room to find that overnight a pressure sore had appeared on his lower back. We were devastated, not only because Ed would be in bed for at least another couple of weeks, but also because according to the nurses the bed had failed to turn him at all during the night. We were counting so heavily on that bed that living without it seemed almost impossible. But if it couldn't be depended on to protect Ed from developing skin problems, we had little choice.

Something was nagging at me. First, on several previous occasions new skin sores had been traced to staff negligence. I was getting more and more upset at these episodes and just one more would have been the breaking point. I'm not sure what I would have done, but everyone knew how I felt and that I would have taken action of some kind. The second thing was the way the nurses were talking. There were small inconsistencies in their account and I was beginning to wonder if they weren't trying to cover up the more likely fact that someone had neglected to turn on the bed the night before.

Even more devastating than the pressure sore would be the effect on the quality of our lives for years to come if we decided not to purchase the bed when the fault was human rather than electrical or mechanical. I had to know, but how? Perhaps a pressure tactic or two was called for.

"What's the point of carrying on?" I said in tears to the nurses. "We take one step forward and six steps back. Just as we seem to be making some progress, someone here does something stupid and we're right back where we started."

"You mustn't talk like that," one of them said.

"Why not? I really don't see the point of carrying on. It's just as well to go jump off a bridge or something."

I could see my words were having quite an effect. I had chosen them deliberately to show how upset and frustrated we were with the situation.

Shortly after that Karen and Ivan arrived. We were walking through the lobby when Karen touched my arm.

"Marion," she almost whispered, "there's a man following us. He's been following us ever since we left your room."

I looked around and saw him immediately. It was Doctor Stratton, the head of the psychology department. I also knew what he was doing here on a Sunday afternoon. Sure enough, when our eyes met he indicated he wanted to talk to me.

Karen and Ivan went on out to the cafeteria and Doctor Stratton and I went into one of the small meeting rooms.

"Okay," I said as we sat down, "who told you I was about to commit suicide?"

He was naturally evasive about that, but I knew who it was and appreciated both their concern and the speed with which Doctor Stratton responded. I assured him that I had no intention of putting an end of to it all, and that I was using that kind of language to indicate how strongly I felt about the situation. Then I unloaded on him.

The scare tactic failed. No one came forward and admitted fault. There was only one other thing I could do. I asked to see the nursing supervisor in private.

"Brenda," I said, "I have to know the truth. If the bed is at fault, that's all we can do about it. But if it isn't and we don't buy it because of this we'll be paying for that mistake the rest of our lives.

She was silent and I pressed on.

"You don't even have to tell me what happened or who's responsible. There won't be any recriminations. I have no intention of suing the hospital or anything like that. Just tell me whether or not we should buy the bed."

There was silence, and I was about to continue my pleading when she spoke quietly.

"Marion," she said, "buy the bed."

The staff psychologist assigned to me is John Williams. Both of us are "sons of the manse," his being Pentecostal and mine United Church, so we have lots to talk about. He says he's the black sheep of the family because he has largely rejected fundamentalism. However he's still interested in spirituality and we spend a fair amount of time discussing our respective views of life and what it all means.

At least twice a week John comes in for a couple of hours. We discuss everything under the sun seemingly at random, although there's no doubt in my mind but that he has carefully structured our sessions.

Marion goes downtown or finds something to do in the library whenever John and I have a scheduled meeting. She says that after our sessions I am unfailingly cheerful and pleasant. I don't doubt it for a moment. Whenever I run into some crisis or frustrating situation, John is there to help me through it. On more than one occasion he and Marion have talked as well, and sometimes he includes both of us in one of the sessions.

"You're not the first to find yourselves at loggerheads with the powers that be," he says after one of our more frustrating family meetings. "It's my observation that patients who take control of their lives and are proactive about their therapies and rehabilitation make the best progress. But inevitably they clash with the various levels of authority."

I remember what Delano had to say along the same lines and feel immeasurably better. We're not the only ones to have that experience.

One of the most painful and least pleasant side effects of a broken neck is what's called referred pain. I don't know how it works. I know only that several times during the day the usual, dull pain in my thumbs flares up to become almost unbearable. The feeling is similar to having a dull blade sawing through all joints at the same time. I've never actually experienced that particular process, but it's the worst pain I can imagine so the comparison is consequently appropriate. It seems grossly unfair that one of the few places in my body I can feel should be the place where a thoroughly confused and demoralized nervous system would choose to send its spare pain. On the other hand, perhaps it's sending pain all over my body and I don't know about it. That thought makes me feel a little better, as if somehow I'm hoodwinking the injury.

In Newfoundland, no one seemed to have any idea of how to go about relieving this condition, although they tried. They even sent in a pain specialist for consultation, but he seemed as much at a loss as the rest of them. Someone did suggest acupuncture, but we were told the powers that be weren't fussy about anyone practicing acupuncture on their premises. Someone else recommended a salve that was applied externally, but my friend the doctor said he had never known it to work on anyone and it would take three months to find out whether or not it would be effective. That didn't seem like much of a recommendation, so I didn't bother to follow it up.

Here in Toronto the pain has become such that I'm willing to try anything. Bearing pain in silence has never been my strong suit. Karen Gill tells me that Ivan has a similar problem which she treats with a concoction called Pain-A-Trate. You can't get it in Canada, she says. It has to be ordered directly from the manufacturer in the States. I'm sure it's obvious that I'm not over-excited by Karen's salve, but I accept—I hope graciously—a tube of it and stick it in the drawer by my bed.

The acupuncturist (if there's any such thing) here at Scarbrae, Kay, is certain she can give me some relief from the thumb pain with her needles, so despite my antipathy to being injected and/or stuck with anything sharp, I agree to try it. I know Marion has had acupuncture. Under intense questioning she sticks to her story that it doesn't hurt—much.

At the appointed time I present myself to this young woman who strips off my shirt and produces several small gleaming needles. If she's impressed with my naked torso, she conceals it well. Before long I feel like the proverbial pincushion, and while it doesn't actually hurt the sensation is distinctly unpleasant.

I endure this for several sessions until the day I get a sharp, stinging pain in my shoulder and I say "oww!" and she says "oops" and I see her take a needle from my shoulder bent at right angles. It's then, as coincidence would have it, that I have an inspiration and tell her I won't be coming back because I have this marvellous new salve that makes the pain go away almost immediately and so I won't be needing the acupuncture anymore. She looks as though she doesn't believe me, but says only that she'd like to see this salve for herself. For a moment, I think "uh oh" and what will I use to cover that little white lie and where will I find it? Then I think of Karen's salve—thank you, Karen!—and tell Kay I'll bring it down first opportunity.

I'm not back in my room too long before the thumbs erupt again. Marion has taken Karen's salve out of the drawer to show Kay, and since it's just sitting there and since nothing else is working I decide to give it a try. Actually, I should put it on just to keep what I told Kay from being a lie. On the other hand, I just might be a little too late to save myself from the effects of that particular sin. Whatever, Marion smears some of the stuff on my thumbs and I lie back prepared to suffer this problem for the rest of my life.

It happens so gradually that I'm hardly conscious of it, but all at once I become acutely aware that the pain has gone from my thumbs, gone completely. It's a miracle! And it's Karen's salve. Thank you, Karen! This time for real. God does work in mysterious ways.

I can't wait to get back to Kay's place of business and show her my miracle ointment. She looks it over carefully and hands it back without comment. I plead the merits of the Pain-A-Trate earnestly, but she shows little reaction. The look on her face says, "you poor gullible fool," but I could be misreading it. To tell the truth, I don't care. This stuff works, ma'am, and that's all that's important.

A couple of days later I meet Doctor Lingworst in the corridor.

"I hear you have a miraculous cure for your thumbs," he says.

No doubt he heard it all from Kay, and no doubt they had a good chuckle about it. What the hell.

"It isn't exactly a cure," I reply, "but it does give excellent temporary relief."

"Could I see it?" he asks.

"Certainly. There's a tube in the bag on the back of my chair."

He digs it out and reads the ingredient list and directions carefully. I wait for his pronouncement. It's not long in coming.

"I see," he says, and walks away.

I guess conventional wisdom at Scarbrae dictates that medical people should be cautious in endorsing miracle cures. Perhaps they should be just as cautious about dismissing them.

Out in the occupational therapy rooms is a large and colourful picture of a young fellow who's just had something called a tendon transfer. Evidently they take a tendon from your forearm, insert it into your hand and that's supposed to give you a grip, something I'm not blessed with at the moment. If one tries not to look at the large, vivid, scarlet scar running from his hand to his elbow, it all looks very promising. I ask Angela about it and why they don't promote it more with their patients.

"Often it's very successful," she says without much enthusiasm. "Sometimes, however, patients are disappointed with the results, which is why we don't push it more than we do. Perhaps you should ask Dr. Lingworst about it."

So I do. His enthusiasm for the operation is only slightly less than Angela's. He professes not to know much about tendon transfers and says I should talk to a specialist. That's fine with me.

"Is there a specialist at Sunnybrook Hospital?"

"Yes," he says after some hesitation, "Dr. Sledge."

"Great! Would you refer me to him, please?"

"If you think this is what you want."

It is, and we settle back to wait for an appointment. Time passes and I approach Dr. Lingworst again about the referral. These things take time, he tells me, so just be patient. I'm not. I lose count of the occasions on which I speak to the good doctor about it but nothing seems to be happening.

It so happens that Marion has an appointment with that same specialist about her wrists and her need for further surgery. She already has the bones in her left wrist fused. When he finishes examining her, Marion decides to hell with protocol and asks him if he's the surgeon who does tendon transfers. He says he is, so she asks if he would see me.

"Certainly," he says. "See my secretary for a time."

The appointment she gets is within a few days.

We tell Dr. Lingworst the good news, but for some reason he doesn't seem all that happy about it. I still need a letter of referral from him, and there isn't much else he can do but provide it. He gives us the letter unfolded and in an open file. We can't avoid seeing it. There's no doubt in my mind but that he meant us to see it.

"I know this patient is not a candidate for a tendon transfer," it says in part, "but he and his family are insisting on this referral."

That part is certainly true, but it isn't exactly a positive note on which to present myself to the Sunnybrook surgeon. Again, I can't believe the attitude.

When we get to Sunnybrook, Dr. Sledge and another doctor see me almost immediately. They roll up my sleeves, examine my arms, and make learned remarks about same. Finally he speaks to me.

"Well, Mr. Smith," he says, "you are an excellent candidate for a tendon transfer."

"Really?" I am genuinely surprised. "Do you do many of those?"

"Oh yes," he replies. "We do hundreds every year."

"Is there much risk involved in the surgery?"

"There's a risk in all surgery," he says, "but with this procedure it's very slight. We've been doing these for a long time without any problems at all."

This is getting better all the time. What can they be thinking over at Scarbrae?

"Where are you going when you leave Scarbrae?" Dr. Sledge asks.

"Back home to Newfoundland," I reply, expecting him to say something like, "If you want this operation you'll have to stay in Toronto until we can schedule you in." Again, I don't expect to hear what he says.

"Excellent! My friend, Dr. Oldford, practices in St. John's. He studied with me and I have every confidence in him. Why don't you go see him when you get home?"

No mention is made of the good doctor's letter of referral and his views on my potential as a tendon transfer candidate, and I feel there's no point in my bringing it up. At the same time, it's very good that I don't have a vindictive streak. Otherwise when I get back to Scarbrae, I'd pin Dr. Lingworst to a wall with my chair and leave him there. Of course that would mean I'd have to stay there, too, and I don't think I could handle that at all.

Dr. Lingworst pretends to have little interest in my announcement that I'm an excellent candidate for a tendon transfer. He murmurs something which I will always choose to believe is "Good," and doesn't hang around to discuss it further. The doctor is a very busy man.

I have one more specialist to see before we go home. Marion keeps reminding me I should be taking advantage of the accessible dental clinic at Sunnybrook. Dentists are not my favourite people. They tend to hurt you, as I explain to Marion, which probably has something to do with my not visiting one in some time. A nurse is doing something or other with me while we're having this conversation, and she looks up with some interest.

"How long since your last checkup?"

"Oh, I don't know. Seven or eight years, I guess."

"You're kidding! You haven't been to a dentist in seven or eight years?"

She sounds as though she finds this hard to believe. Her beliefs are about to be really strained. Marion speaks, although she really doesn't have to.

"Try fifteen years," she says grimly, "and probably more."

The nurse looks as though she's about to fall over. Actually, she looks more like she wants me to open my mouth to see if there are any teeth left.

She says, "When is your appointment with the dentist?"

"Oh, I don't know. Sometime next week, I think."

The date, the hour and the second are firmly fixed in my mind. If that nurse is right, I'm in for a rough time. Now I'm wishing I'd gone every six months or at least every decade. I've been a fool.

The day for the dental appointment arrives. I'm out by the main entrance waiting for the WheelTrans bus to come get us for the short trip to Sunnybrook Hospital when Dr. Lingworst strolls by. He doesn't stand on the niceties.

"I hear you haven't been to a dentist in fifteen years," he greets me.

"Something like that," I confess. My dental situation must now be known all over Scarbrae. The staff is probably running a lottery on how many teeth I'm going to lose. The smart money is on all of them. Dr. Lingworst studies me with satisfaction.

"This is the day you pay," he says, and repeats it. "This is the day you pay."

I'm too miserable to think of a snappy comeback.

The French aristocrats being hauled off to the guillotine in the horse carts were no more apprehensive than I am as we ride over. We aren't in the waiting room five minutes before this young girl of about fifteen comes out and tells me to follow her. If I were here with a heart attack, I think to myself, I wouldn't see a soul for five hours.

I follow the girl into the dentist's office. There is one chair and five hundred tons of gleaming metal instruments, all of them nasty-looking things.

"Where does the dentist want me to park?"

"I'm sure anyplace will do."

I'm sure anyplace won't do, but I may as well wait for the dentist to get more precise. The girl busies herself with some instruments. I'm like a cat in a dog pen. I know it's too soon to ask, but I ask anyway.

"How long before the dentist comes in?" The young girl looks at me brightly.

"Oh," she says, coming over to my chair and obviously enjoying herself by the look on her face, "I'm here. Now, how long since your last dental checkup?"

"I've been a bad boy," I manage to stammer, trying to recover from the shock of having a high-school student practice dentistry on me. "I haven't seen a dentist in... three years, I guess."

"You have been bad," she says in mock severity. Perhaps it isn't mock. She might be thinking I've been depriving some dentist of a livelihood. If she knew the truth I'd be in for one painful session. Perhaps she'll know by examining my teeth, as they do with horses.

"You're too tense," she says. "Relax and let me do the work."

I know I've heard that somewhere before, but for the life of me I can't remember when or where. The dentist is poking around my mouth with a sharp thingy and a little mirror when a grown woman walks in.

"Need any help?" she asks, nodding a smile in my direction. Oh God, they've heard about me even over here. I'm too much work for one dentist to handle alone.

"Sure," my dentist says. "I'm about to take some X-rays. You can give me a hand." Oh God, they have to take X-rays of my jaws. How bad can it be?

Finally the things are hauled from my mouth.

"Now, let's have a little look at these." I wait for a few short moments while she's looking at the mess that I know is in my mouth. She walks back to my chair, chatting with the other woman all the while. Then she looks at me.

"We'll do a little cleaning and polishing here," she says, still brightly, "and then we're all done."

We're all done? We can't be all done. I haven't been to a dentist in three, no make that *fifteen* years. There's a world of work to be done in there. But the dentist is speaking to me again.

"No sign of cavities," she smiles, "and your gums are healthy. Not bad for three years."

I have this insane desire to laugh wildly but I can't because she's busily cleaning away at my teeth, my tremendously healthy and even luckier teeth. And gums, not to forget my gums. I feel like a schoolboy let out for the summer holidays, like a jury member at the close of the O.J. Simpson trial, like a Member of Parliament at the end of a long session. It's over, it's done, and I survived it.

The first thing I do when I get back to Scarbrae is go look for Dr. Lingworst. I have something to say to him. He's nowhere to be found, and someone tells me he's out for the day.

Next morning as the orderlies are getting me ready to get up, in he walks. I've been waiting patiently for twenty-four hours for this moment. I speak before he has a chance to even say good morning.

"Look Doc, no cavities!"

His only response is to smile somewhat weakly and begin asking his normal doctor questions.

I know it's childish of me to take pleasure in these little situations, and perhaps even more childish to be telling them. But hey, there's not a lot of joy in my life right now. I have to take my fun where I find it.

41

So, God, how is it with you and me these days?

After fifteen months of hospitals and rehabilitation centres how do we stand with each other?

I'm about to go home. This long, first phase of recovery and rehabilitation is about over and I'm still a functioning human being. Someway, somehow, I've managed to rise above the demons that assault me by night and sometimes even by day. Sometimes I can pretend for short periods of time they don't even exist.

So how did that happen? How come I can still think rationally on one level while down on the next my gut is Dante's Inferno? It defies logic, you know. The human psyche, brittle and delicate as it is at the best of times, should not be able to absorb this kind of punishment and still function. And yet it does. Three cheers for the psyche that it does not, like the body it inhabits, fold up and die when the neck is broken. Three cheers and too bad.

I suppose you'd say that's how you made us. It was in the blueprints all along that the mind could survive without the body and vice versa. So all credit, along with glory, laud and honour, belongs to you, right? Right.

Thing is, it doesn't always work that way. Sometimes that kind of shock can pretty well destroy the mind so that it refuses to function at all. Happens all the time. Do you also take responsibility for failures? What's happened to the blueprints and the plan then? But you'd probably answer that the blueprints are different for each of us, we humans being unique and all that.

Your long-suffering servants would claim that it's your doing I've made it this far without going off the deep end.

"So many people are praying for you," they tell me often, as if to say that, with all that praying going on, you have no choice but to reach down and help me through this. I hadn't realized that sheer quantity of praying was important. But what do I know? Tennyson's dying King Arthur says to a grieving Sir Bedevere, "Pray for my soul. More things are wrought by prayer than this world dreams of." Perhaps.

Whatever, it seems you want to take credit for my getting this far. Do you also take responsibility for those who drive their wheelchairs over the edge of a nearby city overpass, as some have done? Okay, cheap shot. But the question is still valid. If you're going to take credit when things are going well, you must also take responsibility when they don't. It's a package deal.

Interestingly, those who are quick to say that I wouldn't have gotten this far without your help are reduced to absolute blithering when I ask the next logical question. If sometime in the foreseeable future I do go to pieces—hardly an impossible thought—would that mean you've withdrawn your help from me? In other words, God, do I succeed only with your help and fail when I don't have it? In which case, what must I do to get and keep that help?

One of the responses I get from well-meaning friends is that I must consciously accept your help in order to receive it. You and I both know that there have been times when I couldn't consciously accept a drop of water, let alone the help of Almighty God. Another explanation I'm given is that the prayers of others intercede for me. That's a nice thought, but does it mean that, if no one prays for me and I can't pray for myself, I've had it as far as you are concerned?

The last refuge of those who try to justify your intercession or lack of it is to state with utter finality that we aren't meant to understand these things, which statement is intended to bring closure to the debate. End of discussion. Over and out.

Perhaps for some but not for me. We might be too stupid or too ignorant or too unenlightened spiritually to understand, but I can't accept that we're not *meant* to understand. On the other hand, I might be a little too much like Eve who wanted to know everything and be like God and got herself kicked out of the Garden of Eden. I'm not too worried about that. Where I am now is hardly the Garden of Eden.

I have no memory of asking you for anything since the accident, which surprises me. I always thought that, whatever my intellectual doubts, in a real crisis I'd be on my knees faster than one could say Beelzebub. That would probably still happen if someone I love were in real trouble. But it hasn't worked that way for me. I haven't pleaded for miracles. I haven't asked for strength. I have searched for understanding and even faith, but I haven't gone to you for it.

The reason, I think, is that I haven't blamed you for the accident or the injury. I don't believe you had anything to do with it. Both came about as a consequence of decisions I made for myself. It follows, therefore, that if you had nothing to do with my getting into trouble, you would have nothing to do with getting me out. The response of the faithful to that is that you can make something good happen out of something bad.

That argument always reminds me of the story about the farmer who had worked hard over many years to make a lovely and bountiful garden where once there had been only rocks and weeds. A visitor remarked how wonderful it is that God can create such beauty.

"Yes," said the farmer, "but you should have seen this place when God had it all to himself."

I'm stronger in many ways than I was before, but I believe that strength has come from battles I've fought and won myself with the help of family and friends.

I'll tell you what I think, God. I think I'm on my own as far as you are concerned. Whether one survives a major injury or the emotional turmoil that follows depends largely on how the cookie crumbles—or doesn't crumble—rather than how you've planned it.

That isn't at all to say that I think I'm alone, or that you exist in splendid isolation from your human creation. I simply do not believe that my life is so manipulated by you that my choices are limited only to what you allow me to decide, and that I can avoid the consequences of my actions simply by asking for your help. That's what I believe, but is it enough?

Is it enough to believe we're not alone, especially if that belief is because one *chooses* to believe it? When does choice become conviction and faith?

I believe I am not alone.

42

"April is the cruelest month," wrote T. S. Eliot. Not for us. April is the time for going home.

Home, that most beautiful of all words to us now. Home: Newfoundland, Springdale, 4 Brinex Avenue. Family and friends. After almost seventeen months of hospital rooms and motel rooms, we'll soon be going home. Home, to our own home. I'm putting off thinking about how changed it and I will be.

Originally we were supposed to return to the Hewitt Centre in St. John's, Newfoundland, for three or four weeks before going back to Springdale. Now we've discovered that the O'Connell Centre in Corner Brook has a new rehabilitation wing and they'd love to have me with them for a while for more experience with a spinal cord injury. Even more important, they have a resident physiatrist, someone who specializes in treating injuries like mine and the assorted complications that go with them. I've already spoken to Dr. Scott and made all the necessary arrangements. He sounds really keen and it's only two hours' drive from Springdale as opposed to six to St. John's. I'll stay at the O'Connell for a month or so before going home.

Marion and the social worker are responsible for transportation. The Department of Health in Newfoundland was at first planning to send one of their air ambulance planes to get me. When the measurements for my chair were taken, however, they discovered the chair and the stretcher wouldn't fit into such a small aircraft.

Great heavenly day! The plane is that small? Okay, I know I can handle elevators now, so an airplane should be a cinch, right? Wrong. I'm still not sure about airplanes. I don't like what I'm feeling just thinking about flying, but that might be something left over from a less-than-heroic past. Time to worry about that later.

It's finally agreed that an Ontario air ambulance plane will take us home. It's a little bigger. Hopefully, it's a lot bigger. But the reality is that I'll get on board a herring gull if it's going east as far as Newfoundland.

I discover a trucking company here in Toronto that carries freight to Newfoundland once a month. Evidently it's owned and operated by an expatriate Newfoundlander. Time to give them a call and see what can be done with our few pitiful possessions.

The phone is answered by a male voice that wants to know what it can do for me. The accent is that strange combination of Newfoundland and Toronto dialects which people acquire when they've been away from home too long. It's difficult to describe but unmistakable when it's heard. I tell him I'm returning to Newfoundland in a month or so and I need my stuff carried back at about the same time.

"How much stuff?" He really doesn't seem that interested. "If you leave before our truck leaves you'll need someplace to store it in the meantime. I can't help you there."

"Oh it's not that much. A computer, a small television and a few boxes."

"How many boxes?" I can almost hear him yawning on the other end.

"Not that many." I'm trying to decide between making it sound like a lot and having him think it's too much trouble, or playing down what we have and having him conclude it's not enough to be worth his while. So I straddle the fence and try to avoid any direct reference to the exact amount of freight I have.

"How heavy are the boxes?" he wants to know.

"Not that heavy, actually." Not exactly a definitive answer.

"I need to know how heavy the boxes are so that I can give you an estimate of how much it will cost and tell you whether or not we can take it."

He seems to be getting a tiny bit irritated.

"Well, I don't have any way to weigh them, but they have to be light enough for my wife to lift."

There's a momentary silence on the other end.

"You say your wife has to lift the boxes?"

"Every last one and she has rheumatoid arthritis, so you can see they can't be that heavy."

There is another pause. It's the quiet before the hurricane, the silence before the leopard springs. When he does speak his voice is harsh and the almost-lost Newfoundland accent, mixed with righteous indignation, comes through loud and clear.

"So what's the matter with you, my son? You a cripple or what?"

Okay. I wait for the rage to grab, but nothing happens. I realize I'm not in the least offended by this fellow. He has no way of knowing what I am and he's not trying to be mean. He just objects strenuously to a woman doing all the heavy work while a man sits and watches. Like any good Newfoundlander he's going to say what he thinks about that. But that's not going to stop me from deriving a little perverse pleasure out of this at his expense.

I let a few moments of my own go by. If silence is golden, we are having the richest conversation of all time.

"Well," I say finally, "now that you mention it..." And I proceed to enlighten him in some detail about my physical condition.

Again, there is a long agonizing moment before he speaks in the same reverent tone one would use in the quietness of a little chapel.

"Dear sweet merciful Jesus Christ!"

It isn't a curse. It's more like a plea for forgiveness for sticking both feet in his mouth and cramming them down as far as they can go.

"I'm sorry! My God, I'm sorry! I had no idea..."

Of course not, and I hasten to reassure him that it's okay. That's the kind of gaffe we all make now and then without malice aforethought. But he spends the next twenty minutes apologizing profusely. Before he hangs up, he offers to store our few belongings in his house if we have to leave for Newfoundland before the scheduled departure of his truck. And I think if I had held out for it, he would have taken Marion and stored her, too.

Since I have nothing else to do, I begin to worry about the flight home. The plane is a two-engine prop affair and the question of whether or not it can take Marion, me-on-a-stretcher, a paramedic and the chair is still a burning issue.

The day before we're due to leave, someone from Air Ambulance Services drops by to look at the chair and make a final judgment. He seems to be concerned about mere centimetres, which does nothing for my peace of mind. Apprehensive as I am about the actual flight, I'm even more worried that I won't get on it at all. After measuring the chair from all angles, and carefully sizing up Marion and me, he announces that if they unscrew this and unbolt that—I hope he's talking about the chair—they *should* be able to cram us all aboard. His tone suggests it isn't something he'd want to bet his life on. He obviously isn't making the flight with us.

The next morning is bright and fair. The Gills (what would we do without them) come by to take Marion and our luggage to the little airport on Toronto Island, and I'm lifted onto a stretcher and whisked off to a waiting ambulance. We pass a couple of nurses in the hallway who say goodbye, but that's about all the ceremony there is. Apart from the fact we were probably large thorns in their sides, the staff is used to seeing people coming and going. No big deal about one more.

Two staff people with Newfoundland backgrounds want to make the flight with us, have dinner in Deer Lake and be back that same night. But there just isn't room and they're really disappointed. Even an hour on The Rock is like the balm of Gilead to a native stranded in Toronto.

I'm reminded of my ninety-year-old father-in-law's response when someone asked him if he lived in Toronto.

"No, my son. I'm just marooned here."

That was after more than twenty years.

So it has come at last. We're going home. Seems as though there should be more fanfare, more ceremony, more celebration. But there isn't. The Gills say goodbye with a promise to visit in July, and suddenly we're aboard the plane and taxiing out for takeoff. They've obviously given me drugs to deal with any in-flight anxieties since I don't feel anything other than profound relief. We're going home. We *are* going home.

The pilot tells us it's a four-hour flight on a beautiful clear day, which today is. The pilot reckons without the headwinds, and we have to drop down somewhere in New Brunswick for more gas. The flight takes seven hours.

I can't see out through the windows from my supine position, so I doze most of the time.

Suddenly I hear Marion say, "Ed, we're just passing in over the South Coast!"

Now I'm awake! We're actually over the Island. Only a few more minutes before Deer Lake.

Before long Marion speaks again, although not directly to me.

"What are they looking for?" She's observed both pilots craning their necks out the window and obviously searching for something.

"I don't think," replies the paramedic, "they can find the airport."

It says much for the potency of the drugs they've given me that I find this almost hilarious. They can't find the airport? Don't they have a map? Aren't there any traffic signs? No one will believe this when I write about it, as I most assuredly will.

"Ah, there it is," someone finally says with satisfaction, and we go into a bank to line up for the runway.

I feel the wheels make contact and I know that the first long phase of my battle with paralysis and all its ramifications is about over. Whatever happens from here on in, we're home.

The ambulance from the O'Connell is waiting for us on the Tarmac. I'm trundled aboard and Marion climbs in beside me.

Less than an hour later we're in Corner Brook.

The rehab ward of the O'Connell Centre is on the third floor. A year ago the thought of elevators would have filled me with dread. Now I hardly give it a passing thought.

The staff is friendly and accommodating. They let me have a small room for my computer so that I can continue writing the column. If I want to stay up late watching a ball game on television, no problem. Nurses from one of the other wards will come in and help put me to bed when I'm ready to go. Dr. Scott tries to make me believe I'm doing them all a great favour by being here and acts that way throughout my stay.

I'm at the O'Connell exactly one month. During that time I continue with physiotherapy and occupational therapy. If I were here any longer the staff would have me spoiled completely. Lovely people.

Marion is at Springdale supervising the finishing touches on the house. She comes out weekends. There's a flurry of activity to see that everything is finished by the time I get home. In the meantime, this has got to be the most beautiful spring we've ever had. It's sunny and warm day after day and this intensifies my desire to get back to the house. Friends tell me it's quite nice inside and out.

The day arrives. It is May 22, 1999, exactly seventeen months and nineteen days since the day of the accident. I wish I could say it's been fun.

The Central Health Care Board sends a bus to get me. Again, the day is warm and the skies are blue. Fitting weather to put an end to a forced hiatus that was originally meant to be overnight and from which I intended to return healthy. I'm going home in a wheelchair, paralyzed in almost eighty percent of my body. But I am going home.

Marion and Kathy come with the bus to escort me home. Several nurses and patients are out on the third-floor balcony waving goodbye. The bus moves slowly up the hill and turns east on the Trans Canada Highway. The drive through the magnificent Humber River Valley has never been more impressive.

Since we've been away the new divided highway through Pasadena has been completed and the scenery is unfamiliar. I've always had the need to know exactly where I am when driving, but now someone else is driving and I guess it isn't necessary anymore for me to know where we are.

We stop at the airport in Deer Lake to pick up Jennifer who's flying in from Boston to be with us on this day of days. As she walks across the Tarmac to the arrival entrance I hide behind the doors like a little boy hiding from his sister. She embraces her mother and Kathy, then looks around and spots me behind the door. She cries out and runs to where I am. She is crying. I am crying. We are all crying. Tears of joy? Tears of pain? Who can tell the difference anymore?

This is a big summer for Jennifer. In August she'll be marrying her Australian fiancé, Ian Farrell. Just a friend, remember? Should be quite the wedding: a wet mix of Australians and Newfoundlanders. Hope we all survive it.

We drive by the long and lovely Birchy Lake, one of my favourite scenic spots in the whole Island. Summer after summer I've intended to put my boat off at the bottom of the lake, take a tent and a few supplies, and motor for a few days up Birchy and into the broad expanse of Sandy Lake. Guess I put it off once too often.

We pass by that section of the highway where my hunting trails began. Every fall and winter I used to set my snares in this area and boil up somewhere in those woods. The beauty of the day does nothing to ease the pain in my heart. I don't live there anymore.

"Look, Dad," Kathy calls from her seat farther back, "it's your rabbit country."

But I close my eyes and keep them firmly shut until we turn off the highway to the Springdale access road. Ten minutes.

We turn onto Brinex Avenue. One of our neighbours has a large tree on her lawn festooned with yellow ribbons, a lovely welcome home. We've kept the day and hour of our homecoming a secret because we know our friends were planning a motorcade to meet us at the junction. While I appreciate the thought, I couldn't manage the idea of all that attention. Besides, I don't know how I'm going to react emotionally to wheeling up the driveway to our house, and I'd rather not find out in front of a crowd.

Christopher Reeve says of his homecoming that he sat in the car in his driveway and cried for twenty minutes. Don't think I'll do that. But just in case, our friends have promised Marion they'll keep those first few moments private for the family.

And suddenly, here we are, 4 Brinex Avenue, our home for almost thirty years. I hardly recognize it. The back of the house has been reconfigured with the new extension, there are new and different windows and the old-fashioned yellow aluminum siding has been replaced by modern pale green vinyl. A long wheelchair ramp runs discreetly from the driveway to a new deck.

With the tall birches waving gently over the house, it is lovely indeed.

The bus stops and the doors open. At the top of the driveway are my parents, who've missed very little that's significant in my life since they used to be the only parents watching our ragtag school hockey games. There are Samantha and Robyn holding a banner that reads Welcome Home, and little Nicholas in his father's arms. There are my sister and her husband, determined not to miss this day although they live in St. John's, six hours drive away. Balloons and ribbons hang from the balsams and the birches.

They are all waving.

I need to say something eloquent here, something memorable, something befitting the occasion. Nothing comes. As I wheel out on the bus lift, I'm suddenly almost overwhelmed with emotion, and I understand Chris Reeve's feelings entirely. But I'm not going to give in to it. Everyone's waiting for my reaction so I say the only thing at that moment that I can get past the boulder in my throat.

"That garbage bin by the side of the house has got to go."

Everyone laughs and I relax.

What's that silly little cliché people like to trot out at times like these? Today is the first day of the rest of my life? I guess it is. I know it's the first day of a long and different struggle for Marion and me, in ways we can't even begin to imagine.

Two friends who have become well known for their long walks across the Island have described how they manage to walk several hundred kilometres, often through very difficult terrain.

"We don't set out on a journey that will take several months," they say. "We think only of how far we can go today, and then tonight we'll plan how far we can walk tomorrow."

As the lift lowers me to the pavement and my family rushes to embrace me I know for certain I can make it through this day.

Tomorrow will have to take care of itself.

About the Author

Ed Smith was born in Newfoundland in 1940. His father was a United Church clergyman, so the family moved from one small outport to another, and young Ed and his sister, Pat, found themselves in several different schools for their secondary school education. Ed finished school before he was old enough to attend university and worked in a bank in Sackville, N. B., where his father was attending university preparatory to be ordained. Ed likes to say he put his father through college.

After two years at Dalhousie University in Halifax, Ed was given a Church as a student minister. Three years was enough to convince him that his skills and interests lay in teaching, and he began that career after graduation. In the meantime, Ed and Marion French of St. John's were married in 1963. Ed taught in schools all over Newfoundland, finally settling in Springdale where he and Marion still live. Since that time he has been a high school principal, an assistant superintendent of education, and principal of a college campus in Springdale. Ed retired in 1996, just over two years before the car accident that left him paralyzed from the shoulders down.

It was Marion who encouraged Ed to begin writing a humour column for the local newspaper in 1980. Other papers soon began running the column, so that today "The View from Here" appears in six papers and magazines. He has also written for the *Toronto Star* and *Reader's Digest*. In 2001, Ed prepared a series of short radio clips on life with quadriplegia which he wrote and presented on CBC radio. These earned him The Canadian Nurses' Association award for excellence in broadcasting, and an international Gabriel award for writing that "upholds and uplifts the human spirit." Ed has also been recognized by the Atlantic Community Newspapers Association for "hilarious" material. He has found time to write an autobiography of his childhood, *Some Fine Times*, and *Fish 'n' Ships*, a "brief, twisted history" of Newfoundland. Four collections of his columns have also been published.

Marion and Ed have four adult children and six grandchildren.

Other books by Ed Smith

Fish 'n' Ships
Never Flirt With Your Eyes Shut